Practical Hadoop Migration

How to Integrate Your RDBMS with the Hadoop Ecosystem and Re-Architect Relational Applications to NoSQL

Bhushan Lakhe

Apress®

Practical Hadoop Migration: How to Integrate Your RDBMS with the Hadoop Ecosystem and Re-Architect Relational Applications to NoSQL

Bhushan Lakhe
Darien, Illinois
USA

ISBN-13 (pbk): 978-1-4842-1288-2   ISBN-13 (electronic): 978-1-4842-1287-5
DOI 10.1007/978-1-4842-1287-5

Library of Congress Control Number: 2016948866

Managing Director: Welmoed Spahr
Acquisitions Editor: Robert Hutchinson
Development Editor: Matthew Moodie
Technical Reviewer: Robert L. Geiger
Editorial Board: Steve Anglin, Aaron Black, Pramila Balan, Laura Berendson, Louise Corrigan, Jonathan Gennick, Robert Hutchinson, Celestin Suresh John, Nikhil Karkal, James Markham, Susan McDermott, Matthew Moodie, Natalie Pao, Gwenan Spearing
Coordinating Editor: Rita Fernando
Copy Editor: Corbin Collins
Compositor: SPi Global
Indexer: SPi Global
Cover Image: Designed by FreePik

Distributed to the book trade worldwide by Springer Science+Business Media New York, 233 Spring Street, 6th Floor, New York, NY 10013. Phone 1-800-SPRINGER, fax (201) 348-4505, e-mail orders-ny@springer-sbm.com, or visit www.springer.com. Apress Media, LLC is a California LLC and the sole member (owner) is Springer Science + Business Media Finance Inc (SSBM Finance Inc). SSBM Finance Inc is a **Delaware** corporation.

For information on translations, please e-mail rights@apress.com, or visit www.apress.com.

Apress and friends of ED books may be purchased in bulk for academic, corporate, or promotional use. eBook versions and licenses are also available for most titles. For more information, reference our Special Bulk Sales–eBook Licensing web page at www.apress.com/bulk-sales.

Any source code or other supplementary materials referenced by the author in this text is available to readers at www.apress.com. For detailed information about how to locate your book's source code, go to www.apress.com/source-code/.

Printed on acid-free paper

To my mother....

Contents at a Glance

Contents

Foreword

We are in the midst of one of the biggest transformations of Information Technology (IT). Rapidly evolving business requirements have demanded agility in all aspects of IT. As more and more paper-based business processes are getting digital, rapid application development, staging, and deployment have become the norm. In addition, the data exhaust from these digital applications has become enormous and needs to be analyzed in real time. Growing volumes of historical data is considered valuable for improving business efficiency and identifying future trends and disruptions. Ubiquitous end-user connectivity, cost-efficient software and hardware sensors, and democratization of content production have led to the deluge of data generated in enterprises. As a result, the traditional data infrastructure has to be revamped. Of course, this cannot be done overnight. To prepare your IT to meet the new requirements of the business, one has to carefully plan re-architecting the data infrastructure so that existing business processes remain available during this transition.

Hadoop and NoSQL platforms have emerged in the last decade to address the business requirements of large web-scale companies. Capabilities of these platforms are evolving rapidly, and, as a result, have created a lot of hype in the industry. However, none of these platforms is a panacea for all the needs of a modern business. One needs to carefully consider various business use cases and determine which platform is most suitable for each specific use case. Introducing immature platforms for use cases that are not suited for them is the leading cause of failure of data infrastructure projects. Data architects of today need to understand a variety of data platforms, their design goals, their current and future data protection capabilities, access methods, and performance sweet spots, and how they compare in features against traditional data platforms. As a result, traditional database administrators and business analysts are overwhelmed by the sheer number of new technologies and the rapidly changing data landscape.

This book is written with those readers in mind. It cuts through the hype and gives a practical way to transition to the modern data architectures. Although it may feel like new technologies are emerging every day, the key to evaluating these technologies is to align your current and future business use cases and requirements to the design-center of these new technologies. This book helps readers understand various aspects of the modern data platforms and helps navigate the emerging data architecture. I am confident that it will help you avoid the complexity of implementing modern data architecture and allow seamless transition for your business.

—Milind Bhandarkar, PhD
Founder and CEO, Ampool, Inc.

Milind Bhandarkar was the founding member of the team at Yahoo! that took Apache Hadoop from 20-node prototype to datacenter-scale production system, and has been contributing and working with Hadoop since version 0.1.0. He started the Yahoo! Grid solutions team focused on training, consulting, and supporting hundreds of new migrants to Hadoop. Parallel programming languages and paradigms has been his area of focus for over 20 years. He has worked at the Center for Development of Advanced Computing (C-DAC), National Center for Supercomputing Applications (NCSA), Center for Simulation of Advanced Rockets, Siebel Systems, Pathscale Inc. (acquired by QLogic), Yahoo!, and Linkedin. Until 2013, Milind was chief architect at Greenplum Labs, a division of EMC. Most recently, he was chief scientist at Pivotal Software. Milind holds his PhD degree in computer science from the University of Illinois at Urbana-Champaign.

About the Author

Bhushan Lakhe is a Big Data professional, technology evangelist, author, and avid blogger who resides in the windy city of Chicago. After graduating in 1988 from one of India's leading universities (Birla Institute of Technology and Science, Pilani), he started his career with India's biggest software house, Tata Consultancy Services. Thereafter, he joined ICL, a British computer company, and worked with prestigious British clients. Moving to Chicago in 1995, he worked as a consultant with Fortune 50 companies like Leo Burnett, Blue Cross, Motorola, JPMorgan Chase, and British Petroleum, often in a critical and pioneering role.

After a seven-year stint executing successful Big Data (as well as data warehouse) projects for IBM's clients (and receiving the company's prestigious Gerstner Award in 2012), Mr. Lakhe spent two years helping Unisys Corporation's clients with Big Data implementations, and thereafter two years as senior vice president (information and data architecture) at Ipsos (the world's third-largest market research corporation), helping design global data architecture and Big Data strategy.

Currently, Mr. Lakhe heads the Big Data practice for HCL America, a $7 billion global consulting company with offices in 31 countries. At HCL, Mr. Lakhe is involved in architecting Big Data solutions for Fortune 500 corporations. Mr. Lakhe is active in the Chicago Hadoop community and is co-organizer for a Meetup group (www.meetup.com/ambariCloud-Big-Data-Meetup/) where he regularly talks about new Hadoop technologies and tools. You can find Mr. Lakhe on LinkedIn at www.linkedin.com/in/bhushanlakhe.

About the Technical Reviewer

Robert L. Geiger is currently Chief Architect and acting VP of engineering at Ampool Inc., an early stage startup in the Big Data and analytics infrastructure space. Before joining Ampool, he worked as an architect and developer in the solutions/SaaS space at a B2B deep learning based startup, and prior to that as an architect and team lead at Pivotal Inc., working in the areas of security and analytics as a service for the Hadoop ecosystem. Prior to Pivotal, Robert served as a developer and VP, engineering at a small distributed database startup, TransLattice. Robert spent several years in the security space working on and leading teams in at Symantec on distributed intrusion detection systems. His career started with Motorola Labs in Illinois where he worked on distributed IP over wireless systems, crypto/security, and e-commerce after graduating from University of Illinois Champaign-Urbana.

Acknowledgments

This is my second book for Apress (the first being *Practical Hadoop Security*) continuing the *Practical Hadoop* series, and I want to thank Apress for giving me the opportunity to write it. I would like to thank the Hadoop community and the user forums that bring innovation to this technology and keep the world interested! I have learned a lot from the selfless people in the Hadoop community who believe in being Good Samaritans.

On a personal note, I want to thank my friend Satya Kondapalli for making a forum of Hadoop enthusiasts available through our Meetup group Ambaricloud. I also want to thank our sponsors Hortonworks for supporting us. Finally, I would like to thank my friend Milind Bhandarkar (of Ampool) for taking time from his busy schedule to write a foreword and a whole section about his new Butterfly architecture.

I am grateful to my editors, Rita Fernando, Robert Hutchinson, and Matthew Moodie at Apress for their help in getting this book toegther. Rita has been there throughout to answer any questions that I have, to improve my drafts, and to keep me on schedule. Robert Hutchinson's help with the book structure has been immensely valuable. And I am also very thankful to Robert Geiger for taking time to review my second book technically. Bob always had great suggestions for improving a topic, recommending additional details, and of course resolving technical shortcomings.

Finally, the writing of this book wouldn't have been possible without the constant support from my family (my wife, Swati, and my kids, Anish and Riya) for the second time in the last three years, and I'm looking forward to spending lots more time with all of them.

Introduction

I have spent more than 20 years consulting for large corporations, and when I started, it was just relational databases. Eventually, the volumes of accumulated historical data grew, and it was not possible to manage and analyze this data with good performance. So, corporations started thinking about separating the parts (of data) useful for analaysis (or generating insights) from the descriptive data. They soon realized that a fundamental change was needed in the relational design, and a new paradigm called data warehousing was born. Thanks to the work done by Bill Inmon and Ralph Kimball, the world started thinking (and designing) in terms of Star schemas and dimensions and facts. ETL (extract, transform, load) processes were designed to load the data warehouses.

The next step was making sure that large volumes of data could be retrieved with good performance. Specialized software was developed, and RDBMS solutions (Oracle, Sysbase, SQL Server) added processing for data warehouses. For the next level of performance, it was clear that data needed to be preprocessed, and data cubes were designed. Since magnetic disk drives were slow, SSDs (solid state devices) were designed, and software that cached (or held data in RAM) data for speed of processing and retrieval became popular. So, with all these advanced measures for performance, why is Hadoop or NoSQL needed? For two reasons.

First, it is important to note that all this while, the data being processed either was relational data (for RDBMS) or had started as relational data (for data warehouses). This was structured data, and the type of analysis (and insights) possible was very specific (to the application that generated the data). The rigid structure of a warehouse put severe limits on the insights or data explorations that were possible, since you start with a design and fit data into it. Also, due to the very high volumes, warehouses couldn't perform per expectations, and a newer technology was needed to effectively manage this data.

Second, in recent years, new types of data were introduced: unstructured or semi-structured data. Social media became very popular and were a new avenue for corporations to communicate directly with people once they realized the power behind it. Corporations wanted to know what people thought about their products, services, employees, and of course the corporations themselves. Also, with e-commerce forming a large part of all the businesses, corporations wanted to make sure they were preferred over their competitors—and if that was not the case, they wanted to know why. Finally, there was a need to analyze some other types of unstructured data, like sensor data from electrical and electronic devices, or data from mobile devices sensors, that was also very high volume. All this data was usually hundreds of gigabytes per day.

Conventional warehouse technology was incapable of processing or managing this data. So, a new technology had to be designed to process it, and with good performance (since total volumes were in terabytes). In some cases, as the unstructured data (or insights from it) needed to be combined with structured data, the new technology needed to support interfacing with data warehouses or RDBMS.

Hadoop offers all these capabilities and in addition allows a schema-on-read (meaning you can define metadata while performing analysis) that offers a lot of flexiblity for performing exploratory analysis or generating new insights from your data.

This gets us to the final question: how do you migrate or integrate your existing RDBMS-based applications with Hadoop and analyze structured as well as unstructured data in tandem? Well, you have to read rest of the book to know that!

Who This Book Is For

This book is an excellent resource for IT management planning to migrate or integrate their existing RDBMS environment with Big Data technologies or Big Data architects who are designing a migration/integration process. This book is also for Hadoop developers who want to implement migration/integration process or students who'd like to learn about designing Hadoop applications that can successfully process relational data along with unstructured data. This book assumes a basic understanding of Hadoop, Kerberos, relational databases, Hive, Spark, and an intermediate level understanding of Linux.

Downloading the Code

The source code for this book is available in ZIP file format in the Downloads section of the Apress Web site (www.apress.com/9781484212882).

Contacting the Author

You can reach Bhushan Lakhe at blakhe@aol.com or bclakhe@gmail.com.

CHAPTER 1

▨ ▨ ▨

RDBMS Meets Hadoop: Integrating, Re-Architecting, and Transitioning

Recently, I was at the Strata + Hadoop World Conference, chatting with a senior executive of a major food corporation who used a relational solution for storing all its data. I asked him casually if they were thinking about using a Big Data solution, and his response was: "We already did and it's too slow!" I was amazed and checked the facts again. This corporation had even availed of the consulting services of a major Hadoop vendor and yet was still not able to harness the power of Big Data.

I thought about the issue and possible reasons why this might have occurred. To start with, a Hadoop vendor can tune his Hadoop installation but can't guarantee that generic tuning will be valid for specific type of data. Second, the food corporation's database administrators and architects probably had no idea how to transform their relational data for use with Hadoop. This is not an isolated occurrence, and most of the corporations who want to make the transition to using of relational data with Hadoop are in a similar situation. The result is a Hadoop cluster that's slow and inefficient and performs nowhere close to the expectations that Big Data hype has generated.

Third, all NoSQL databases are not created equal. NoSQL databases vary greatly in their handling of data as well as in the models they use internally to manage data. They only work well with certain kind of data. So, it's very important to know the type of your data and select a NoSQL solution that matches it.

Finally, success in applying NoSQL solutions to relational data depends on identifying your objective in using Hadoop/NoSQL and on accommodating your data volumes. Hadoop is not a cure-all that can magically speed up all your data processing—it can only be used for specific type of processing (which I discuss further in this chapter). And Hadoop works best for larger volumes of data and is not efficient for lower data volumes due to the various overheads associated.

Electronic supplementary material The online version of this chapter (doi:10.1007/978-1-4842-1287-5_1) contains supplementary material, which is available to authorized users.

© Bhushan Lakhe 2016   1
B. Lakhe, *Practical Hadoop Migration*, DOI 10.1007/978-1-4842-1287-5_1

So, having defined the problem, let's think about a solution. You are probably familiar with the myriad design methodologies and frameworks that are available for use with relational data, but do you know of similar resources for Hadoop? Probably not. There is a good reason for that—none exists yet. Lambda is being developed as a design methodology (Chapter 12), but it is not mature yet and not very easy to implement.

So, what's the alternative? Do you need to rely on the expertise of your data architects to design this transition, or are there generic steps you can follow? How do you ensure an efficient and functionally reliable transition? I answer these questions in this book and demonstrate how you can successfully transition your relational data to Hadoop.

First, it is important to understand how Hadoop and NoSQL differ from the relational design. I briefly discuss that in this chapter and also discuss the benefits as well as challenges associated with using Hadoop and NoSQL.

It is also important to decide whether your data (and what you want to do with it) is suited for use with Hadoop. Therefore, factors such as type of data, data volume, and your business needs are important to consider. There are some more factors that you need to consider, and the latter part of this chapter discusses them at length. Typically, the four "V"s (volume, velocity, variety, and veracity) separate NoSQL data from relational data, but that rule of thumb may not always hold true.

So, let me start the discussion with conceptual differences between relational technology and Hadoop. That's the next section.

Conceptual Differences Between Relational and HDFS NoSQL Databases

Database design has had a few facelifts since E.F. Codd presented his paper on relational design in 1970.[1] Leading relational database systems today (such as Oracle or Microsoft SQL Server) may not be following Codd's vision completely; but definitely use the underlying concepts without much of modification. There is a central database server that holds the data and provides access to users (as defined by Database Administrator) after authentication. There are database objects such as views (for managing granular permissions) or triggers (to manipulate data as per data 'relations') or indexes for performance (while reading or modifying data).

The main feature, however, is that relations can be defined for your data. Let me explain using a quick example. Think of an insurance company selling various (life, disability, home) policies to individual customers. A good identifier to use (for identifying a customer uniquely) is customers' social security number. Since a customer may buy multiple policies from the insurance company and those details may be stored in separate database tables, there should be a way to relate all that data to the customer it belongs to.

Relational technology implements that easily by making the social security number as a primary key or primary identifier for the customer table and a foreign key or referential identifier (an identifier to identify the parent or originator of the information) for all the related tables, such as life_policies or home_policies. Figure 1-1 summarizes a sample implementation.

---

[1] www.seas.upenn.edu/~zives/03f/cis550/codd.pdf "A Relational Model of Data for Large Shared Data Banks"

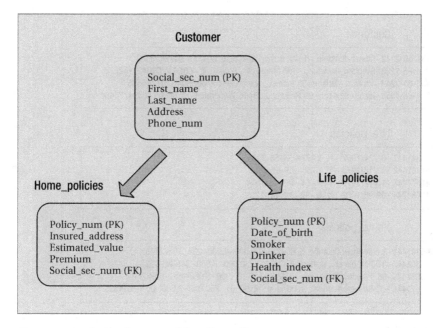

Figure 1-1. *Relational storage of data (logical)*

As you can see in Figure 1-1, the policy data is related to customers. This relation is established using the social security number. So, all the policy records for a customer can be retrieved using their social security number. Any modifications to the customer identifier (social security number) are propagated to maintain data integrity.

Next, let me discuss Hadoop and NoSQL databases that use HDFS for storage. HBase is a popular NoSQL database and therefore can be used as an example. Since HDFS is a distributed file system, data will be spread across all the data nodes in contrast to a central server. Kerberos is used for authentication, but HBase has very limited capability for granular authorization as opposed to relational databases. HBase offers indexing capabilities, but they are very limited and are no match for the advanced indexing techniques offered by RDBMS (relational database management systems). However, the main difference is absence of relations. Unlike RDBMSs, HBase data is not related. Data for HBase tables is simply held in HDFS files.

As you can see in Figure 1-2, the policy data is not related automatically with a customer. Any relating that's necessary will have to be done programmatically. For example, if you need to list all the policies that customer "Isaac Newton" holds, you will need to know the tables that hold policies for customers (here, Hbase tables Life_policies and Home_policies). Then you will need to know a common identifier to use (social security number) to match the rows that belong to this customer. Any changes to the identifier can't be propagated automatically and will need to be implemented manually.

Customer

234-56-2243~Albert~Einstein ~1 oak drive, Palatine, IL 60421~ 8472453333
345-86-1223~Stephen ~Hawking ~100 Maple ct. , Darien , IL ~60561~6304271623
453-65-2244~Thomas ~Edison~55 Pine st., Naperville , IL 60660~6307246565
294-85-4553 ~Isaac~Newton~99 Redwood drive, Woodridge, IL 60561~6304275454

Life_policies

45341441 ~01/24/1962 ~N~Y~72~234-56-2243
41441442 ~03/18/1972 ~Y~Y~60~294-85-4553
41671443 ~10/12/1976 ~Y~N~64~453-65-2244
41489744 ~09/06/1968 ~N~N~82~345-86-1223

Home_policies

45341441~1 oak drive, Palatine, IL 60421~500,000~4,000~234 -56-2243
45356442~ 100 Maple ct. , Darien , IL 60561~750,000~5,000~345-86-1223
45987443~55 Pine st., Naperville , IL 60660~1,100,000~8,000~45 3-65-2244
45671444 ~99 Redwood drive, Woodridge, IL 60561~300,000~2,000~29 4-85-4553

Figure 1-2. NoSQL storage of data

So, for example, if an error in social security number is discovered, then all the files containing that information will need to be updated separately (programmatically). Unlike RDBMS, HDFS or HBase doesn't offer any utilities to do that for you. The reason is that HBase (or any other HDFS-based NoSQL databases) doesn't offer any referential integrity—simply due to their purpose. HBase is not meant for interactive queries over a small dataset; it is best suited for a large batch processing environment (similar to data warehousing environments) involving immutable data. Till recently, updates for HBase involved loading the changed row in a staging table and doing a left outer join with the main data table to overwrite the row (making sure the staging and main data table had the same key).

With the new version of HBase, updates, deletes, and inserts are now supported, but for small datasets these operations will be very slow (compared to RDBMS) because they're executed as Hadoop MapReduce jobs that have high latency and incur substantial overheads in job submission and scheduling.

Starting with a large block size used by HDFS (default 64 MB) and distributed architecture that spreads data over a large number of DataNodes (helping parallel reads using MapReduce or Yarn), HBase (and other HDFS based NoSQL databases) are meant to perform efficiently for large datasets. Any transformations that need to be applied involve reading the whole table and not a single row. Distributed processing on DataNodes using MapReduce (or Yarn on recent versions) provides the speed and efficiency for such reads. Again, due to the distributed architecture, it is much more efficient to write the transformed data to a new "file" (or staging table for HBase). For the same reason, Hadoop and NoSQL databases are better equipped to store (and process) large image or video files, large blocks of natural language text, or semi-structured as well as sensor data.

Compare this with a small page size for RDBMS (for example, Microsoft SQL Server uses a page size of 8 KB) and absence of an efficient mechanism to distribute the read (or update) operations and you will realize why NoSQL databases will always win in any scenarios that involve data warehouses and large datasets. The strength of RDBMS, though, is where there are small datasets with complex relationships and extensive analysis is required on parts of it. Also, where referential integrity is important to be implemented over a dataset, NoSQL databases are no match for RDBMS.

To summarize, RDBMS is more suited for a large number of data manipulations for smaller datasets where ACID (Atomicity, Consistency, Isolation, Durability) compliance is necessary; whereas NoSQL databases are more suited for a smaller number of data manipulations to large datasets that can work with the "eventual consistency" model. Table 1-1 provides a handy comparison between the two technologies (relational and NoSQL).

Table 1-1. *Comparative Features of RDBMS vs. NoSQL*

	Feature	HDFS-based NoSQL	RDBMS
1	Large datasets	Efficient and fast	Not efficient
2	Small datasets	Not efficient	Efficient and fast
3	Searches	Not efficient	Efficient and fast
4	Large read operations	Efficient and fast	Not efficient
5	Updates	Not efficient	Efficient and fast
6	Data relations	Not supported	Supported
7	Authentication/Authorization	Kerberos	Built-in
8	Data storage	Distributed over DataNodes	Central Database server
9	ACID compliant	No	Yes
10	Concurrent updates to dataset	Not supported	Supported
11	Fault tolerance	Built-in	Not built-in
12	Scalability	Easily scalable	Not easily scalable

Figure 1-3 shows the physical data storage configurations (for the preceding example) including a Hadoop cluster (Hive/NoSQL) and RDBMS (Microsoft SQL Server).

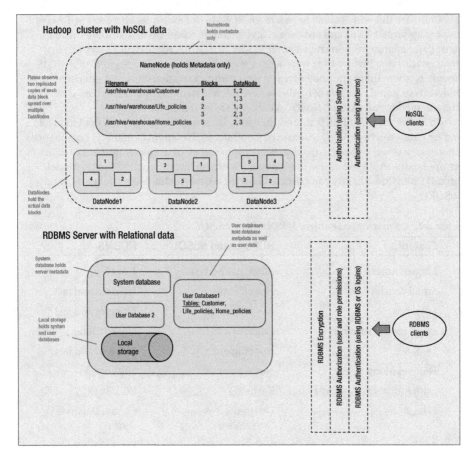

Figure 1-3. *Physical data storage configurations (NoSQL and RDBMS)*

Relational Design and Hadoop in Conjunction: Advantages and Challenges

The preceding section talked about how different these two technologies are. So, why bother bringing them together? What's the effort involved, and is it worth that effort? I'll discuss these questions one at a time.

I will start with the advantages of combining these two technologies. If you review Table 1-1, you will realize that these technologies complement each other nicely. If a large volume of historical data is gathered via RDBMS, you can use NoSQL databases to analyze it. That;s because Hadoop is better equipped to read large datasets and transform them—the only condition being that transformation is applied to the whole dataset (for efficiency). So, how best can you leverage use of Hadoop/NoSQL in your environment? Here are a few ideas:

- **Transform data into (valuable) information:** Data, by itself, is just numbers (or text). You need to add perspective to your data in order for it to be valuable for your business needs. Hadoop can assist you by generating a large number of analytics for your data. For example, if Hadoop is used for analyzing the data generated by auto-sensors, it can consolidate, summarize, and analyze the data and provide reports by time-slices (such as hourly, daily, weekly, and so on) and provide you vital statistics such as average temperature of the engine, average crankshaft RPM, number of warnings per hours, and so forth.

- **Gain insights through mapping multiple data structures to a single dataset:** When using RDBMS for your data needs, you are aware of the need to specify a data structure before using it. Referring to the example in the last section, if SQL Server is used to store Customer and policy data, then you need to define a user database and Customer as well as policy table structures. You can only store data after that. In contrast, Customer data within HDFS is simply held as a file, and structure can be attached to it while it is read. This concept, known as *schema on read*, offers a lot of flexibility while reading the data. A good use of this concept might be in a case where a fact table holds the sales figures for a product and can be read as "Yearly sales" or also can be read as "Buying trends by region."

- **Use historical data for predictive analysis:** In a lot of cases, there is a large amount of historical data to be analyzed and used for predicting future trends. Hadoop can be (and is) successfully used to churn through the terabytes of data, consolidate it, and use it in your predictive models. For example, past garment-buying trends in spring and fall for the prior ten years can assist a departmental store in stocking the right type of garments; spending habits of a customer over the last five years can help them mail the right coupons to him.

- **Build a robust fault-tolerant system:** Hadoop offers fault tolerance and redundancy by default. Each data block is replicated thrice as default configuration and can be adjusted as per the needs. RDBMS can be configured for real-time replication, but any solution used to implement replication needs extensive setup and monitoring and also impacts performance due to replication overheads. In addition, due to the way updates are implemented for Hadoop, there is fault tolerance for human mistakes, too, since updated data is mostly written to a new file, leaving original data unchanged.

- **Serve a wide range of workloads**: Hadoop can be used to cater to a wide range of applications. For example, a social media application where eventual consistency is acceptable or low-latency reads as well as ad-hoc queries where performance is paramount. With components (such as Spark) offering in-memory processing or ACID compliance (Hive 0.14), Hadoop is now a more versatile platform compared to any of the RDBMS.

- **Design a linearly scalable system:** The issue with scaling an RDBMS-based system is that it only scales up—and that too not easily. There is downtime and risk involved (since the server needs to be supplemented with additional hardware resources) and though newer versions (of RDBMS) support distributed computing model, the necessary configuration is difficult and needs complex setup and monitoring. Hadoop, in contrast, scales out easily without any downtime, and it is easy and fast to add or remove DataNodes for a Hadoop cluster.

- **Design an extensible system:** A Hadoop cluster is easily extensible (features can be added easily without downtime). Troubleshooting is easy due to extensive logging using the flexible and comprehensive Log4j API and requires minimal maintenance or manual intervention. Compare that with RDBMS, which requires extensive monitoring and setup for continued normal operation.

If Hadoop deployment has so many advantages, why doesn't everyone implement it in their environment? The reason (as explained earlier) is that Hadoop is not the best solution for all types of data or business needs. Additionally, even if there's a match, there are a number of challenges in introducing Hadoop to your organization, which I discuss in the next section.

Type of Data

The following are things to consider, depending on the type of data you are dealing with:

- **Workload:** Hadoop is most suited for read-heavy workloads. If you have a transactional system (currently using RDBMS), then there is extra effort involved in deriving a denormalized warehouse-like version of your database and having it ingested via an appropriate Hadoop tool (such as Sqoop or Flume) into HDFS. Any updates to this data have to be processed as reads from source file, applying updates (as appropriate) and writing out to a staging file that becomes the new source. Though new versions of some NoSQL databases (Hive 0.14) support updates, it is more efficient to handle them in this manner.

- **High Latency:** With most NoSQL databases, there is an increase in latency with increasing throughput. If you need low latency for your application, you will need to benchmark and adjust your hardware resources. This task requires a good understanding of Hadoop monitoring and various Hadoop daemons and also expertise in configuring a Hadoop cluster.

- **Data dependencies:** If your relational data is column oriented or nested (with multiple levels of nesting), you have more work ahead of you. Since there is no join in NoSQL, you will need to denormalize your data before you store it within a NoSQL database (or HDFS). Also, cascading changes to dependent data (similar to foreign key relationships within RDBMS) needs to be handled programmatically. There are no tools available within NoSQL databases to provide this functionality.

- **Schema:** Your schema (for data stored within RDBMS) is static and if you need to make it semi-dynamic or completely dynamic, you need to make appropriate changes in order to adapt it for NoSQL usage.

Data Volume

Hadoop is not suitable for low data volumes due to the overheads it incurs while reading or writing files (these tasks translate to MapReduce jobs and incur substantial overheads while performing job submission or scheduling). There is a lot of debate about the "magic number" you can use as critical volume for moving to Hadoop, but it varies for the type of data you have and, of course, for your business needs. From my personal experience, Hadoop should only be considered for volumes larger than 5 TB (and with a high growth rate).

Business Need

If your business need for moving to Hadoop doesn't match your existing data, then there is work involved—especially if it is the type of data Hadoop/NoSQL are not good at processing. For example, if your business need is complex analytics for subsets of normalized relational data with frequent updates, then you need to denormalize your data and also establish a policy and timeline to apply the updates (once a day, twice a day, and so on). There is also additional work involved in separating the fact data from dimensional data as the need may be. If, however, you want to use Hadoop for analyzing the browsing habits of thousands of your potential customers and determine what percentage of that converted to actual sales, then the work involved may be minimal—because you probably have all the required data available in separate NoSQL tables—albeit it may be in unstructured or semi-structured format (which NoSQL has no problems processing).

Of course, there may be more specific challenges for your environment, and I have only discussed challenges in moving the data. There may be additional challenges in modifying the front-end user interfaces (to work with Hadoop/NoSQL) as well!

Deciding to Integrate, Re-Architect, or Transition

Once you have decided to introduce Hadoop/NoSQL in your environment, here are some of the next questions: how do you make Hadoop work best with your existing applications/data? Do you transition some of your applications to Hadoop or simply integrate existing applications with Hadoop? A slightly more drastic approach is to completely re-architect your application for Hadoop/NoSQL usage.

Unfortunately, there is no short answer to these questions, and the decision can only be made after careful consideration of a number of relevant factors. The next section discusses those factors.

Type of Data

The type of data you currently have (within your applications) can have an impact in multiple ways:

- **Structured/Unstructured data:** If most of your application data is structured and there is no possibility of adding any semi-structured or unstructured data sources, then the best approach is integration. It is best to integrate your existing applications with Hadoop/NoSQL. You can either think about designing and implementing a data lake, or if you only need to analyze a small part of your data, then simply have a data-ingestion process to copy data into HDFS and use Hive or HBase to process it for analysis and querying. Alternatively, if you have a semi-structured or unstructured data sources, then depending on their percentage (to structured data), you can either transition your application completely to NoSQL or re-architect your application partially (or completely) to NoSQL if you have a large percentage of semi-structured/unstructured data currently (or expected in the immediate future).

- **Normalized relational data:** If a large percentage of your data is highly normalized relational data, then probably you have a complex application with a high amount of data dependency involved. Since NoSQL databases are not capable of supporting data dependencies and relations, you can't really think about re-architecting or transitioning your application to NoSQL. Your best chance is integration, and that too with additional effort. You can think of a data lake but need to de-normalize and flatten your data (remove hierarchical relationships) and remove all the data dependencies. The concept is similar to building a data warehouse, but instead of a rigid fact/dimensional structure of a dimensional model, you need to simply de-normalize the tables and try to create flat structures that (ideally) need no joins or very few joins, since Hadoop/NoSQL is not good at processing joins.

Type of Application

As you have seen earlier, NoSQL is suited for certain types of applications only. Here is how it impacts the decision to integrate, transition, or re-architect:

- **Data mart/Analytics:** Hadoop is most suited for single write/ multiple read scenarios, and that's what occurs in a data mart. Data is incrementally loaded and read/processed for analysis multiple times after. There are no updates to warehouse data, simply increments. That works well with Hadoop's efficiency for large read operations (and also inefficiency with updates). Therefore, for data mart applications, it's best to re-architect and transition to Hadoop/ NoSQL rather than integrate. Again, it may not be possible to move a whole enterprise data warehouse (EDW) to Hadoop, but it may certainly be possible to re-architect and transition some of the data marts to Hadoop (I discuss details of data marts that can be transitioned to Hadoop in Chapters 9 and 11).

- **ETL (batch processing) applications:** It is possible to utilize Hadoop/NoSQL for ETL processing effectively, since in most cases it involves reading source data, applying transformations (to the complete dataset), and writing transformed data to the target. This again can use Hadoop's ability for efficient serial reads/writes and applying transformations unconditionally and uniformly to a large dataset. Therefore, for ETL applications, it is best to re-architect and transition to Hadoop rather than integrate. The caution here is making sure there are very few (or ideally no) data dependencies in the data that is being transformed. Given NoSQL's lack of join capability and inability to process relations within normalized data, either the data-lookup tasks should be maintained within RDBMS, or, if not possible, transition to NoSQL should be avoided.

- **Social media applications:** Currently, use of social media is increasing every day, and corporations like to use social media applications for everything, starting with product launches to post-mortems of product failures. Most social media data is unstructured or semi-structured. NoSQL is good at processing this data, and you should definitely think about re-architecting and transitioning to Hadoop for any such applications.

- **User behavioral capture:** Many e-commerce websites like to capture user clicks and analyze their browsing habits. Due to the large volume and unstructured nature of such data, Hadoop/NoSQL are ideally suited to process it. You should certainly re-architect/transition these applications to NoSQL.

- **Log analysis applications:** Any mid-size or large corporation uses a large number of applications, and these applications generate a large number of log files. In case of troubleshooting or security issues, it is almost impossible to analyze these log files. Other important information can be derived from log files, like average processing time for batch processing tasks, number of failures and their details, user access and resource details (accessed by the users), and so on. Hadoop/NoSQL is ideally suited to process this large volume of semi-structured data, and you should certainly design new applications based in Hadoop/NoSQL for these purposes or re-architect/transition any existing applications to Hadoop. You are certain to see the benefits,

Business Objectives

Last but not least, business objectives drive and override any decisions made. Here are some of the business objectives that can impact the decision to integrate/re-architect/transition:

- **Provide near-real time analytics:** There may be situations where a business needs to have strategic advantage by providing ways to analyze its data in near real time for higher management. For example, if the Chief Marketing Officer (CMO) has access to up-to-date sales of the new product launched by region (or city), he can probably address the sales issues better. In these cases, designing a data lake can provide quick insights into the sales data. Therefore, integrating existing application(s) with Hadoop/NoSQL is the best strategy here.

- **Reduce hardware cost:** Sometimes an application is useful for an organization but it needs proprietary or high-cost hardware. If there are budgetary constraints or simply organizational policy that can't be overridden, Hadoop can be useful for cost reduction. There is of course time/effort/price involved in re-architecting/transitioning an application to Hadoop; but cost analysis of hardware ownership/rental (as well as maintenance) compared to one-time re-architect/transition cost and hosting on cheaper hardware can help you make the right decision.

- **Design for scalability and fault-tolerance:** In some situations, there may be a need for easy scalability (for example, if a business is anticipating high growth in the near future) and fault tolerance (if demanded by functional need or a client). If this is a new requirement, it may be cost-prohibitive to add these features to existing applications, and Hadoop/NoSQL can certainly be a viable alternative. A careful cost analysis of additional hardware, software, and resources (to support the new requirements) compared to one-time re-architect/transition cost and hosting on cheaper hardware can help you make the right decision.

I have only introduced the preceding criteria briefly here and will discuss it in much more detail in later chapters. The next section talks about what each of these techniques involves.

How to Integrate, Re-Architect, or Transition

I discuss these approaches in detail in later chapters. The objective of this section is just to introduce the concepts with quick examples. Let me start with the least intrusive approach: integration with existing application(s).

Integration

Think of a scenario where a global corporation has its data dispersed in large applications, and it is almost impossible to analyze the data in conjunction while maintaining it at the same granularity. If doesn't offer the flexibility to derive new insights from it, what is the use of such data held on expensive hardware and employing resources to maintain it? The *data lake* is a new paradigm that can be useful in these scenarios. Pentaho CTO James Dixon is credited with coining the term. A data lake is simply the accumulation of your application data held in HDFS without any transformations applied to it. It typically is characterized by the following:

- **Small cost for big size:** A data lake doesn't need expensive hardware to implement a large Hadoop cluster. Use of commodity hardware provides a big cost saving (and implementation at fraction of the cost) compared to traditional data warehouses (implemented using RDBMS).

- **Data fidelity:** While in a data lake, data is guaranteed to be preserved in its original form and without any transformations applied to it.

- **Accessibility:** A data lake removes the multiple silos that divide the data by application, departments, roles, and so forth and make it easily and equally accessible to everyone within an organization.

- **Dynamic schema:** Data stored in a data lake doesn't need to be bound by a predefined rigid schema and can be structured as per need, offering flexibility for insightful analysis.

Broadly, data lakes can be categorized as follows:

- **Data reservoir:** When data from multiple applications is held without silos and organized using data governance as well as indexing (or cataloging) for fast retrieval, it constitutes a data *reservoir*. Data here is organized and ready for analysis, but no analysis is defined, although a reservoir may consist of data from isolated data marts along with data from unstructured sources.

- **Exploratory lake:** Organizations with specialized data scientists, business analysts, or statisticians can perform custom analytical queries to gain new insights from data stored in a data lake. Many times this doesn't even involve IT and is a purely exploratory effort followed by visualizations (presented to higher management) in order to verify the relevance and utility of the analytics performed. Due to the way data is held in a data lake, it is possible to perform quick iterations of these analytics to the satisfaction of decision makers.

- **Analytical lake:** Some organizations have an established process to feed their analytical models for advanced analysis, such as predictive analysis (what may happen) or prescriptive analysis (what we should do about it) and use data from a data lake as input for those models. A data lake (or its subset) can also act as a staging area for a data mart or enterprise data warehouse (EDW).

Data *governance* is an important consideration for implementing data lakes. It is important to establish data governance processes for a data lake lest it turn into a data "swamp." For example, the fact that metadata can be maintained separately from underlying data also makes it harder to govern—unless uniform metadata standards are followed that help users understand data interrelations. Of course, that still doesn't eliminate the danger of individual end users ascribing data attributes to data (from the data lake) that are only relevant in their own business context and don't follow organizational metadata standards or governance conventions. The same issue may arise about consistency of semantics within the data. Here are some important aspects of data governance:

- **MDM integration:** For a data lake, MDM integration is a bidirectional process. Master data for an organization can be a good starting point, but metadata in a data lake can grow and mature over time with user interaction since individual user perspectives and insights can result in new ways to look at (and analyze) the same data. This is an important benefit of maintaining the metadata and underlying data separately within a data lake. Additionally, tagging and linking metadata can help organize it further and assist in generating more insights and intelligence.

- **Data quality:** The objective of data quality is to make sure that data (within a data lake) is valid, consistent, and reliable. Quality of incoming data needs to be accessed using data profiling. *Data profiling* is a process that discovers contradictions, inconsistencies, and redundancies within your data by analyzing its content and structure. Correctional rules need to be set up to transform the data. The corrected output needs to be monitored over time to ensure that all the defined rules are transforming the data correctly and also to modify or add rules as necessary.

- **Security policy:** It is a common misconception that since data within a data lake doesn't have any silos, the same applies to access control, and it is unrestricted as well. Data governance needs processes performing authentication, authorization, encryption, and monitoring to reduce the risk of unauthorized access as well as updates to data.

- **Encryption:** Due to the distributed nature of Hadoop, there is large amount of inter-node data transfer as well as data transfer between DataNodes and client. To prevent unauthorized access to this data in transit as well as data stored on DataNodes (data at rest), encryption is necessary. There are a number of ways encryption "at rest" can be implemented for Hadoop, and doing so is necessary. As for inter-node communication, it can be configured to be encrypted.

- **Masking of PII (Personally identifiable information) and other sensitive data:** Encryption can help prevent unauthorized access, but even users who are authorized to access data may not be permitted to access certain sensitive information such as personal information for clients, their healthcare data, and so on. Also, federal regulations for certain industries (such as insurance, healthcare, financial) prevent such access to all employees. Therefore, any such sensitive data needs to be masked and protected by additional passwords.

If you consider the features (described earlier in this section) and considerations for a governed data lake, the design will look something like Figure 1-4.

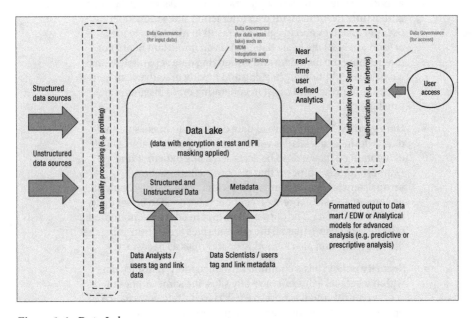

Figure 1-4. *Data Lake*

Re-Architecting Using Lambda Architecture

Re-architecting an application for Hadoop/NoSQL environment involves redesigning the data and query layers completely for HDFS/NoSQL storage and processing. Typically, Hadoop is used for batch processing, which means that for an interactive application that needs ad hoc queries executed, re-architecting for Hadoop can pose a problem. Especially if the functionality needs low latency for data retrieval, Hadoop/NoSQL won't be able to deliver it.

Nathan Marz has provided an architectural solution to counter this problem known as *Lambda architecture*. It suggests that you build your Big Data system as a series of layers with each layer providing specific functionality and the next layer building upon functionality provided by earlier layer (as shown in Figure 1-5). This architectural solution can be used for re-architecting an application for Hadoop or designing a new application meant to be used with Hadoop/NoSQL.

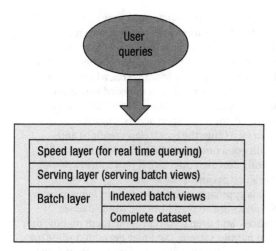

Figure 1-5. *Layers of Lambda architecture*

There are three layers. The batch layer is the first layer that computes views used for querying. The serving layer is the second layer that indexes the view created in first layer and serves them. The speed layer is the third layer that provides real-time querying functionality within Lambda architecture.

Batch Layer

Executing queries on a huge dataset (the highlight of Hadoop-based systems) requires a large amount of resources and can be very slow. Sometimes it may even abort due to lack of resources. A smart workaround can be to precompute data in advance and make it ready for queries. The precomputed data can be indexed to speed up random reads (since Hadoop is not very good at them). This concept is not very different from the RDBMS materialized views that can be indexed. However, for the Hadoop world it is new, and these precomputed views or batch views constitute the batch layer for Lambda architecture.

When you want to execute a query, you can design and run a function on that batch view instead of on the whole dataset. The indexed batch view facilitates a quick retrieval of values (you need) since it is indexed and a subset of the data. You can create multiple batch views for your dataset covering varied functionalities and suited for varied analytics as per your need. In addition, parallelism for data retrieval is always guaranteed due to the distributed nature of Hadoop.

For example, a clothing web retailer collects data through a Hadoop-based system that records all user clicks (including sales transactions). For them, a batch view that isolates all the sales transactions by geographical locations may be useful for the sales department, and another batch view with user clicks and dates might be useful for data scientists to analyze product interest by season or time of year.

In some cases, if your dataset is enormous, even the batch views may be huge, and you can think about breaking them up further. For example, the clothing web retailer has user clicks and sales generating billions of records per month. If you have your batch views by quarter, the volumes may still be large for quick processing of queries, and you may want to design an additional batch layer with views by month. That will reduce your processing time (since you will only process the latest month, as opposed to a quarter) but may complicate your retrieval strategy since you will need to determine the correct view to query, and multiple views if need be (if durations span across months).

Indexing the views is a very important step (after the batch view creation) and will need to be performed by someone with good understanding of your data as well as functional needs (analytics and frequently executed queries). If your indexes do not coincide with your queries, you will experience performance issues.

The obvious question one has with this approach is about the time or latency for creating such batch views. Because these views are created from the whole dataset, clearly they will use of lot of system resources, and even if you compute them nightly, they are not going to have all the data collected by your system. Data may get added while (or after) these views are computed, and your query results will be outdated by many hours. The next layers of Lambda deal with that issue.

Serving Layer

The serving layer serves the views. The indexed batch views that were created in the batch layer need to be "hosted" somewhere they can be accessed without much latency.

Therefore, the serving layer needs to be a specialized distributed database that can load the batch views and support good performance for random reads as well as sequential data retrieval. The serving layer also needs to be capable of swapping a batch view with a newer version when it is made available by the batch layer so that user queries can return up-to-date results (it needs to support batch updates).

But because user queries are not going to update the batch views, the serving layer doesn't need to support random writes, and because random writes cause most of the complexity in databases, the serving layer distributed databases can be extremely simple. That simplicity gives them robustness, predictability, and ease of configuration (as well as operation). It concurs with the philosophy of the Lambda architecture which believes in moving the complexity from batch and serving layers to the speed layer, which essentially is discardable.

One last point to remember about the serving layer is that no single distributed database can be recommended or used. You need to consider the nature of your data before deciding on the serving layer, because each distributed (or NoSQL) database has its own strengths, and you need to make sure it matches your data.

Speed Layer

The serving layer updates after the batch layer finishes processing a batch view. This means that the only data not included in the updated batch view is the data that was added while the update (for batch view) was processing. The purpose of the speed layer is to make that data available—and quickly (as the name suggests).

The basic functionality of a speed layer is similar to the batch layer, since it also produces views based on data it receives. The difference is that the speed layer only processes new or recent data that's not processed by the batch layer, whereas the batch layer uses all the data for computing the views. Another difference is that the batch layer updates a view by recomputing (or rebuilding) it, whereas the speed layer performs incremental processing on a view and only processes the delta (or difference) by comparing it with the last time incremental processing was done.

So, for example, if a view in speed layer was processed at 10:45 p.m. and the next processing is done at 11:00 p.m., then only the data received between 10:45 and 11 will be processed. These processing differences help the speed layer in achieving the smallest latencies possible. Because the speed layer views are almost real time (depending on your processing latency, you may process every five minutes, resulting in processing or data latency of five minutes), you can also term them as real-time views.

Therefore, you see that you have a system that is almost real time and can answer any queries correctly, yet it offers all the benefits of a Hadoop-based system. Figure 1-6 shows how a query can provide results at almost real time using the workflow of Lambda architecture.

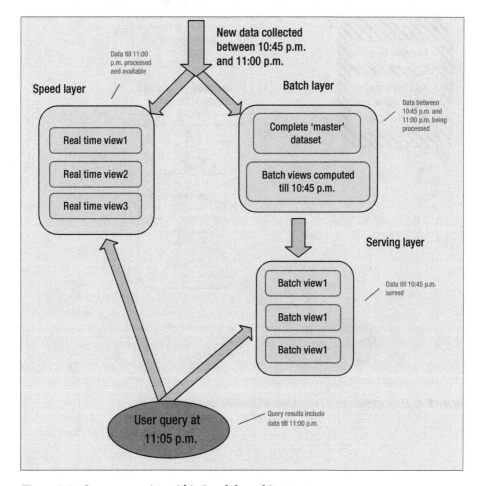

Figure 1-6. Query processing within Lambda architecture

The last thing to remember (about the Lambda architecture) is that the speed layer is disposable. Any new data also triggers processing within the batch layer, and while the real-time views are being used (from the speed layer), recomputation of views continues within the batch layer. Once those batch views (from the batch layer) are recomputed and served by the serving layer, parts of real-time views are not needed (because that data is already available through batch views) and can be discarded. So, for the preceding example, if the batch views are completely processed by 11:15 p.m., then any query after 11:15 p.m. will be processed as shown in Figure 1-7.

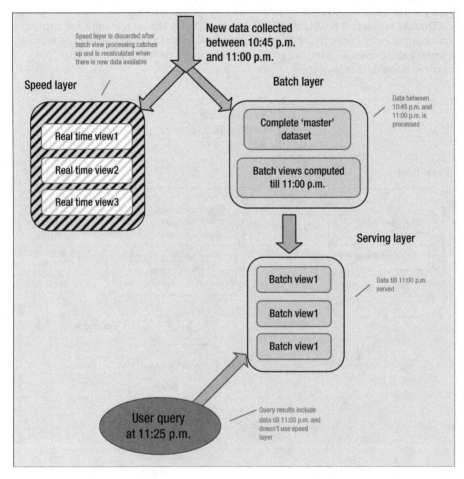

Figure 1-7. Disposable speed layer within Lambda architecture

Lambda architecture supports a property called *complexity isolation*, which pushes processing complexity to layers whose results are temporary. Because the speed layer involves much more processing complexity (compared to the batch or serving layers), the fact that speed layer results are temporary agrees philosophically with the architecture. Also, in case of any data or processing issues, the entire contents of the speed layer can easily be discarded and rebuilt quickly.

I discuss Lambda architecture in more detail in Chapter 8, and there is also a case study in Chapter 15.

Transition to Hadoop/NoSQL

Transition implies migrating an existing application (possibly using RDBMS for data storage and processing) to a Hadoop/NoSQL-based environment. You can leverage the re-architecting technique described in the last section, but there's an additional step involved: data migration. Also, you don't have to use Lambda architecture for your new system. You can select a suitable NoSQL database for use (based on your functional need and data volumes) and simply have your application front-end interface write to it. Of course, you have to make sure your front end can write data in a format acceptable to the NoSQL database and can also read data from it.

A large number of NoSQL databases are available (about 150 as listed by `nosql-database.org`), and they vary greatly in functionality and features. This section talks about some of the criteria you can use to select the most appropriate NoSQL database for your purposes.

Type of Data

You need to consider the type of data you plan to collect and store within your NoSQL database. Unlike RDBMS, NoSQL databases don't have a uniform way of storing data. Actually, they don't even use the same model for data storage. For example, NoSQL databases like MongoDB are document stores or document databases. It is important to choose a NoSQL database that matches the type of data you have.

Broadly, there are four types of NoSQL databases:

- **Key-value store:** These databases store data as key-value pairs with a hash table to index and manage the data. Prominent examples include Riak and Amazon DynamoDB.

- **Document store:** A *document* is a set of key-value pairs. These database systems store data as documents within databases (collection of documents). Examples: MongoDB and CouchDB.

- **Column store:** Data is held and processed in storage blocks that contain data by columns (or groups of columns called column *families*). Examples: HBase and Cassandra.

- **Graph databases:** These databases allow you to store entities (nodes) and relationships (edges) between these entities. Nodes and edges have properties, and edges also have directional significance. A graph lets the data be stored once and then interpreted in different ways based on relationships between nodes. Examples include Neo4J, OrientDB, and FlockDB.

Data Volume

You need to consider the data volume because some NoSQL databases (for example, MongoDB) use memory-based computations for speed (and therefore do not scale horizontally) whereas others do not and therefore can easily scale out. If your data volumes are high, it is probably better to use a solution like Cassandra that can scale out easily.

Data Distribution

You need to consider how widely the data needs to be distributed geographically from a performance perspective. Some NoSQL databases use master/slave (or "primary/secondary") architectures, which can only scale read operations versus peer-to-peer architectures that can scale both reads and writes. So, depending on your application behavior, you can decide which architecture would match your needs.

Migrating the Data

After you decide on an appropriate NoSQL solution, you need to design ETL to migrate the data from your application(s) to the target database. Sometimes it is necessary to build a transition model or a staging database and move the data to it, before migrating to its ultimate destination. There may be multiple reasons for this approach such as a difference in data models of source and target databases or need for denormalizing or transforming the data or simply for performance reasons—the source may have too much data that the target probably can't load in a single iteration or entity. Chapter 7 discusses construction of a transitional model. For now, Figure 1-8 summarizes the steps for transition to Hadoop/NoSQL.

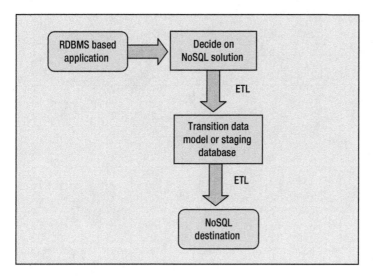

Figure 1-8. *Transition to Hadoop/NoSQL*

Summary

Everyone wants to utilize the power of Big Data in their environment. Unfortunately, decision makers often don't consider all the parameters before concluding that Big Data is right for their organization. Sometimes the lack of proper experience on the part of the technical staff (that provides technical evaluation) is an issue.

Moreover, lack of understanding of NoSQL databases and their nuances is a major issue. It doesn't help that there are no formal frameworks or design methodologies for Hadoop implementations. Lambda is just introduced, but it may not be applicable or useful in all possible scenarios (besides not being easy to implement).

The Hadoop/NoSQL world is ever evolving, innovative, and driven by a lot of smart people. It offers useful technologies and clever solutions for a large variety of problems. You just need to be cognizant of the implementation issues and carefully consider your individual environment and needs before you introduce NoSQL in it—that's all.

In this chapter, I have tried to summarize the pros and cons of Hadoop/NoSQL implementations, and hopefully they will guide you in making the right decisions. Later chapters elaborate on the concepts introduced here.

PART I

Relational Database Management Systems: A Review of Design Principles, Models and Best Practices

CHAPTER 2

■ ■ ■

Understanding RDBMS Design Principles

I always enjoy interviewing the junior members of our database architecture community. I asked someone if he had ever used or heard of "SSADM" (structured systems analysis and design method). The answer was negative, and honestly, it didn't surprise me. I thought the term was probably before his time, or maybe it never got popular in the US (I had used it in earlier part of my career in the UK). But even some of my senior colleagues and friends had not heard of SSADM, or even about Accenture's METHOD/1—which is very American.

My experience working in Chicago clued me in to the lack of awareness and understanding that most corporations have when it comes to database design methodologies. The buzzwords *top-down*, *bottom-up*, and *conceptual to physical model* were the extent that most of the corporate database designers (that I knew) indulged in. Subsequently, I have also seen the effects of that apathy when it comes to making design changes to an application or tracking the origin of some of the changes made.

Database design, however, is not all about the methodologies. It's about the implementation of these frameworks. More importantly, it's about creating the best design for automating and accurately representing a business process and collecting/storing the data that's the result of executing that business process. Design methods should be used as a reference, and any variations needed for effective implementation should be made. For example, you may know that none of the leading RDBMS (Oracle or Sybase or Microsoft SQL Server) can strictly qualify as "relational" databases because they don't satisfy all the criteria as specified by E.F. Codd in his paper "A Relational Model of Data for Large Shared Data Banks."

So, it's good to follow the frameworks as guidelines. But functional accuracy and performance of a system are more important—and a good database designer knows that. For almost 50 years now, "relational" databases are the most popular databases, and the new NoSQL technology can't offer some of the design flexibility and ease of use that are the highlight of RDBMS. Of course, NoSQL has many advantages too, but it helps to understand the strengths of RDBMS through the robustness and descriptiveness of its frameworks—the design methodologies.

What exactly are these methodologies, and how do they facilitate design? I will start with some of the popular design approaches (which can't be termed *methodology*) and then discuss some more extensive and descriptive design methodologies.

B. Lakhe, *Practical Hadoop Migration*, DOI 10.1007/978-1-4842-1287-5_2

27

One last thought before I start with the overview of design methodologies. Why spend time understanding the older relational technology and design if the ultimate aim is to work with the cutting edge distributed NoSQL database technology? Well, in my opinion, it will assist you in transitioning your applications better. A lot of technical resources don't get a chance to understand relational design techniques (especially with the advent of newer technologies), and the initial chapters provide an overview that will provide a quick information refresh, in some cases. In others, they provide concise discussion enabling a good understanding of relational design methodologies.

Overview of Design Methodologies

Design methodologies provide a framework around which you can "build" and implement your database designs. You can start with a business requirement, understand business processes, and then build process and data flows. That will lead you to a conceptual and thereafter a logical data model. Finally, implement the logical model to a physical database. Done!

Can you sum up database design in four sentences any better? Well, there's much more to designing a database, since it summarizes the data processing of a certain functional area of your organization. All the entities (tables) map to results of (execution of) a single or multiple business processes, and the process inter-relations are symbolized by relations between entities and their attributes (columns). For example, consider an inventory management system. The Customer tables corresponds to a business process that manages (adds, updates, or deletes) customer details. Sales table corresponds to the sales transactions that customers perform. Subsequently, the relation between Customer and Sales tables accurately corresponds to the relation between processes that manage customer details and ones that manages sales details.

Let me start with a simple design method and then discuss some more complicated ones.

Top-down

The top-down design method starts (as the name indicates) at the top. The system design starts with an overview or list of objectives defining the purpose of the system. This is followed by design of first-level subsystems or modules and then the subsequent level of modules till you reach the last modular level—the entities themselves. A module may have multiple submodules or no modules at all. The details for each of the modules are filled in as last steps, after the whole modular structure is decide on. This design approach is more suitable for new application development or bigger (modular) enhancements to an application.

A good example is an insurance company's requirement of designing a claims archival system. The objectives are: moving claims older than two years to slower, long-term storage (thereby releasing high-speed storage for more productive purposes), modifying reporting and an ad hoc querying system to access archival database for older claims, and shrinking the claims database and rebuilding indexes for better performance. The next section discusses the various levels (of modules) required to achieve our objectives.

Bottom-up

The bottom-up design method starts at the bottom level, or at a lowest business process level. The individual business processes and thereby entities and their groupings derive functionality of a "module" or subsystem level and subsystems (corresponding to business processes for a department or division of an organization) combine to form a logical model. A conceptual model is derived from the logical model and provides a modular view of the system, thereby making it easy to add or modify functionality.

Because this design is developed with modular (or subsystem) isolation, there is always a risk associated with data mismatch or data duplication between the modules. But it is a faster design approach and may save time in some cases. It is more suited for scenarios where new functionality is added to an existing application or there is a need to reuse code or design fragments for quick development.

If you are to implement the claims archival system mentioned earlier using a bottom-up design approach, you will start by designing the actual entities that are required to hold archived data. I discuss this example in greater detail in the next section.

SSADM

Structured systems administration and design methodology is a design methodology every bit as extensive as its name sounds. It starts with a feasibility study and culminates in a physical design accurately depicting the functional need that facilitated the design. The methodology discusses specific details for performing each of the design steps that makes the implementation easy and successful. SSADM was developed by the Office of Government Commerce of British Treasury in early 1980s and follows the waterfall software process model.

The main design steps for SSADM are as follows:

- Feasibility study

- Investigation of the current environment

- Business system options

- Requirements specification

- Technical system options

- Logical design

- Physical design

Again, if you want to use SSADM to design a claims archival system, you will need to start with a feasibility study that will involve evaluation of available disk space and time required for moving the claims data. Investigation of the current environment will involve checking the volume of data that needs to be moved. Business and technical system options are not relevant in this case, as the functionality of the same system (or application) is being extended. Requirements specifications will have details of the functionality required—design details for new archival objects and queries to archive data, modifications to query/reporting system to use new archival objects as needed, and instructions for shrinking/reindexing the claims database. Logical and physical design will have the structures for newly designed archival objects.

Exploring Design Methodologies

The objective of a design method is to accurately represent the business processes and their data storage needs for a business. There are a number of ways to make sure that your approach results in a correct model: the data-driven model, process-driven model, blended (combination of data- and process-driven), object-oriented, prototyping (RAD—rapid application development), and agile. In practice, object-oriented design is not used for databases any more (because object-oriented databases are not used), and mostly blended models are used, unless the organization is in a hurry and wants a prototype ready quickly. A combination of top-down and bottom-up is usualy used, rather than one method.

Top-down

Top-down design approach is about planning and achieving a good understanding of the objectives for designing the system. It was conceptualized in the 1970s by Harlan Mills and Niklaus Wirth at IBM. Pros and cons to this approach are as follows. First the pros: it starts with objectives/overview of the system and thus helps in designing a more cohesive system, it develops better interfacing between modules, and design modularity facilitates a complete and documented coverage of necessary functionality. Now the cons: the main issue with this design approach is the development time needed. Also, until the modules have reached the final or entity level, design activities can't start.

A design method usually starts at the requirements phase (because unless a database is "required," you can't design it). I have seen two extremes for the requirement phase. Either the client wants to start with a conceptual model right away and skip the requirement gathering and documentation, or the client spends too much time gathering requirements to make sure there is no need to refer back to the users of the system being designed. You need to make sure high-level requirements are documented, but don't spend too much time on the details because they are bound to change.

Of course, it might also help to broadly classify them. For example, some requirements can't be implemented directly, like "system needs to be easily extensible without redesigning it." These are the "not implementable" requirements. The second category is the "implementable" ones—"The system needs to automatically include a new product in appropriate product catalog." The last one is 'conflicting' requirements like "every new product needs to be included in the main catalog" and "seasonal products should not be included in the main product catalog." Finally, if your development phases are already planned, it helps to classify requirements by phases as well. For example, "row level security is only needed in phase 2."

The next step is using the requirements to document the objectives and build a first level of modules or subsystems that will lead toward building a conceptual model (since the top-down approach involves starting with a generic model that covers all the high level requirements or objectives). In this case, the objectives are as follows:

1. Moving claims older than two years to slower, long-term storage (thereby releasing high speed storage for more productive purposes)

2. Modifying reporting and ad hoc querying system to access archival claims objects for older claims (since now the claims data is distributed in two sets of entities)

3. Shrinking claims database and rebuilding indexes (for better performance)

So, the first level modules will be:

- Archival system

- Modifications to query and reporting system

- Database maintenance

For modules "modifications to query and reporting system" and "database maintenance," the second level modules will be modified scripts and new scripts for database maintenance (shrinking, rebuilding indexes, and so on) respectively.

The second level modules for "archival system" will be:

- Designing new archival objects

- Designing queries to archive data

The third and lowest level will be designing the actual archival objects and queries themselves. For that purpose, it will help to have a conceptual model. But how do you build a conceptual model?

For a top-down design approach, you can start with a generic model that covers all your high level requirements. But how can you choose a generic model that matches your requirements? Well, to start with, you can use a conceptual model (available for your organization) for a functional area that broadly matches your requirements or objectives. If no such model is available, you can review the enterprise conceptual model (covering all application areas) and choose a part of it that matches your requirements or objectives.

Assuming that either of the previously mentioned models is available, you can choose appropriate "entity groups" (for matching "subject areas" that cover your objectives or business requirements). If you consider the claims archival system example from the previous section, you can use the "claims processing" subject area as a generic model to start with. Figure 2-1 shows the conceptual model for claims processing.

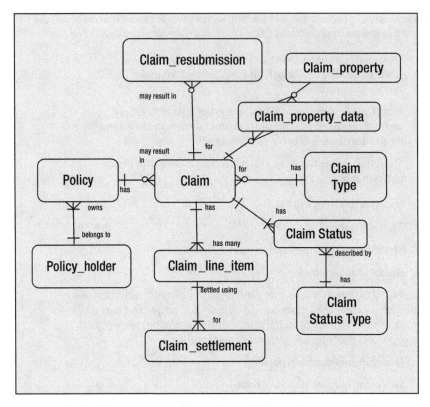

Figure 2-1. *Conceptual model for claims processing*

As a next step, you can remove the processing from the generic model that does not concur with your requirements or objectives. In this case, you simply need to archive all the claims data that is more than two years old. So, you need to focus on the group of entities that hold claims data. Also, because claims data is related and distributed in normalized entities, it is important to make sure that all the related entities are archived and all related records are archived. In the conceptual model, you can safely start with all the entities starting with Claim and evaluate them.

Consider Claim (claim details), Claim_resubmission (resubmitted claims), Claim_ line_item (claim lifecycle details), or Claim_settlement (settlement details for a claim). All these entities are related and hold time-bound claim details. Therefore, they should be considered for archival. Claim_type, Claim_property_data, Claim_property, and Claim_ status_type are static reference values that are not time-bound, but they may change in the future, and it is still important to archive them. So, if you decide that and create a logical model (the next step per the design methodology), it will look like Figure 2-2.

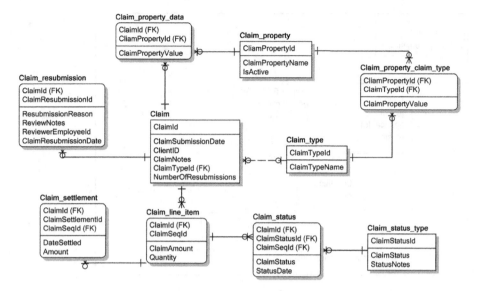

Figure 2-2. *Logical model for claims processing*

The last step for this design methodology is generating a physical model using the logical model. Because you want to differentiate between the regular Claims entities and the ones used for archival, you might want to consider adding a prefix like arch for the entities used for archival. Case tools such as Erwin can help you forward engineer (or transform) your logical model to a physical model depending on the RDBMS of your choice.

For example, if Microsoft SQL Server is chosen as the target RDBMS, then SQL Server data types will be used. Again, Erwin can generate Transact-SQL scripts to create the tables (along with primary and foreign keys for referential integrity) within your SQL Server database. That's the final task for the module "Designing new archival objects." The other module "Designing queries to archive data" will have tasks to write queries for moving the data to the newly created archival objects.

If you are familiar with software process models, you will notice that the top-down design methodology works similarly to the software process model build-and-fix. As with the build-and-fix model, you start with business requirements and build the first version of a system. By the time your detailed modular design and individual tasks are complete along with build, business requirements may change and you need to iteratively modify your system to incorporate all the latest requirements as well as changes to previous ones. Figure 2-3 shows the process model.

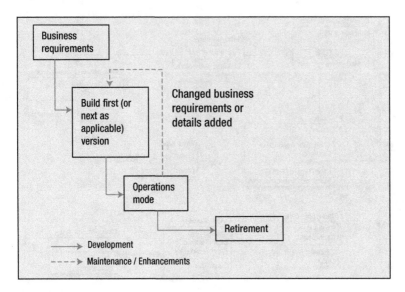

Figure 2-3. *Software process models: build-and-fix model*

Bottom-up

If you review the project plans of projects you have recently worked on (as well as the design task details), you will realize that you can't determine the design approach that was used. Even after you have a discussion with the data architect or enterprise architect, it will be evident to you that a single design approach was not used. Rather, a mixed design approach was employed, most probably a combination of top-down and bottom-up.

Big software projects start with specific high level business requirements and objectives and proceed with module design, following the top-down approach. However, the strategy disintegrates quickly since the module leads want to complete their individual tasks within the stipulated time and hence want to reuse existing code and sometimes even existing modules. This adds the bottom-up approach to the mix. In some cases, the functionality of an operational system is expanded to match the objectives of the system being designed.

Using the bottom-up design approach, the initial focus is on the lowest modular level or individual entities that form the basis of higher level modules. After designing these entities, they are grouped to form next level modules. This process is continued till a hierarchical or modular system is complete that delivers the necessary functionality. This is like knowing broadly what a machine is supposed to do and designing individual modules in great detail that provide parts of the required functionality. In the end, you hope that the combined functionality provided by the individual modules matches what is required as the machine's functionality—and that the modules interface with each other perfectly.

A big advantage of this approach is reusability and the time/money it might save. Of course, the designer needs to have the necessary experience (or intuition) to decide on modular functionality.

Let's talk about how you can implement the claims archival example (discussed in the last section) using a bottom-up approach. To start with, you will need to review the claims processing conceptual model and decide which entities need to be archived. Once you have decided that, you need to design the archival entities. Prefixing them with arch (to differentiate from regular claims entities), you can design entities such as arch_claim_item, arch_claim_resubmission, arch_claim_settlement, and so on. You can validate (start/end validity) to all the reference or metadata entities like Claim_type or Claim_status_type.

Next will be the design of the process required to populate these entities and removing the archived records from associated claim tables, claim_item, claim_resubmission, and claim_settlement. After that, the new entities can be added to the logical model and finally to the conceptual model as grouping Archival.

Now, since any claim-related query or report needs to read from regular as well as archived claims data, the reporting system needs to be modified to read from the correct objects based on dates the report is requested for. That will be the next module of this new system.

Finally, because a large amount of data is removed from existing database objects and added to the new ones, database maintenance must be performed to ensure that database performance is not affected. That will be the last module of the new system. So, finally, the claims-processing system can have a new top level module called Archival.

If you review carefully, you will realize that we have designed the same system, but by performing the same steps in opposite order. This design method resembles a software process model called incremental, shown in Figure 2-4.

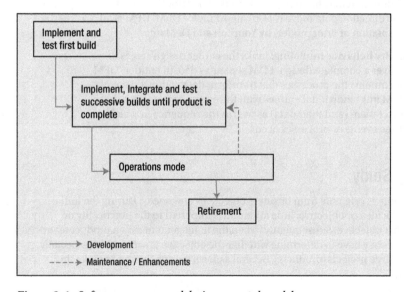

Figure 2-4. *Software process models: incremental model*

As you can see from Figure 2-4, sthis ystem is built incrementally using successive builds till you complete all the development (required to provide the necessary functionality). You can think of this approach as a sequence of agile scrums, too.

SSADM

In the 1970s, the initial attempts for establishing design methods or frameworks were simply an attempt to automate the manual systems. They just imitated the logical business flow and thus didn't add much value. These semi-formal design methods contained redundant and duplicate information, lacked clarity of method (no well-defined steps), and had a number of inconsistencies. SSADM was the first attempt toward formalizing the design strategy. Initiated in 1981, the current version of SSADM is V4.2 launched in 1995. SSADM uses three main techniques for design:

- **Logical data modeling:** During this LDM stage, the data needs of the system (being designed) are identified and documented. Next, a model is designed by separating data into entities (specific information that a business process generates and needs to be recorded) and relationships (the association between entities).

- **Data flow modeling:** As the names suggests, focuses on data movements within a system. More specifically, data flow modeling (DFM) depicts the processes or activities that transform data while considering all the data stores as well as external entities that may be sources or targets of data for the system. The direction data move is also important for DFM. DFM is an adaptation of prior models by Yourdon and DeMarco.

- **Entity behavior modeling:** Links the earlier design stages to deliver a complete design. LDM separates data in entities. DFM documents the processes that transform data within a system. EBM links individual entities with the events or processes that affect them (and their data) as well as the sequence in which these events or processes occur.

Feasibility Study

Projects or products originate from business objectives and needs. During the initial discussion of the idea or objective, little attention is imparted to the practicality or feasibility of that objective. Subsequently, when the management asks a product team to implement it, they have to determine whether the objective is achievable (especially for potentially large projects/products). Several aspects are considered to make this determination:

- *Technical*—Is the product or project technically viable?

- *Monitory*—Does the organization have the necessary budget available to execute the project?

- *Compatibility*—Will the new product interface easily with existing systems within the organization?

- *Integrity*—Will the new product compromise the professional (or moral) integrity of the organization in any way?

The output from this stage is a feasibility study document. As per SSADM guidelines, this document should also contain details of all the options that were considered for a feasibility study (including the ones that were rejected and the reason for rejection).

Investigation of the Current Environment

This involves referring to existing application documentation, exploring the current application, and conducting discussions with application users, developers, and administrators to develop a good understanding of the system. This helps in the following:

- Understanding business terminology

- Understanding frequently used application features and how they are used

- Developing a data model

- Defining the scope of the application

The outputs from this stage are requirement details (for the new system or application), existing services and user details, logical and physical data models, data flow diagram, and a data dictionary (all for the existing system).

Business System Options

At this stage, the analyst compares the requirements and objectives (for developing the new system) with the functionality of the existing system. It may be possible to modify the existing system slightly to match the objectives, or it may be necessary to develop a completely new system to achieve the objectives and satisfy the requirements.

As an output from this stage, the analyst develops and presents a number of possible business system options to achieve the necessary objectives.

Requirements Specification

This is arguably the most important and most complex step. One reason is that the analyst needs to have all the details of logical specifications of the proposed system. It is of course important to have these specifications error-free, unambiguous, consistent, and concise.

Another reason this step is complex is that the analyst needs to build a logical data model (at least the entity-relationship diagram) as well as a data flow diagram (DFD) to make sure that the logical specifications are accurate, even though they are not the expected outputs from this stage.

The output from this stage is a comprehensive requirements specification document.

Technical System Options

In an earlier stage, the analyst had enough information to propose possible business options. Now with the technical requirements ready and available, it is possible for the analyst to present a number of technical system options that can be used. These options are evaluated, and the best possible option is selected before moving on to the next stage.

Logical Design

This design stage specifies the logical map of processes pertaining to the proposed application and also the entities affected by those processes. Information about the data and inter-relationships is included as well.

The outputs from this stage are:

- Data dictionary

- Logical data model

- Logical process model

Physical Design

The final stage of SSADM uses the logical design specifications (from the last stage) and translates them into physical database structures (for the proposed implementation target like Oracle or Microsoft SQL Server). This involves:

- Attaching database-specific datatypes for columns

- Implementing referential integrity constraints using primary keys, foreign keys or triggers (discussed in the next section), and nullability

- Defining indexes and specifying function details (structure as well as implementation)

- Listing the hardware and software requirements

The output from this stage is complete physical design that the implementation team (including administrators) can use to build the required system.

So, these are the stage details for SSADM. I will discuss an example (and complete design) using SSADM as a design method. As with any other design method, there are pros and cons to using SSADM.

Pros and Cons of SSADM

SSADM provides the following advantages:

- Excellent isolation between logical and physical design of the system. Benefits are:

  - Freedom to implement logical design using the database of your choice.

  - Isolation of issues between logical and physical designs. In fact, if you identify issues with your logical design after physical implementation, you can modify the physical implementation to resolve the issues.

- Clearly defined and well-documented steps that lead to a complete design

- Involvement of a wide range of resources (analysts, business users, administrators, application users, and developers) offers a good perspective that reflects in design and also reduces possibility of error (in understanding or implementing the requirements)

Now the cons:

- The implementation time for SSADM is long, and any changes need to be processed through all the stages. For example, if requirements change while the physical design is being worked on, you need to start with checking feasibility of those requirements, check whether they are already implemented in existing system, change requirement specifications, and then apply changes to logical/physical data models.

- There is considerable cost and time involved in training resources to use SSADM and implement using it.

As a closing thought, I want you to review the waterfall software process model and consider the similarities between it and SSADM. Similar to SSADM, the waterfall model is comprehensive with a large number of steps. As you can see in Figure 2-5, changes to requirements or specifications involve rework to all the subsequent stages, which can be time consuming (although it does help maintain consistency within your system—at any stage, requirement specifications match the existing physical system).

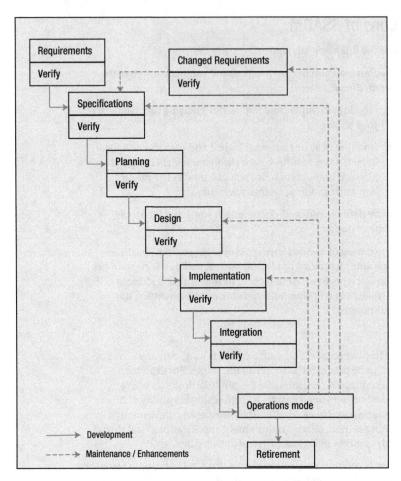

Figure 2-5. *Software process models: waterfall model*

Components of Database Design

It's time to focus on primary constructs used for relational database design. You will need to use them at the conceptual and logical design stage. I am sure you have used primary keys or foreign keys or triggers for some database development project before, but it is still interesting to see where these components fit in the scope of relational design. Constructs like supertypes or subtypes are not very frequently used (or at least not understood), and constructs like cardinality or self-referencing relationships need to be completely understood in order to design well.

The most discussed relational concept is *normal forms*. It is a highlight of relational design but sadly is still not very clear to a lot of designers. I will discuss the three normal forms with an example. I will also cover Boyce Code normal form (BCNF) briefly for your understanding, even though it's mostly theoretical and rarely used in practice.

Finally, you need to understand that holding your data in third normal form is not always the best option. For reporting or warehousing, you need to denormalize data. I discuss that concept with an example too.

Normal Forms

Normalization is a process that efficiently organizes data by identifying and removing any data redundancy, keeping cross-references (within data) intact. The objective is to remove data redundancy completely and gain better organization of data. Normalization is a multistep process, and depending on how much of this process is applied to the data, it is said to be in *first*, *second*, or *third* normal forms.

There are higher forms of normalization, such as BCNF, fourth normal form, and fifth normal form, although they are theoretical and rarely used in real world.

First Normal Form

The objective of first normal form is to identify and isolate any repeating groups of data to separate tables, of course, keeping cross-references to source data intact. A data row may have one or more repeating groups, and as a first step you need to identify them. Here's an example. Consider an insurance company that sells health insurance. Customers who own valid policies file claims using a toll-free phone number answered by the company's call center. Based on a short conversation, here's what's captured typically for a claim:

```
ClaimId, ClaimSubmissionDate, CustomerName, DateOfBirth,
SocialSecurityNumber, CustomerAddress, ClaimNotes, ClaimType,
ClaimShortDesc1, PhysicianId1, ClaimShortDesc2, PhysicianId2,
ClaimShortDesc3, PhysicianId3, NumberOfResubmissions
```

ClaimId is a system-generated number that increments for each new claim. ClaimType indicates type of the claim (such as dental, vision, medical, and so forth), ClaimShortDesc (1–3) have short descriptions of the actual complaints as the claim progresses and the complaint is referred to another physician or a specialist. PhysicianId (1–3) are identifiers for the physicians involved in the treatment of the patient. A claim may have one or more (up to three) medical conditions and physicians associated with it. NumberOfResubmissions has a count of how many times this claim has been resubmitted for processing. Here is some sample data:

13666969, 6/1/2015 09:30:13, Bobby Simpson, 02/12/1964, 219-44-3211, 1 Oak st. Darien IL 60561, Consulted Physician out of network since closest and then a specialist, Medical, **Severe stomach pain, 43211, Cramp of abdominal muscles, 12456, NULL, NULL,** 0

13666970, 6/1/2015 10:00:23, Alan Border, 03/22/1961, 239-32-5674, 21 Maple st. Naperville IL 60563, Cause of pain still not determined, Medical, **Pain in left shoulder, 31341, Left shoulder dislocation, 11232, Physiotherapy, 54543,** 1

13666971, 6/1/2015 10:05:11, Steve Waugh, 12/14/1970, 246-56-9867, 32 Madison ct. Woodridge IL 60517, Most probably seasonal allergies, Vision, **Dry itchy eyes, 73443, Eye infection, 33342, NULL, NULL,** 0

13666972, 6/1/2015 11:29:16, Ricky Ponting, 10/03/1965, 223-43-7658, 54 Argyle st. Westmont IL 60559, Dentist recommended removing tooth; but patient not agreeing, Dental, **Severe pain in maxillary first molar, 41414, NULL, NULL, NULL, NULL,** 1

13666973, 6/1/2015 12:09:18, Bobby Simpson, 02/12/1964, 219-44-3211, 1 Oak st. Darien IL 60561, Referred to Ophthalmologist by regular Optometrist, Vision, **Double vision, 33562, Change of prescription, 25251, NULL, NULL,** 0

13666974, 6/1/2015 14:06:41, Ricky Ponting, 10/03/1965, 223-43-7658, 54 Argyle st. Westmont IL 60559, Most probably seasonal allergies, Vision, **Dry itchy eyes, 63462, NULL, NULL, NULL, NULL,** 0

A quick review of the data will make you realize that this data has a repeating group (marked in bold) and subsequently data duplication. It has some other issues as well (which I discuss a little later). The repeating block of data is medical conditions and physician details associated with a claim.

Also, with this table design, there's a provision to capture up to three medical conditions and associated physicians. But what happens if more than three medical conditions are associated with a claim? Since it happens rarely, designers of this system asked call center representatives to open a new claim and refer to that new number in the notes section of the current claim! That is a bad workaround, and this design issue needs to be resolved.

To get this table in first normal form, you need to move the medical condition data to a separate table. Will that resolve the other issue (of associating more than three medical conditions with a claim) too? Let's see.

Now, before we move the repeating data to a new table, you need to make sure you can cross-reference it and also that it still relates to the correct claim. First, see if you can you identify each row of data uniquely for your Claims table. In this case, you can; since the ClaimId is a system-generated unique number and can be used to identify a row uniquely. Such an identifier is known as a *primary key*, and the column can be designated as such.

Next, you need to identify rows uniquely for the new table. Since there are multiple medical conditions associated with a single claim, just the ClaimId won't suffice as a primary key. You will need to add a sequence number additionally to make the primary key unique. Besides, in this case, sequence does have significance (since it stores the sequence in which the medical conditions were diagnosed for a claim) and may be useful for analysis.

So, after moving data to a new table (call it ClaimMCdata), the new tables will look like Figures 2-6 and 2-7.

Claims

ClaimId	Claim Submission Date	Customer Name	DateOf Birth	Social Security Number	Customer Address	ClaimNotes	ClaimType	NumberOf Resubmis sions
13666969	6/1/2015 09:30:13	Bobby Simpson	02/12/1964	219-44-3211	1 Oak st. Darien IL 60561	Consulted Physician out of network since closest and then a specialist	Medical	0
13666970	6/1/2015 10:00:23	Alan Border	03/22/1961	239-32-5674	21 Maple st. Naperville IL 60563	Cause of pain still not determined	Medical	1
13666971	6/1/2015 10:05:11	Steve Waugh	12/14/1970	246-56-9867	32 Madison ct. Woodridge IL 60517	Most probably seasonal allergies	Vision	0
13666972	6/1/2015 11:29:16	Ricky Ponting	10/03/1965	223-43-7658	54 Argyle st. Westmont IL 60559	Dentist recommended removing tooth; but patient not agreeing	Dental	1
13666973	6/1/2015 12:09:18	Bobby Simpson	02/12/1964	219-44-3211	1 Oak st. Darien IL 60561	Referred to Opthalmologist by regular Optometrist	Vision	0
13666974	6/1/2015 14:06:41	Ricky Ponting	10/03/1965	223-43-7658	54 Argyle st. Westmont IL 60559	Most probably seasonal allergies	Vision	0

Figure 2-6. *Claims data in first normal form*

ClaimMCdata

ClaimId	CMCdataSeqNum	ClaimShortDesc	PhysicianId
13666969	1	Severe stomach pain	43211
13666969	2	Cramp of abdominal muscles	12456
13666970	1	Pain in left shoulder	31341
13666970	2	Left shoulder dislocation	11232
13666970	3	Physiotherapy	54543
13666971	1	Dry itchy eyes	73443
13666971	2	Eye infection	33342
13666972	1	Severe pain in maxillary first molar	41414
13666973	1	Double vision	33562
13666973	2	Change of prescription	25251
13666974	1	Dry itchy eyes	63462

Figure 2-7. *Medical condition data moved to a separate table*

After the removal of repeating groups from Claims, you can see that the data is more manageable (as shown in Figures 2-6 and 2-7). Also, you must have observed that the new table ClaimMCdata doesn't need to have multiple columns like ClaimShortDesc1, PhysicianId1, and so on. You can simply add a row per medical condition for a claim, without being limited by three medical conditions. So, the design issue for a claim having more than three medical conditions is resolved as well.

The table Claims is now in first normal form, but you do need to think about the next normal form—and how to get there.

Second Normal Form

The formal definition for an entity to be in second normal form is if all of its non-key attributes are individually dependent on the group of key attributes only and not dependant on a part of that key attribute group. In other words, an entity is in second normal form if its non-key attributes are free from any partial-key dependencies or no part of the key determines a non-key attribute.

So, it is easy to see that entities with a single attribute as key are automatically in second normal form (as there are no partial-key dependencies possible). That is also the reason a system-generated sequential number (used as an identifier) serves well as a primary key.

For the entity (or table) Claims, since the system generated identifier (ClaimId) is used as a primary key, it is automatically in second normal form. For the other entity ClaimMCdata, the primary key is a combination of ClaimId and CMCdataSeqNum, and it is easy to see that there are no partial-key dependencies, and it is in second normal form too.

Third Normal Form

An entity is in third normal form if and only if no non-key column (or group of columns) determines another non-key column (or group of columns), and all the non-key columns are determined by (or functionally dependent on) the group of key columns only. In other words, both these conditions need to be satisfied:

- All non-key items dependent only on group of key columns

- No non-key columns (or group) dependent on another non-key column (or group)

Are the entities Claims and ClaimMCdata in third normal form? For the entity Claims, if you review columns sequentially, you will observe that fourth column DateOfBirth functionally depends on non-key column SocialSecurityNumber instead of the key column ClaimId. The columns CustomerName and CustomerAddress depend on column SocialSecurityNumber too. Because this violates the requirements for third normal form, you need to move these columns to a separate entity. Call it CustomerDetails. Now, if you move all the customer information columns to a separate entity, how will you cross-reference it for a claim? You need an identifier for each customer record that can be placed within a claim record and reference the customer information located in CustomerDetails. You can use a system-generated sequential number as identifier and call it CustomerId.

If you review the ClaimMCdata entity, you will realize that it is already in third normal form. The non-key attributes ClaimShortDesc and PhysicianId are dependent on the key attributes ClaimId and CMCdataSeqNum only and no other non-key attributes.

So, after moving the customer data columns from the Claims entity, Figure 2-8 shows how Claims and CustomerDetails will look.

Claims (third normal form)

ClaimId	ClaimSubmission Date	CustomerId	ClaimNotes	ClaimType	NumberOfResubmissions
13666969	6/1/2015 09:30:13	63678348	Consulted Physician out of network since closest and then a specialist	Medical	0
13666970	6/1/2015 10:00:23	97769325	Cause of pain still not determined	Medical	1
13666971	6/1/2015 10:05:11	52562723	Most probably seasonal allergies	Vision	0
13666972	6/1/2015 11:29:16	98428998	Dentist recommended removing tooth; but patient not agreeing	Dental	1
13666973	6/1/2015 12:09:18	63678348	Referred to Ophthalmologist by regular Optometrist	Vision	0
13666974	6/1/2015 14:06:41	98428998	Most probably seasonal allergies	Vision	0

CustomerDetails

CustomerId	CustomerName	DateOfBirth	SocialSecurity Number	CustomerAddress
63678348	Bobby Simpson	02/12/1964	219-44-3211	1 Oak st. Darien IL 60561
97769325	Alan Border	03/22/1961	239-32-5674	21 Maple st. Naperville IL 60563
52562723	Steve Waugh	12/14/1970	246-56-9867	32 Madison ct. Woodridge IL 60517
98428998	Ricky Ponting	10/03/1965	223-43-7658	54 Argyle st. Westmont IL 60559

Figure 2-8. *Claims and CustomerDetails data in third normal form*

If you review the entities again (Figure 2-8), you will discover that you can apply both the conditions for third normal form successfully to entities Claims, ClaimMCdata, and CustomerDetails.

Keys in Relational Design

Keys have special usage and purpose within relational design. A *key* is an alphanumeric pattern or a column value that identifies (or references) a data row uniquely either partially or completely. So, a key can be used to identify a data row (primary key), serve as alternate or candidate key (columns that can be possibly used as whole or part of primary key), be a foreign key (cross-reference), or a surrogate key (system-generated sequential or random numbers, transparent to users).

Let's go through each of these using the entity design from the last section. In case you are new to IE notation for logical models, the columns above the line (within the entity box) are primary key columns. As you can see in Figure 2-9, ClaimId is the *primary key* for entity Claims, and CustomerId is the primary key for entity CustomerDetails. These (as mentioned) are system-generated numbers guaranteed to be unique for that column and hence can be used for identifying a data row uniquely. As per the definition for a *surrogate key*, ClaimId and CustomerId are good examples of surrogate keys, which are used (or generated) in cases where no *natural key* (combination of columns that can uniquely identify a data row) exists.

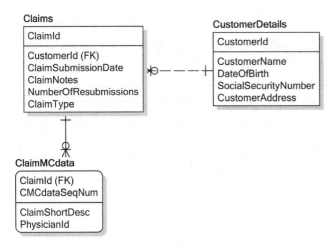

Figure 2-9. *Primary and foreign keys for claims processing*

In the case of `ClaimMCdata`, since a claim can have multiple medical conditions associated with it, I added `CMCdataSeqNum` (sequence number) as part of the primary key to make it uniquely identify a data row.

The `CustomerDetails` entity has an example of *alternate key* or *candidate key* as shown in Figure 2-9. As you are aware, a system-generated identifier called *CustomerId* is used as primary key. But it is also possible to use the `SocialSecurityNumber` column as a key, since it can uniquely identify a customer. In this case, you don't need to worry about moving the column to a separate table, as there are no attributes only dependent on `SocialSecurityNumber`.

You may recall that before I moved all the customer information to a separate entity `CustomerDetails`, I placed an identifier called `CustomerId` within a claim record, so that you can cross-reference information for the customer who filed it using it. `CustomerId` is of course the primary identifier or primary key for entity `CustomerDetails`. This key that's used for cross-referencing information from another entity is known as a *foreign key*. For IE notation, a foreign key column is marked with `FK` within parentheses. Another foreign key you can see is `ClaimId` for entity `ClaimMCdata`. It references the claim information the medical condition information belongs to.

Optionality and Cardinality

Optionality and cardinality are diagramming conventions for describing relationships. For example, consider the following relation between `Claims` and `ClaimMCdata`. The crow's foot means many and the absence of it means one. That's the cardinality of a relation. Also, the circle means optional and the bar means mandatory. That's the optionality of a relation.

Subsequently, the relation can be read as "a claim may result in none or many medical condition records." It can also be read as "a claim medical condition record will always have a corresponding claim record exist for it."

While considering dependencies, a relationship that "identifies" the records in the child table or dependent table is an identifying relationship. The child table inherits the primary key of the parent and may need to supplement it with an attribute for uniqueness. In Figure 2-10, Claims has an identifying relationship with ClaimMCdata and as you see, ClaimMCdata had to supplement its primary key with a sequence number for uniqueness (since a claim record may be inherited by many ClaimMCdata records).

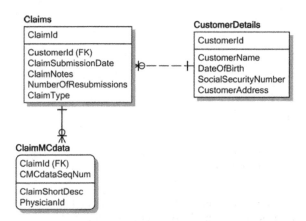

Figure 2-10. *Optionality and cardinality in Claims processing*

There are non-identifying relationships too. For example, the relation between Claims and CustomerDetails entities discussed earlier is a non-identifying relation. A CustomerDetails record is not inherited by a Claim record; the foreign key attribute CustomerId simply acts as a pointer or cross-reference to customer details for the customer who filed the claim. The non-identifying nature of the relationship is indicated by a dotted line (instead of solid) and by CustomerId not being a part of the primary key for Claim.

Now, all the relations from the preceding model are of one-to-many or zero-to-may cardinality. What happens if there's a relation that has "many-to-many" cardinality? You need to use a mapping table to break that relation into two one-to-many' relations. Consider the following part of claims processing logical model shown in Figure 2-11. The entities Claim and Claim_property have a many-to-many relationship, since a property may be applicable to many claims and a claim may have many properties. To represent this relation within a logical model, you need to create a mapping table Claim_property_ data and map claims with their respective properties and vice versa.

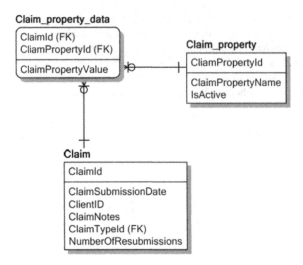

Figure 2-11. *Resolving a many-to-many relationship*

To summarize, optionality and cardinality bring clarity to the relations and help document them better. They also make the logical model more readable and understandable.

Supertypes and Subtypes

Supertypes and subtypes are among the most useful logical constructs for relational design. Supertypes correspond to entity classes (a group or type of multiple entities usually associated with the same business process or used for providing same business functionality) and subtypes represent a different level of entity class too. You can think of supertypes and subtypes as supersets and subsets with respect to entities.

Supertypes and subtypes are best used at the conceptual modeling stage and therefore are well-suited for the top-down design approach. They assist in providing concise documentation of business rules as well as exploring alternative data models. Because subtypes and supertypes are not directly implemented by any RDBMS, you need to break them up in separate entities before the logical or physical data modeling stage.

Here's an example to discuss the concepts of supertype and subtypes. Consider the following part of claims processing logical model (again), as shown in Figure 2-12. To recapitulate, Claim holds the claim data, Claim_type holds all the types for claim (Auto, Health, Home, and so on), and Claim_property holds all the possible properties for claims.

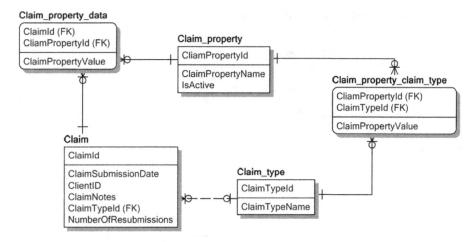

Figure 2-12. *Use of mapping entities to assign properties based on claim type*

As I already explained, the entities Claim and Claim_property have a many-to-many relationship, and Claim_property_data is a mapping table that maps claims with their respective properties. Similarly, Claim_property and Claim_type have a many-to-many relationship, and Claim_property_claim_type is a mapping table that maps claim types with their respective properties.

The purpose of these four tables (Claim_property, Claim_property_data, Claim_type, and Claim_property_claim_type) is to make sure that a specific type of claim only has the necessary properties available to it that are governed by the claim type. For example, a home insurance policy won't have VIN as a property, and an auto policy won't have estimated reconstruction cost as a property.

Is it possible to redesign this part of the logical model using supertypes and subtypes? Yes, if Claim is used as a supertype and the various types of claims (Auto, Health, Home) as subtypes, this part can be redesigned, and the four tables that were added (to accommodate the specific properties of a type of claim) can be removed. The design will look like Figure 2-13.

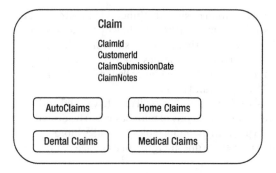

Figure 2-13. *Use of supertypes/subtypes to assign properties based on claim type*

49

The expanded logical model will look like Figure 2-14.

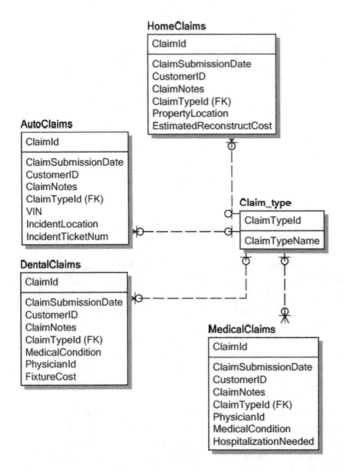

Figure 2-14. *Logical model using supertypes/subtypes for claims processing*

The supertype Claim has a number of common or shared attributes (ClaimId, CustomerId, ClaimSubmissionDate, ClaimNotes) that will be inherited by all the subtypes (AutoClaims, HomeClaims, DentalClaims, MedicalClaims), and the subtypes will have their own specific attributes. So, AutoClaims may have attributes like InsureeVIN, OtherVehicleVIN, IncidentLocation, and TicketNumber, whereas MedicalClaims may have attributes like MedicalCondition, Physician, and so on.

This is another way to ensure that a specific type of claim will only have valid and applicable properties stored for it. There are pros and cons of both designs. The design with separate entities for properties and type (with mapping tables) provides more flexibility, and any addition or removal of properties doesn't result in a change to the logical model. But it is harder to understand and maintain. The design with supertypes and subtypes is much easier to understand and maintain; but inflexible. Any changes to properties of a specific type of claim will result in changes to the entity structure and will be difficult to implement. You can choose the approach that suits your environment.

There are a few things to be noted about supertypes and subtypes that will help you understand these concepts better:

- Subtypes for a (supertype) should be mutually exclusive (non-overlapping) and exhaustive. In the given example, the subtypes (`Auto`, `Home`, `Medical` claims) are mutually exclusive. But if there's a functional overlap, it complicates the design and you need to find ways to remove the overlap.

- Creating partitions is a technique used sometimes to remove overlaps, especially since some CASE tools allow multiple breakdowns (partitions) into complete, non-overlapping subtypes. For example, if the auto and home policies both cover third-party liability and have difference in coverages, it will cause an overlap and possibly need a resolution through partitions (such as auto policies with home coverage, auto policies without home coverage, and home coverage without auto coverage).

- Subtypes and supertypes can participate in relationships (just like entities), but only for a conceptual model (not for logical/physical model, since supertypes/subtypes are not supported directly by any RDBMS).

- Subtypes can be used with several levels of nesting and can form a hierarchy.

I hope this chapter gave you a good orientation of the critical building blocks of relational design. We will be using all these constructs to analyze a real-world business scenario and design a logical/physical model to store the outputs from execution of relevant business processes.

Summary

A lot of people might question coverage of relational database design in this era of NoSQL databases with cutting edge technology and distributed architecture. I personally feel that since most of the database world is still operating within the structure, constraints, and regularity of relational databases, there is relevance to this discussion. Unless you understand what you are using, you can't transform it to what you want it to be. Most of the existing applications were designed a while back and use relational design features extensively. To migrate these applications to a newer technology, you certainly need a good understanding of what features were used and what do they do.

More importantly, there are no tools available for NoSQL design specifically and most of the architects use relational design tools for creating data models that are targeted for NoSQL databases. For example, re-architecting RDBMS data involves denormalization and aggregation of entities (since NoSQL databases are not very good at processing joins). These tasks need to be (and are) performed using relational database modeling tools. Also, unless you understand the concepts of denormalization and aggregation, you can't modify your model to fit a NoSQL solution. That's why it is important to familiarize yourself with the relational design concepts covered in Chapters 2 and 3. As another example, it will be difficult to understand column-based storage of Columnar NoSQL databases or embedded document structure of Document-oriented NoSQL databases unless you understand how normalized data is organized in rows for relational databases. That also means you need to understand the concept of normalization.

Many of the time-tested and useful concepts of relational design are adopted for NoSQL. Knowing and understanding the relational concepts will certainly help you draw parallels with the corresponding NoSQL features and make the learning process easier and more interesting. I will demonstrate how the relational design changes to a more flatter, data duplicated version for implementation into Columnar or Document databases in the later chapters (Chapter 6). Though the data volumes increase (with duplication), you can see how performance enhances for NoSQL solutions.

On a different note, one important thing to remember about frameworks or methodologies is that they are design guidelines or suggestions. You don't need to follow them verbatim, and it is best to adopt them as well as you can for your environment. I have often seen the best designs where architects have used their creativity to supplement the formal design steps with something specifically useful for their purpose.

This chapter summarized the leading design methods and useful components of relational design. I am sure this will assist you in understanding the process of database design using the method SSADM, the topic of the next chapter.

CHAPTER 3

■ ■ ■

Using SSADM for Relational Design

I worked for a British computer company in the 1990s, and it was company policy to use SSADM (Structured Systems Analysis and Design Method) for any new projects. At the time, we were working on a part of the London Underground (also called the *Tube*) automation. I went to my manager with the time estimate for a new module that I was designing. The estimate was high, and he asked, "What are all these tasks for gathering requirement specifications and technical system options?" I said those were SSADM-based tasks. He replied: "We can do the documentation later. Right now, get on with the database design and front-end development." A lot of years later, that attitude has not gone away.

Now for some obvious questions. What's the relevance of SSADM for Hadoop migration? Can you use SSADM with NoSQL databases? Why does it need to be a part of this Hadoop book? Think about this: most of the systems that you may want to interface with or migrate to Hadoop may have used a subset of SSADM for their design. Having a good understanding of SSADM helps you grasp the source system design better.

More importantly, the logical design process remains the same for a system whether you implement it using relational technology or a NoSQL solution. Only the physical implementation steps differ per your chosen target technology. Besides, SSADM is a superset of most of the design techniques used today. So, it will definitely help you to understand the extensive design steps specified by SSADM and will ultimately help you present your design in an organized manner that's also self-documenting.

Because the logical design process is independent of target technology used for implementation, you can use any SSADM-based tools (or in general any relational design tools) for system design—even if you plan to use NoSQL to implement your design. That's also the reason why no specific NoSQL design tools are available.

Getting back to SSADM (and design methodologies in general), formal design methodologies are sometimes intimidating, and the reason is very simple. Architects and modelers try to fit in their designs into the specific steps that a design method has elaborately described. Instead, a designer should use the method as a framework or guideline and supplement the design with specific requirements that are necessary in their environment (and also feel free to omit the steps that are redundant). In case of SSADM, too, the documentation clearly mentions the need to apply (or omit) steps depending on your need.

© Bhushan Lakhe 2016

B. Lakhe, *Practical Hadoop Migration*, DOI 10.1007/978-1-4842-1287-5_3

Moreover, if you think carefully, you will realize that the development process you follow (based on your development/design experience) is not very different from SSADM. It's just not formalized or categorized into specific steps or modules (as in the case of SSADM). For example, you may not do a "feasibility study" and come with a feasibility report, but you will (most probably) make sure that the system (you plan to develop) is technically feasible, required by your organization, and that the management is ready to spend money for its development. This may also be true about most of the SSADM steps.

SSADM is not very popular in the Americas, but the reason I am using it as an example of design methodology is because of its extensiveness and exhaustiveness. I feel it will give you a good understanding of the (formal) process of software development. What you need to be careful about is making sure that you drive the process and not let the process drive you.

You already know the steps that SSADM involves and what they do (at a high level). In this chapter, I discuss a real-world scenario and use the SSADM framework to design a database solution that will efficiently hold the data that the business processes generate (for the scenario I am discussing). So, let's start with the first SSADM module: feasibility study.

Feasibility Study

Informally, you (or your management) always make sure that the system you plan to implement is practically possible. You also make sure your organization is ready to pay the bill. SSADM simply formalizes this process and also helps you create documentation that may be useful in future to record what the business need for this development was.

When you rely on making decisions in an informal manner or when you rely on experience of involved resources, it is possible that you may overlook some aspects that may impact your decision. SSADM makes sure you don't. Also, it will be useful to conduct a feasibility study, irrespective of your implementation target being a RDBMS-based system or a NoSQL-based solution. Therefore, this design stage can be used even for a NoSQL-based system.

So, how do you apply SSADM to conduct a feasibility study for a real-world business scenario? Let me discuss the scenario first.

"YourState Insurance" is a leading insurance company that sells health insurance to its US-based customers. The company's dynamic vice president of marketing, being a former baseball player, wants to add a "Loss of Play" policy for active baseball players and their clubs. Subsequently, he directs his research department, risk management group, and IT architecture group to determine if this new line of business can be profitable. The following are the salient features of the new policy he wants YourState insurance to sell:

- Policy will insure an active player's contract.

- Policy will exclude coverage for any chronic or pre-existing conditions a player is known to have.

- Policy will consider the player's age, past injuries, and schedule while deciding premium.

- Policy will offer coverage within two-year intervals only (for long-term contracts) and price will be adjusted after every two years.

Using SSADM techniques, the IT architect as well as business users from the research department and risk management group have started the feasibility study.

Project Initiation Plan

To start with, an IT project manager (along with the architect) prepared a project initiation document. It contained the following sections:

1. *Introduction*: This section provided the following information:

    a. *Background of the project*: History and what exactly prompted to research the feasibility of this new "Loss of Play" policy

    b. *Goals*: SMART (specific, measurable, achievable, realistic, and time-bounded) objectives

    c. *Project authorization*: Formal email from marketing VP, mandating this project and confirming its sponsorship

2. *Project definition*: Defined all aspects of the project such as the following:

    a. *Key deliverables*: This project will deliver the following key deliverables:

        • Business case (benefits and risk of the new policy) and business system options

        • Requirements specifications

        • Technical system options

        • Data flow diagram

        • Logical data model

        • Logical process model

        • Physical data model (target database)

    b. *Constraints*: This project has the following constraints:

        • Financial budget for this research is capped at $250,000, and this includes employee time

        • The research for this policy will be limited to the state of New York (to start with)

        • This research will be limited to coverage of contracts of $10 million or more (for individual players)

c. *Assumptions*: The following assumptions are made:

- Injury and precondition data for players (to be insured) is available

- Club schedule (for the player to be insured) for next two years is available

d. *Exclusions*: Any baseball club registered or headquartered outside the state of New York is excluded

e. *Interfaces*: This project will have the following interfaces:

- "Baseball Loss of Play" graphical user interface (internal)

- Claims processing system (internal)

f. *External dependencies*: Current dependencies are the following:

- Accessibility to player contracts

- Accessibility to medical history of the player

g. *Tolerance*: Project manager is authorized to expenses up to $250,000, use of three resources for three months starting with commencement of the project.

h. *Benefits*: The main benefit of this project is a possible addition of a new line of business. If found feasible, it will provide expansion to the types of policies offered by YourState insurance company.

i. *Costs*: Initial costs for this project are $160,000

Area	Cost
Project management	$50,000
Infrastructure (hardware/software)	$20,000
IT resources	$40,000
Business resources	$50,000

j. Approach/Process/Execution and milestones:

- *Approach*: The approach for analysis will be based on design methodology SSADM, and the deliverables will closely follow the SSADM modules and corresponding deliverables

- *Milestones*: Again, the milestones correspond closely to SSADM deliverables and are as follows:

  - Feasibility study report

  - Requirements specification

  - Technical system options

- Data and process flow diagrams

- GUI specifications

- Logical data model

- Physical data model

- Graphical user interface

k. *Contingency plans*: In case of any contingencies, a packaged solution (that can be customized for our needs) will be sought

l. Project organization structure:

- SRO (senior responsible owner) for the project is vice president (marketing)

  - Project manager reports to SRO and is also answerable to project board

  - Project team has following members:

Name	Division/Organization
Solution architect	IT
Senior analyst	Research department
Senior analyst	Risk management group

m. Communication and stakeholders:

- *Communication method*: The key communications channels are:

  - Weekly reports

  - Weekly meeting

- *Stakeholders*: The stakeholder map in Note A has the details

n. *Reporting cycle*: Following are the details about reporting for this project:

- *Project initiation*: The project will formally start when the SRO and project board have approved this project initiation document

- Reporting periods:

    - Project team with project manager—weekly

    - Project manager with SRO—monthly

    - SRO with project board—quarterly

- *Decision points*: Key decisions must be taken after each of the milestones

- Exception reporting will be performed by project manager in case agreed tolerances are exceeded

- Project issues will be available in the issue log attached to Note B

- The project will be formally closed by SRO on completion of all milestones or after feasibility study report (if it is not deemed feasible)

- Note A: Stakeholder map

Stakeholder	Interest	Information Requirements
SRO	Sponsor	Details on how milestones are progressing
Business development	Sponsor	Details on how the new policy will benefit the business
IT	Development	Technical details needed to develop the system
Claims department	User	How the new system is used

- Note B: Issue Log

Issue #	Issue title	Description	Logged by	Owner	Action & Progress	Action Date	Status

Requirements and User Catalogue

The requirement and user catalogues serve a very important purpose of documenting functional requirements for a system and the prospective users (along with their roles). These catalogues also provide a quick overview for designers (and users) to make sure all the requirements are documented and accurately reflect the required functionality.

Requirements Catalogue

A requirements catalogue lists all the functional requirements and the non-functional requirements that originate from it. The catalogue entries also list out benefits, related documents, and related requirements for each of the functional requirements. For the current project, here are the entries from the requirements catalogue:

Project: Loss of Play policy	Author BL	Date 6.19.15	Version 1	Page 1 of 3
Source: Discussion with VP, Marketing	Priority High		Owner ST	Req ID 01

Functional Requirement:
A Loss of Play policy needs to be added for active baseball players and their clubs. The policy should insure an active player's contract excluding coverage for any chronic or pre-existing conditions a player is known to have. It should also consider the player's age, his past injuries, and his schedule while deciding premium and offer coverage within two-year intervals only (for long-term contracts). Premium should be adjusted every two years.

Benefits
This policy will be a new line of business that may result in a substantial amount of profit since there are not many such policies available currently.

Comments/suggested solutions
A team of IT architect and business analysts is performing a feasibility study to determine whether this project is viable and beneficial for YourState insurance company.

Related documents
Project initiation plan, interview, and observation notes (gathered by the team performing the feasibility study), current and proposed environment descriptions.

Related requirements
02

Resolution
Accepted by VP, marketing and project board

Project: Loss of Play Policy	**Author** BL	**Date** 6.19.15	**Version** 1	**Page** 2
Source: Discussion with VP, marketing		**Priority** High	**Owner** ST	**Req ID** 02

Functional requirement:
A web interface needs to be developed for the proposed Loss of Play policy if the feasibility study finds the project viable and YourState management decides to add the new policy as a new line of business. This interface will need to store the policy data within the central Claims database and be a part of the YourState Claims application used by the claims department.
Business event: Loss of Play web interface added

Non-functional requirements

Description	**Expected response**	**Acceptable range**	**Comments**
Claim submitted through web interface	Immediately	Under five seconds	Claim needs to be stored within the database within five seconds and confirmation received (to the agent inputting it)

Benefits
The web interface is necessary for the claims department to enter the claim information or view/modify claim status.

Comments/suggested solutions
The development of this interface depends on the outcome of a feasibility study (requirement id 01) and if the project proceeds, then a team will develop the necessary web interface as per the design specifications (please refer to the project initiation plan for details).

Related documents
Project initiation plan, current and proposed environment descriptions.

Related requirements
01

Resolution
Accepted by VP, marketing and project board, but subject to a viable feasibility report.

User Catalogue

The user catalogue lists out the possible users with their job titles (for the proposed system) and descriptions of their job activities. Following is the user catalogue for this project:

User	Activity
Claims adjuster	View or modify existing claims
IT	System administration and technical support
Marketing	View claims
Call center representative	Create new claims

Current Environment Description

This section describes the existing environment in detail and is helpful in providing an overview of the existing system. It covers the hardware and software configurations, data flow, and logical data model. It is necessary to know what exists before designing a new system that is meant to supplement the current system's functionality.

Current System Description

Hardware: Windows 2008 R2 (Datacenter edition) server-based physical cluster with 64 CPUs, 1 TB RAM, and 20 TB SAN storage. Database used is SQL Server 2008 R2 (Datacenter edition). The Claims database is one of the largest databases with a size of 10 TB and covers claims for last three years. Earlier claims are archived in the archival database. The daily volume of claims is between 2,000 and 3,000 and includes claims filed using YourStates' toll-free phone number as well as the web-based claim filing system. Every night, an automated process allocates claims to claims adjusters based on several parameters (such as type of claim and the adjusters' expertise, number of claims an adjuster is working on, location, and so on).

Current Physical Data Flow Model

A data flow model provides functional details of how data flows within the existing system. Figure 3-1 shows data flow for the Policy and Claims processing system for YourState insurance company.

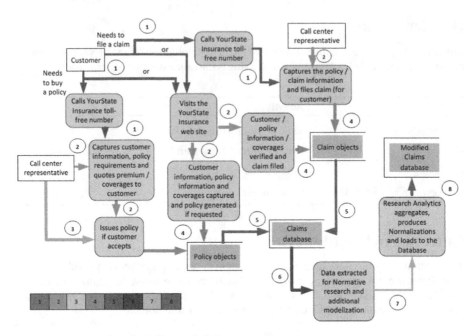

Figure 3-1. *Data flow for Policy and Claims processing system*

As you can see, a policy can be bought or a claim can be filed either online or by calling the YourState toll-free phone number. Customer, policy, and coverage information is accessed and verified before filing a claim. If a customer has the necessary coverage, then a claim is filed (record inserted in Claims database).

Current Logical Data Model

The logical model shows how the key entities within a system are interrelated and also provides details of those relationships. The logical data model in Figure 3-2 shows the relationships for key entities within the Claims processing system.

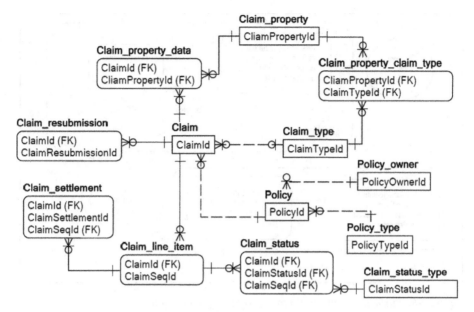

Figure 3-2. *Claims processing logical data model*

Proposed Environment Description

This section describes the three important aspects of the proposed new system: event flow, data flow, and functional logic that events employ to capture data. I will discuss each of these in detail. Let me start with the business activity model that outlines the business processes along with the details of the activities that make up a process and show the process/activity interconnections as well as interactions.

Business Activity Model

A business activity model focuses on critical business processes and models the essential activities within these processes. Activities can be further divided into tasks (for clarity). It also shows the business events that invoke the business processes and the business rules involved in invoking and performing the required activities.

In Figure 3-3, events are represented by circles, activities by rectangles, business processes by dotted rectangles, and diamonds represent a decision point. So, the event "request for a quote" from a prospective client invokes the business process "policy quote" that has underlying activities such as documentation review by risk management group and issual of quote, client review (of quote), and in case the client has any queries or reservations, the quote is sent back to risk management group for another review and modification(s). Client acceptance of the quote invokes the next event "request for issual of policy." That in turn invokes the next business process "policy issual" and culminates in issual of a policy and capture of information to appropriate databases within the YourState insurance company.

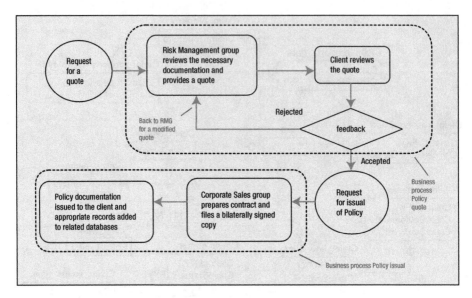

Figure 3-3. *Business activity model for Loss of Play policy issual*

To summarize, this business activity model captures the complete business requirement of issuing a Loss of play policy to prospective clients.

Data Specification

This section describes the new entities that are required to store data for the proposed system. In this case, a few new entities are required to support the new Loss of Play policy, and they are as follows:

- PlayerInjuries: This entity records past baseball injuries for a player and is used in conjunction with a player's medical history to determine the premium for Loss of Play policy for a baseball player.

- PlayerSchedule: This entity stores the schedule details for current and next season for a baseball player.

- PlayerChronicConditions: This entity records existing chronic health conditions for a baseball player and is used to determine the premium for Loss of Play policy for a baseball player.

- PlayerContracts: This entity records details of the contract a baseball player has with his club (the club that's requesting policy coverage) and is used to determine the premium for Loss of Play policy for a baseball player.

Function Specification

This section specifies the new functions and events required to implement the new system. A data flow model shows where these events and functions fit in with respect to the whole system. For the proposed Loss of Play policy, the new events are as follows:

- Request for a Loss of Play policy quote

- Request for a Loss of Play policy issual

- Request for a Loss of Play policy cancellation

- Request for a Loss of Play policy claim

The new functions required to support the new policy are as follows:

- GetPlayerInjuryInfo: Load past injury information for a baseball player in entity PlayerInjuries

- GetPlayerChronicCondInfo: Load information about a baseball player's chronic medical conditions in entity PlayerChronicConditions

- GetPlayerContractDetails: Load information about a baseball player's contract in entity PlayerContracts

- GetPlayerScheduleInfo: Load information about a baseball player's schedule for current and next season in entity PlayerSchedule

- CalculateLossOfPlayPremium: To calculate the premium for a contract using the supplied documentation and the information collected by functions GetPlayerInjuryInfo, GetPlayerChronicCondInfo, GetPlayerContractDetails, and GetPlayerScheduleInfo

- **EvalLossOfPlayClaim:** To evaluate a Loss of Play claim filed by a client

Problem Definition

The *problem* or need for this project is discussed in great detail in the project definition sub-section of the project initiation plan. Also, the requirements catalogue defines the necessity of the project, thereby discussing the problem at hand. However, to recapitulate, here are the requirements in order of priority (highest priority first):

- Feasibility of a new policy Loss of Play that will insure an active baseball player's contract (excluding coverage for recurrence of any chronic or pre-existing conditions a player is known to have)

- Consider technical, financial, legal, and organizational feasibility and also consider that this policy will offer coverage for a maximum of two years only (policy renewable after revaluation of premium)

- Feasibility of implementation of this policy (in terms of design and development by IT)

Feasibility Study Report

A feasibility report is the final outcome or deliverable of the feasibility study module of SSADM. It usually has the following sections and subsections; although some of these sections might be excluded as per your individual need and applicability:

- Management or executive summary
- Introduction
  - Purpose
  - Project history
  - Methodology
- General information
  - Current systems and processes
    - Current operations
    - Physical environment
    - User organization
  - System objectives
  - Issues
  - Assumptions and constraints
  - Alternatives
  - Alternative1
    - Description
    - Benefits and costs
  - Alternative2 (and so on for more alternatives)
  - Comparison of Alternatives
  - Recommendations and conclusions

A careful review of earlier sections will confirm that the information needed in introduction section is already provided by corresponding sections within the project initiation plan and the information required by the general information is covered by the current environment and proposed environment sections discussed earlier. Subsequently, let me focus on the sections not covered, starting with the alternatives section:

- *Alternatives*: Based on extensive study of the current environment, proposed system requirements, and constraints defined by the project initiation plan, the following alternatives are feasible:
  - *Alternative1*: Develop a new subsystem that will work seamlessly with the existing Policy and Claims processing system using business and IT resources.

- *Alternative2*: Have business analysts and IT architects prepare detailed specifications of the proposed system and hire a software development company to do the development.

- *Alternative3*: Buy a software application that provides similar functionality and have IT resources customize it to match the necessary functionality.

- *Comparison of alternatives*: The first alternative (in-house development) may be slow and may lack in quality (depending on the resources), but it is the most affordable and offers the most control. The second (custom development by a software development vendor) is fast, may offer better quality, but is expensive and also may lack adequate control over development and functionality and may require changes (to developed system). The third alternative (customized package solution) might be the most expensive, but offers technical support and ease of change.

- *Recommendation and conclusion*: After comparing the available alternatives, recommendation is to use the first alternative and develop the subsystem in-house using IT resources.

The other section that's not covered earlier is the management summary or executive summary. Let me discuss that now:

- *Management summary*: Provides a brief summary that describes the purpose, methods, issues, and results of the feasibility study.

Following is the management summary for this feasibility study:

The purpose of this feasibility study was to determine if introducing a new Loss of Play policy (that will insure an active baseball player's contract excluding coverage for recurrence of any chronic or pre-existing conditions a player is known to have) for YourState insurance company is feasible (considering technical, financial, legal and organizational feasibility).

Method used for conducting this feasibility study was SSADM (and the feasibility module). Techniques and deliverables were used as defined by SSADM documentation.

There were no issues encountered while conducting this study and three alternatives were evaluated. The alternative involving in-house development of the necessary subsystem and train internal (YourState) resources to manage the system was recommended due to its affordability as well as best control over development and functionality.

This concludes the feasibility study module. Next up: requirements analysis.

Requirements Analysis

This module uses the outputs from the feasibility study module and continues the design process using SSADM guidelines and techniques. The main focus of this module is to perform a detailed analysis of the current environment through available documentation and also interviews with users performing varied roles to support the current system. This analysis leads to extensive documentation of the current environment and covering the details of services provided by the current system, users and their roles (as well as activities), logical data model, and physical data flow. As a result of this analysis, it is possible to specify the business system options for the proposed system.

Subsequently, there are two main stages for this module: investigation of current environment and business system options. Please note the independence of this SSADM stage from the implementation target (RDBMS or NoSQL). Therefore, this design stage can be used even for a NoSQL-based system.

Investigation of Current Environment

This stage focuses on conducting a thorough analysis of the existing environment and documenting the scope or boundaries of the current system (to start with). The next task is documenting the functionality or services provided by the current system along with user roles and activities. There are a number of outputs or deliverables from this stage that provide extensive information as needed and that also help in designing the business system options.

As you may recall, some of the deliverables (such as logical data model or physical data flow) were already discussed while conducting the feasibility study, though not in much depth. I will discuss additional details for those deliverables and also discuss the additional ones that I have yet to mention. Let me start with a list of outputs (or deliverables) for this stage:

- Current data flow model
- Current logical data model
- Requirements catalogue
- User catalogue
- Logical data store/entity cross reference
- Logical view of current services and system scope

Current Data Flow Model

YourState insurance company has an existing system that processes new policies for new or existing customers and also manages them. It also stores claims (that the customers file) and the up-to-date status for them. Figure 3-4 shows the data flow model (presented earlier in the last module) with more details.

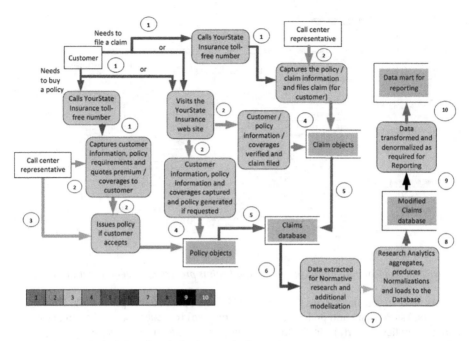

Figure 3-4. *Detailed data flow for Policy and Claims processing system*

Let me discuss the data flow briefly. A new customer can buy one of the policies offered by YourState online (using the website) or call the toll-free number. In either case, customer information is captured within the `policy-holder` entity and the policy-related information is captured within the `policy` entity. A temporary policy is issued subject to verification of the information provided as well as payment information. If all the information is verified to be correct and payment processes successfully, then a policy is issued and mailed to the customer.

A claim can be similarly filed online or by calling YourState's toll-free number. Customer information and claim details are captured (in both cases) and the assigned claims adjuster verifies coverage (for policy against which a claim is filed) and then assigns a field agent (if necessary) to investigate the claim. If that's not necessary, then documentation is requested from customer as necessary. A claim is settled in accordance with the company's norms and of course following the county, state, and federal laws.

Current Logical Data Model

Figure 3-5 is the logical data model for the existing Policy and Claims processing system. It shows the major entities and their inter-relationships.

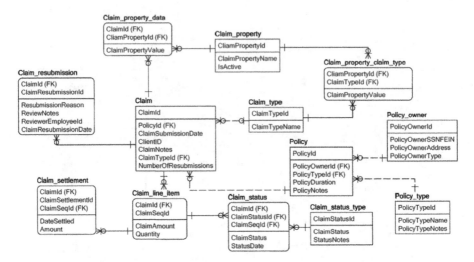

Figure 3-5. *Logical data model for Policy and Claims processing system (attribute level)*

As you can see, the entities Claim and Policy are central to the processing. They (of course) store claim and policy details. The entity Policy_owner stores information about the policy owner(s)—individual or corporate. Policies and claims can be of different types, and Policy_type and Claim_type store the details. Status of claim is stored within Claim_status and Claim_line_item as well as Claim_settlement hold settlement details for a claim. If a claim is rejected and resubmitted for evaluation, those details are stored within entity Claim_resubmission. This model uses the *crows feet* or *information engineering notation* to show the relationships between different entities.

Requirements Catalogue

This requirement catalogue pertains to the development of the existing Policy and Claims processing system and dates back to 2010 when this system was developed. Earlier, YourState insurance used a packaged solution which was customized for its needs, but didn't provide all the functionality it needed and also cost them in licensing fees as well as delays for getting technical support.

Project: Policy/Claims processing system	**Author** BL	**Date** 4.22.10		**Version** 3.3	**Page** 1
Source: Approved requirement by VP, business development		**Priority** High	**Owner** ST		**ReqID** 01

Functional requirement:

A comprehensive policy and claims processing system needs to be developed by IT for our internal use. This system needs to be able to capture customer and policy information and also support filing and processing of a claim throughout its lifecycle. Most recent claim status needs to be displayed and updateable easily. Business logic (specified in requirements specifications) needs to be applied while issuing policy, calculating premium, and also processing claims.

Non-functional requirements

Description	**Expected response**	**Acceptable range**	**Comments**
Policy/Claim information submitted through web interface	Immediately	Under 5 seconds	Policy or Claim needs to be stored within the database within 5 seconds and confirmation received (to the agent inputting it)
Policy/Claim retrieved for display and update	5 seconds	Under 10 seconds	It is imperative that an agent has this information available as quickly as possible

Benefits

This system will help manage our policies and claims more effectively (as compared to the packaged application in use currently) and will also save $500,000 per year in licensing fees for the current software application and additional expenses for support. Lastly, it will reduce the delays in bug fixes and technical support.

Comments/suggested solutions

A team of IT architect and business analysts is performing a feasibility study to determine if this project is viable and beneficial for YourState insurance company

Related documents

Project initiation plan, interview, and observation notes (gathered by the team performing feasibility study), current and proposed environment descriptions

Resolution

Accepted by VP, business development and project board

User Catalogue

The user catalogue lists out the users with their job titles (for the existing system) and descriptions of their job activities. Following is the user catalogue for this project:

User	Activity
Claims Adjuster	View or modify existing claims
IT	System Administration and technical support
Marketing	View customer information, policies, and claims
Call center representative	Create new policies and claims
Business development and support	View and modify customer and policy information

Logical Data Store/Entity Cross-Reference

This process involves comparing the LDM with DFM and resolving the inconsistencies. Several checks are used for this purpose:

1. *Matching DFM processes with LDM entities*: You need to verify that all the entities in your LDM have a corresponding process within DFM that modifies them. Following is an example of such a match (I have not displayed all such matches, but it will be a good exercise to identify the ones that I have left out).

    Please note that the entities like Policy_type hold static reference data and may have a process like static data maintenance (not shown in DFM) associated with them.

DFM Process	LDM Entities Affected
Customer and Policy data transformed using business logic and then inserted in the database	`Policy`, `Policy_owner`

2. Data stores in logical DFM should have a one-to-one relationship with entities in LDM. A data store may have many entities within it, but an entity should only exist in a single data store. If there any exceptions, they should be justified individually.

   In this case, there is a single data store (Claims) and all the entities within LDM are a part of it.

3. Ensure that the elementary processes defined in the DFM can get the data they require by navigating through the data model.

   This is a reverse check (compared to # 1), as it makes sure that the DFM processes access entities from LDM. For the Policy and Claims processing system, all the processes within DFM write to Policy and Claim entities only and therefore pass this check.

Logical View of Current Services and System Scope

The prime purpose of this step is to convert the current physical DFM into a logical DFM by eliminating external physical factors, duplication, and redundancy, using the LDM (which by definition is already logical) as a reference for validation. What does this mean?

A data flow model has combination of processes—logical and physical. Also, there are some data stores that only service the physical implementation of the current system and don't contribute to the logical implementation. For example, there may be a data store dedicated to logging performing data and there may be processes populating that data. These kinds of processes and data stores need to be eliminated from the data flow model (to convert it to a logical DFM). Lastly, processes/data stores that are duplicated need to be considered for combination.

In case of the Policy and Claims processing system, I have not shown any processes catering to physical implementations. Also, as mentioned earlier, there are processes for maintaining static reference data, but I have not shown them in the DFM as well. Subsequently, the DFM is already a logical DFM, and it is easy to prepare a logical view of services provided:

- Add or modify customers and policies (using YourState web-site or toll-free phone number)

- File and process claims for customers (using YourState web-site or toll-free phone number)

As you can see, the scope of this system is also automatically documented (by specifying the services provided).

To summarize, what is the purpose or benefit of creating this logical view of services? Well, a logical view can be useful in providing the thinking or strategy behind the physical implementation of a system. So, in case the situation changes and a particular decision is questioned, the logical view has a record of the logic behind that decision and makes it easy to cross-check.

Business System Options

At this stage, having completed the feasibility study, as well as investigation of the existing system, and having reviewed the requirements and user catalogue, there are a number of possibilities for the required logical system. The functionality within each of the BSOs is based on the following implementation strategies:

1. Don't add the Loss of Play policy.

2. Try to buy an off-the-shelf package that provides required functionality for adding Loss of Play policy.

3. Develop the necessary system using internal IT resources.

4. Hire expert resources on contract to develop the system.

5. Have a software development company develop the application for a predetermined price.

None of the BSOs associated with the preceding strategies offered an ideal solution, and all of them had pros and cons. Ultimately, after much deliberation, three options (options 3, 4, 5) were shortlisted and forwarded to the project board with detailed analysis:

- *Alternative1*: Develop a new subsystem that will work seamlessly with the existing Policy and Claims processing system using business and IT resources. The call center and policy department will need to provide additional training to resources who will manage the new policy. IT will develop the sub-system that will consist of the additional database entities and a web interface.

  - *Benefits and costs*: The main benefits are cost and complete control over development/functionality. With in-house development, total cost will only be about $200,000.

- *Alternative2*: Hire expert resources on contract to develop a solution that provides necessary functionality and have knowledge transfer to IT resources for maintaining and supporting it (also training to call center and policy deptartment).

  - *Benefits and costs*: The main benefits are time, quality of development, and ease of modifications. Although, with contract resources, total cost will be little higher (compared to *alternative1*) at $275,000.

- *Alternative3*: Have business analysts and IT architects prepare detailed specifications of the proposed system and hire a custom software development company to do the development. The call center and policy department will still need to provide additional training to resources who will manage the new policy.

  - *Benefits and costs*: The main benefits are time and quality of development. Although, with custom development, total development cost will be higher at about $325,000.

- *Comparison of alternatives*: The first alternative (in-house development) may be slow and may lack in quality (depending on the resources), but is the most affordable and also offers the most control. The second (custom development by contract resources) is fast and may offer better quality, but is a little expensive and also may lack adequate control over development. The third alternative (customized package solution) might be the most expensive but offers technical support and ease of change.

- *Project board decision and conclusion*: After comparing the available alternatives, the project board decided that the second alternative is the best option for YourState insurance and decided to develop the subsystem in-house using a combination of IT resources and expert contract resources.

Requirements Specification

This is the most complex module because it involves full logical specifications as a deliverable. The requirements specified in the feasibility study module are used as a starting point and the business system option from the requirement analysis module is used as a framework to develop an accurate, unambiguous, and consistent logical specification document. This specification focuses on system functionality rather than implementation.

The architect prepares the following deliverables to effectively produce the logical specification:

- Data-flow model (DFM)

- Logical data model (LDM)

- Function definitions (of all functions required for functioning of the system)

- Entity life-histories (ELHs) that describe all events through the life of an entity

- Effect correspondence diagrams (ECDs) that describe how each event interacts with all relevant entities

Note that this stage is useful and necessary regardless of implementation target (RDBMS or NoSQL). Therefore, this design stage can be used even for NoSQL-based system. I will discuss content and notations for all these deliverables using the new Loss of Play policy as an example, starting with the data flow model.

Data Flow Model

I discussed the current Policy and Claim processing system in detail in the last section. That gives you a good idea about the processing of a claim or creation of a new policy for a customer. Subsequently, when a new policy is added to the repertoire of the YourState insurance company, the new processing needs to match the existing business processes (since the Loss of Play policy is just a new policy for the same company) and standards, since there shouldn't be a need to design a new process for each new policy added. However, there are a few things to remember about the new policy:

- *Additional processing*: A number of requests for information need to be generated since the premium relies on it.

- *No online or phone issual*: The premiums (as well as insured amount) involved are relatively large, and there is a need for manual verification and signing. Therefore, policy will need to be issued after both parties sign the agreement.

- *No automated claim processing*: Any claims need to be processed as per predetermined logic and also subject to thorough manual investigation (since the claim amount is expected to be high).

So, to summarize, there is a combination of manual processes and automated logic for issuing the Loss of Play policy as well as processing claims associated with it. Noting that, Figure 3-6 is the data flow model for the Loss of Play policy.

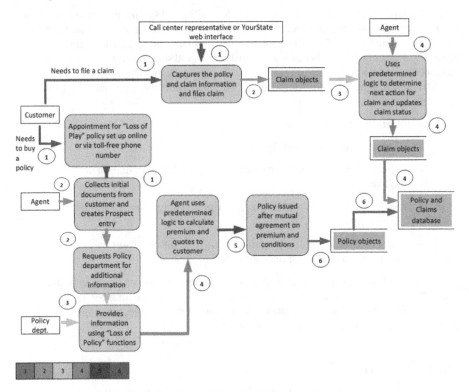

Figure 3-6. *Data flow model for "Loss of Play" policy and claim processing*

You can see that there are two separate streams of processing for buying a policy and filing a claim, and they both use a mix of manual and automated processing.

Logical Data Model

The logical data model inherits entities used by Policy and Claims processing, but that's expected and works well. There are five new entities: LossOfPlayProspect, PlayerInjuries, PlayerContracts, PlayerChronicConditions, and **PlayerSchedule**. The model in Figure 3-7 shows their inter-relations.

The entity LossOfPlayProspect is central to the Loss of Play policy processing, and you can see that the primary key (ProspectId) is propagated as reference (foreign key) to other related entities. When a prospective customer (club holding a baseball player's contract) requests a Loss of Play policy, certain data is collected about the player (whose contract needs to be insured) and stored within entities PlayerInjuries, PlayerContracts, and PlayerChronicConditions. The player's schedule (for current and next season) is also stored within an entity called PlayerSchedule. All this information is used to quote a premium for insuring a player's contract. Again, the quoted premium may be negotiated by the customer and final premium may be different (hence separate columns in entity LossOfPlayProspect). Also, since all the prospects may not materialize as customers, the relationship between entities Policy and LossOfPlayProspect is zero-to-one (on both sides, since every policy may not start as a Loss of Play prospect).

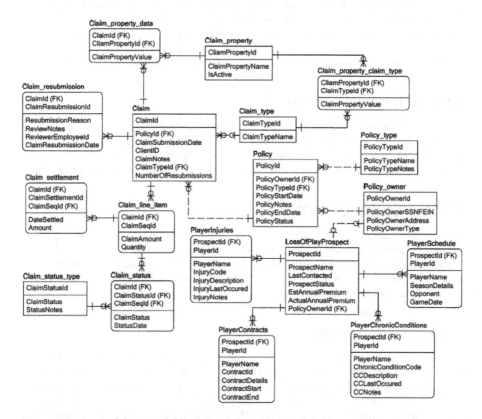

Figure 3-7. *Logical data model for Loss of Play policy and claim processing*

Lastly, the player contracts are also captured (for review) in entity `PlayerContracts` and actual contracts are scanned and stored as images.

Function Definitions

This section defines all the functions that are required for making the new Loss of Play policy available to the customers. Some of these functions may be implemented within a database, and others may be implemented at the web-interface (used by customers and agents). I will mark the functions accordingly.

GetPlayerInjuryInfo

This function loads past injury information for a baseball player in entity `PlayerInjuries`. Data comes from two sources: media and player's medical history. Since it takes time for a player's injury to be reported on his medical history (or sometimes an injury is not even recorded if a player is treated privately), data from media is also leveraged to cross-check. The gathering of data from media is a mix of automated and manual processing. Raw data gathered using keyword searches is reviewed manually, and relevant data is input via web-interface in a temporary table. Data received through medical history is also input via web interface into the same temporary table. A supervising agent reviews the data and then invokes the function `GetPlayerInjuryInfo`, which loads the data in entity `PlayerInjuries`. Input to this function is `ProspectId` and name of the player.

GetPlayerChronicCondInfo

This function loads information about a baseball player's chronic medical conditions in entity `PlayerChronicConditions`. Similar to `GetPlayerInjuryInfo`, data from multiple sources is input into a temporary table, reviewed, and then loaded to entity `PlayerChronicConditions`. Input to this function is `ProspectId` and name of the player.

GetPlayerContractDetails

This function loads information about a baseball player's contract in entity `PlayerContracts`. A scanned image is stored within the database along with contract details such as start and end dates. Contract data is first loaded to a temporary table and upon successful review, loaded to entity `PlayerContracts`. Input to this function is `ProspectId` and name of the player.

GetPlayerScheduleInfo

This function loads information about a baseball player's schedule for current and next season in entity `PlayerSchedule`. Information about a player's schedule is requested from his club (club holding his contract and requesting coverage for it) and cross-checked with published schedule (by media). Schedule is first loaded to a temporary table and, upon review, loaded to entity `PlayerChronicConditions`. Input to this function is `ProspectId` and name of the player.

CalculateLossOfPlayPremium

This function is used to calculate the premium for a contract using the information collected by functions `GetPlayerInjuryInfo`, `GetPlayerChronicCondInfo`, `GetPlayerContractDetails`, and `GetPlayerScheduleInfo` in conjunction with (a confidential) algorithm. Upon invocation, the inputs (to this function) `ProspectId` and name of the player are used to retrieve necessary information (from appropriate entities) and calculations performed to get the magic number (premium for Loss of Play policy).

EvalLossOfPlayClaim

This function pre-evaluates a Loss of Play claim filed by a client based on certain proprietary (for YourState insurance company) logic. Only certain types of claims can be pre-evaluated and still need manual intervention to check the outcome. The purpose of this function is to filter out trivial or frivolous claims and save time for agents to who are assigned to evaluate a claim. Inputs are `ProspectId` and name of the player.

There's a very interesting (and exclusively SSADM-based) concept called *entity-event modelling*. An entity-event model is a graphic representation of how business events affect the entities within an information system. Business events trigger processes, which in turn affect entities. An entity-event model consists of a set of:

- Entity life histories (ELHs)

- Effect correspondence diagrams (ECDs)

I will start with ECDs and discuss the concept along with notations. I will then provide ECDs for the major events for Loss of Play policy.

Effect Correspondence Diagrams (ECDs)

ECDs describe how each event interacts with all relevant entities or how a particular business event affects specific set of entities. An ECD captures a snapshot of the part of system state which is updated by an event. Because ECD deals with a single event, it is more static than ELH and therefore acts as a bridge between LDM and more dynamic modelling of event sequences by ELH.

The possible major events for Loss of Play policy are as follows:

- Request for a Loss of Play policy quote

- Request for a Loss of Play policy issual

- Request for a Loss of Play policy cancellation

- Request for a Loss of Play policy claim

I will provide ECDs for these events and discuss notations simultaneously.

The ECD for a policy quote is easy to follow (see Figure 3-8). When the process (Policy Quote) starts, an identifying instance of LossOfPlayProspect is created and that is followed by creation of multiple instances of PlayerInjuries, PlayerChronicConditions, PlayerSchedule, and a single instance of PlayerContracts. The star in the upper right corner denotes iterations or multiple instances.

Policy Quote

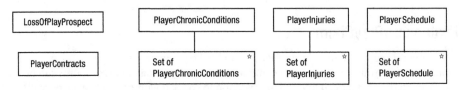

Figure 3-8. *ECD for event "quote for Loss of Play policy"*

When a new policy needs to be issued, it is checked whether the prospect exists as a policy owner. If the policy owner doesn't exist, a single instance of policy owner is created, and the PolicyOwnerId is updated for the corresponding prospect instance (see Figure 3-9). Next, a single instance of Policy is created.

Policy Issual ·

Figure 3-9. *ECD for event "issual of Loss of Play policy"*

When a policy is cancelled, the status is updated for relevant instance of Policy to mark it inactive or cancelled (Figure 3-10).

Policy Cancellation

Figure 3-10. *ECD for event"cancellation of Loss of Play policy"*

While filing a claim, a single instance of object Claim is created, and multiple instances of Claim_property_data are created along with appropriate values for the properties added. See Figure 3-11.

Claim filing

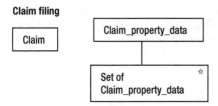

Figure 3-11. ECD for event "claim filing for Loss of Play policy"

Entity Life Histories (ELHs)

For an entity, ELH shows the effects caused by various business events sequentially. ELHs are drawn using the structured design constructs of sequence, selection, iteration, and parallelism. Notation used is almost the same as ECDs with addition of levels. The first level is the entity itself, and the second level is the type of events. The third level contains individual events that modify the (data for an) entity. The last level contains the processing operations that modify the entitiess. Levels two and four may not be necessary in some cases and may be eliminated.

I will now present and discuss ELHs for more frequently used entities such as `Policy`, `Claim`, and `LossOfPlayProspect`.

The lifecycle for the `Policy` entity is very simple. It is either created by an agent (resulting from a call from customer via YourState toll-free number) or by a function activated through online request for a policy (and after the basic checks are performed). The circle on the upper right corner of second level rectangles denotes a selection or option. The policy is modified by authorized agents as per the need. A function is provided for that purpose on the internal web interface. A policy cancellation is update of status to *inactive* or *closed*. See Figure 3-12.

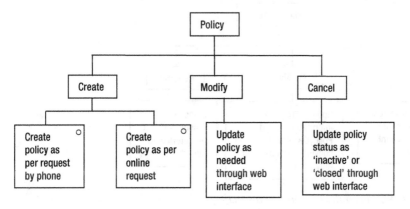

Figure 3-12. ELH for entity Policy

The lifecycle of a claim is similar to policy as far as the creation (or filing) is concerned, but modification involves adjustment or evaluation of a claim. A claims adjuster does that and updates the status (approved or rejected). If approved, the next processes modify claim settlement–related entities (`claim_line_item`, `claim_settlement`). If rejected and resubmitted for review, the status is updated accordingly and details are captured in a claim resubmission–related entity (`claim_resubmission`). See Figure 3-13.

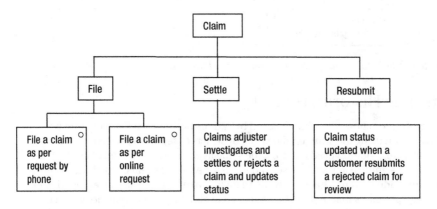

Figure 3-13. *ELH for entity Claim*

Last, for entity `LossOfPlayProspect`, an entry is created after the initial meeting with an agent and the relevant documents are received. This process is a little different (compared to other policies) due to the high amounts (for premium as well as claims) involved. If a prospect buys a Loss of Play policy, then `PolicyOwnerId` is updated for that prospect. Any other updates to prospect information are accommodated similarly. If a prospect doesn't buy a policy within 6 months, his details are removed. See Figure 3-14.

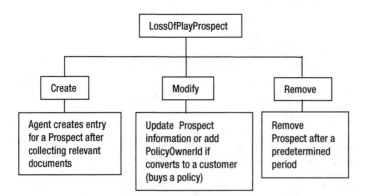

Figure 3-14. *ELH for entity LossOfPlayProspect*

Logical System Specification

This module is about assembling, linking all the design deliverables and preparing for a physical implementation. However, before a final listing is prepared, technical system options (for implementation) are explored, and a choice is made by the project board regarding the option to be used. I will briefly discuss the possible technical system options for the new Loss of Play policy discussed in this chapter and then discuss the deliverables for the logical design stage. Almost all the deliverables are already discussed earlier in this chapter, so I will focus on the ones that are not.

Again, note that even this stage is independent of implementation target (RDBMS or NoSQL). Only the possible technical options are discussed here. Target technology can still be chosen depending on your need. Therefore, this design stage can be used even for NoSQL-based systema.

Technical Systems Options

The Loss of Play policy discussed in this chapter extends the type of policies offered by the YourState insurance company and since it already offers a large number of policies, it has an existing information system to sell and support these policies via a web interface (as well as a toll-free phone number). Therefore, the following technical systems options were presented to the project board:

- *Option 1*: Design a separate web interface and database for the new policy. Use separate database and web servers.

- *Option 2*: Use the existing web interface and add functionality to sell and manage the new policy. Also, add the new database objects (as needed) to the existing database (used by all other policies). Last, scale out the existing database and web servers to handle additional data and user traffic.

- *Option 3*: Design a separate web interface to sell and manage the new policy, but share the existing database for policy and claim processing. Last, scale out the existing database and web servers to handle additional data and user traffic.

The project board evaluated these three options and chose the third option. Subsequently, it was decided to use the existing database, but develop a new web interface for processing the Loss of Play policies and claims. One of the reasons was a mix of manual and automated processing that would be hard to handle for the existing interface (since all the processing for existing policies is automated).

Next, reviewing the hardware (Windows 2008 R2 Datacenter edition, server-based physical cluster with 64 CPUs, 1 TB RAM, and 20 TB SAN storage), it was decided to add 100 GB RAM and 2 TB of storage. The operating system and database (SQL Server 2008 R2 Datacenter edition) was determined to be capable of handling the additional connections.

Logical Design

This is a very important stage where all the design deliverables are consolidated, cross-checked, and linked to facilitate a successful physical implementation of the system. Any design gaps are identified and resolved. Explanations and notes (that will help implementation) are added. As per SSADM guidelines, the following deliverables are expected as output (from this stage):

- The logical process model
  - Update processing model (ECD)
  - Enquiry processing model (EAP)
  - The dialogues
  - Function definitions
- The menu and command structures
- The requirements catalogue
- The data catalogue
- The system LDM

Update Processing Model

Typically, the update processing model brings together the operations that constitute the update function (for an information system). The model is then presented in form of a structure chart accompanied by descriptions of operations that constitute it. Function definitions and ECDs are used to construct these models since they provide information about events and how an event affects the entities within LDM. I discuss functions and ECDs earlier in this section, and it will be good exercise to segregate update functions, prepare ECDs for them, and then construct an update processing model using these ECDs as a starting point. Please remember that the update processing models are at event level, not function level.

Enquiry Processing Model

An enquiry processing model differs from the UPM as there are no events (to define processing around them) and the enquiry constitutes a single function. So, EPMs are at function level. Enquiry access path or EAP (which shows how an enquiry interacts with the logical database) is used as a basis to construct the EPMs. Figure 3-15 shows an EAP for the Loss of Play policy search.

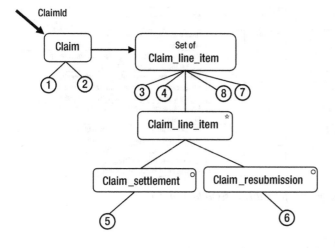

1. Get input ClaimId
2. Retrieve Claim record, on error fail with error message
3. Get all the Claim_line_items associated with the Claim
4. Check if the claim_line_item is settled or resubmitted for review
5. If settled, get details of settlement
6. If resubmitted for review, get details of resubmission
7. Output details of settled line items
8. Output details of resubmitted line items

Figure 3-15. *EAP for claim status enquiry*

You may have already observed that the notation for EAP is exactly same as for ELH or ECD. A star in the upper right corner for iteration or multiple instances and a circle in upper right corner for optional relationship (either-or relationship). The beginning of search processing is indicated by the inclined downward arrow. ClaimId (for which details are sought) is input, and a search is made in the Claim entity. If a match is found, the claim record is retrieved along with corresponding line item records. Multiple line items may exist for a Claim (as indicated) and for each of them, status is checked to determine whether that line item is settled or resubmitted for review (in case it was rejected). Accordingly, the details are output to be displayed.

The EAPs for search functions can be developed for other entities as required.

As far as the GUI (graphical user interface) is concerned, dialogues, menu and command structures are beyond the scope of this discussion (as the focus here is use of SSADM for database design) and the GUI deliverables are pertaining to front-end web-interface. The only other deliverable left to discuss is data catalogue or data dictionary. Let me discuss it briefly.

Data Catalogue

Data catalogue is the data dictionary most of us are familiar with. The following format is recommended for the logical data dictionary. Note that the attribute types and sizes do not refer to a particular physical database implementation and therefore may change as per the database system used as a target for physical implementation. Figure 3-16 uses the LossOfPlayProspect entity as the only example (I'm not including the whole data dictionary for brevity and relevance to the discussion), as it will ably demonstrate the concept and provide necessary understanding.

Entity	Attribute	Type	Size	Description
LossOfPlayProspect	ProspectId	Number	5	Unique sequential number used as identifier or primary key
	ProspectName	Text	100	Name of the person or organization interested in buying the "Loss of Play" policy
	LastContacted	Date	10	Date a prospect was contacted most recently
	ProspectStatus	Text	50	Status of the Prospect indicates his interest in buying a policy; viz. "Active", "Not interested" etc.
	EstAnnualPremium	Number	20	Estimated annual premium that was initially quoted to a prospect
	ActualAnnualPremium	Number	20	Actual annual premium that was mutually agreed (valid only if a prospect buys a policy)
	PolicyOwnerId	Number	5	If a prospect buys policy, then he becomes a policyholder. This is a foreign key linking the Prospect and Policy Owner records

Figure 3-16. *Data dictionary entry for entity LossOfPlayProspect*

Physical Design

The final module of SSADM provides guidelines for physical implementation of the logical design completed using techniques discussed in the earlier modules. Essentially, SSADM being a design methodology, can't get into the finer details of the implementations, but it does provide high level guidance and attempts to make the implementation as efficient as possible. There are two aspects of the implementation:

- Physical data design
- Physical process specification

Since the focus of this chapter is database design, I will focus on the physical data design. An important thing to note is that a physical implementation always relies on the expertise of the implementer (for the platform or software used for implementation). The following steps are followed:

- Transformation from logical data model (LDM) to physical data model
- Initial space estimation and provision for growth
- Optimization of physical design and regular maintenance

At this stage, the details of physical implementation will change depending on the target technology you choose for your implementation (RDBMS or NoSQL).

Logical to Physical Transformation

This transformation involves substituting appropriate data types for the logical attributes, implementing the referential integrity constraints, and adding relevant supporting objects to the physical database to support the relationships specified within a logical data model.

A number of case tools (for example, ERwin) can be used to implement this transformation. Of course, you need to choose your target database system and then make sure that the case tool you plan to use supports it. The process of transforming a logical model to physical is known as *forward engineering*, and a case tool can accept a logical model as input and "forward engineer" it to a physical model. Output is provided as scripts (using the target RDBMS query language), that can be executed on the target server to create the necessary database objects within the database of your choice. This includes database tables, indexes, keys (primary/foreign), and triggers (if necessary). Logical data types are translated into physical data types and implemented by the RDBMS. After completion of this process, the physical database structure is ready for use.

Space Estimation Growth Provisioning

A physical data structure (resulting from the last step) will occupy space, and you need to estimate your initial storage needs. For the Loss of Play policy, it was decided to add 2 TB of storage to account for the additional space needed to store policy and claim data, as well as scanned documentation (required to determine the premium) and player contracts. That is a good start, but what happens next year? Or the year after?

You need to know the growth rate for the additional data created by the new policy. For example, if you determine that the growth rate is 15%, then 15% space will be required additionally each year. So, each year 300 GB (15% of 2 TB) will be required to support the growth. You have to make sure that this additional disk space is added annually.

Optimizing Physical Design

Optimizing your physical design depends largely on the target RDBMS of your choice because optimization is specific to the architecture of your database system. However, a part of the optimization is SQL-specific and that tuning can be applicable to any database system supporting SQL. Broadly, optimization or tuning can be performed at the following levels:

- *Server level*: This tuning involves adjusting the server configuration parameters to support the type of expected processing. For example, for an OLAP or warehousing environment, a large amount of data is read (and not updated). So server can support reads without any locks (with the most lenient isolation level) that will provide speed for read access.

- *Database level*: This involves tuning the database settings. Using the same example of a warehousing environment, since there are no update transactions expected, transaction logs can be small and without any mechanism for recovery.

- *Application level*: This tunes the application database and involves adding appropriate indexes or statistics and making sure all the frequently executed queries use indexed scans (for performance). Also, target database system-specific tuning is performed. For example, if SQL Server is the target database, frequently used queries should use a clustered index (since that is the order data is stored physically in) for performance.

Important thing to note about the tuning is that it's not a one type setup. You need to review it periodically and adjust as necessary. Your system may be operating optimally right now, but that doesn't guarantee that it will continue to be optimal after six months, when 2 TB of data is added or 1 TB is updated. Therefore, you need to review all your settings periodically and adjust them. Also, indexes or statistics need to be rebuilt frequently for guaranteeing sustained performance levels. That constitutes database maintenance and preferably needs to be automated or scheduled by your database administrator.

Summary

In this chapter, I have discussed SSADM and all the possible deliverables following the SSADM design methodology. SSADM is quite old, and there are no attempts to modify it for use with the latest database design techniques. However, that doesn't mean it's not relevant anymore. In fact, it represents one of the most extensive and logical design methods for relational database design, which is a major reason I used it as an example. It's just that some of the techniques can be replaced with more efficient ones that were not available at the time SSADM was designed.

If you have a quick look at the design methods used today, you will realize that they represent subsets of SSADM. None of them is so thorough in design tasks or covers all the deliverables SSADM did a lot of years back.

That leads to the second thing to note about SSADM. I have discussed all the deliverables, but obviously they may not be necessary for your environment. You need to make a conscious decision about what deliverables are relevant and only present those as part of your design.

Also, since some of the techniques that SSADM describes are now replaced by better and more efficient ones, you should feel free to combine them with SSADM guidelines. After all, even the SSADM documentation clearly says that the techniques described are guidelines and not rules required to be followed verbatim.

If you are still questioning why you just read a long chapter discussing SSADM and its deliverables, it will be useful for any migrations that you plan from RDBMS to NoSQL databases. This chapter is meant to help you understand the design documentation (and the logical/physical design) for a relational application effectively and ultimately help you perform a successful migration. Also, as I have discussed at every SSADM design stage, SSADM design techniques are independent of implementation target (RDBMS or NoSQL) and therefore are useful for design of any systems that you plan to implement.

CHAPTER 4

■ ■ ■

RDBMS Design and Implementation Tools

It was 2001 and since the dot-com bubble was completely deflated, budgets were tight. I was redesigning a claims-reimbursement system for a major insurance company in downtown Chicago and needed a good CASE tool. I mentioned that to my manager, and the blank look prompted me to explain what it does. "Well, can't you use Word?" I explained that I couldn't do what was needed using a word processor. The next question was whether there was any open source or "free" software available. It was surprising to see that a corporation ready to spend millions for consulting was not willing to spend a few thousand dollars for a necessary database tool.

I have frequently seen a general level of apathy and lack of understanding for many specialized database tools. Also, with the advent of technology and new techniques and tools crowding the market on a daily basis, it is hard for the new database professionals to understand or gain expertise with database tools used for design, monitoring, or diagraming (flow-charting). I feel it will be helpful to understand the types of tools available for RDBMS implementation and their features.

The popular RDBMS implementation tools range from design to administration and monitoring. Any RDBMS implementation starts with design. There are two types of tools used for design. The first is a CASE tool that assists with conceptual and logical design as well as transformation to a physical database structure. The second is a diagraming or flow-charting tool that assists with drawing the different types of models associated with database design. I discuss both if these tools in this chapter.

There is another set of applications sometimes used by developers to transition RDBMS data to an object-oriented model. These frameworks are referred to as object relational mapping (ORM) frameworks. They are useful if you plan to represent your relational database as an ODBMS (object-oriented database). Hibernate and Spring are popular frameworks that can be used for this purpose. They offer features like high performance, scalability, reliability, extensibility, and idiomatic persistence (ability to develop persistent classes that follow object-oriented idioms including inheritance, polymorphism, association, and composition) that assist in a successful, fast, and easy ORM transition that reduces your development time.

© Bhushan Lakhe 2016
B. Lakhe, *Practical Hadoop Migration*, DOI 10.1007/978-1-4842-1287-5_4

Getting back to RDBMS, after a database is designed and implemented as a physical structure (for a target RDBMS), it needs to be managed and maintained on a daily basis. New databases may need to be created, allocated space (for databases) may need to be expanded, or users may need to be added or provided access to new objects. Database administration tools help to perform all these tasks easily and quickly.

Finally, a database (and the database server) needs to be monitored for performance, unauthorized access, and any kind of failures that may result in service interruption. In many cases, the tools used for database administration also provide monitoring functionality, but some cases do warrant use of specialized monitoring tools that provide a wider range of features and flexibility.

Database Design Tools

Chapter 3 discusses the database design process using SSADM as a method. As you may note, a large number of models and deliverables are produced as part of the design process. These models/deliverables are related, and it is necessary to show the relationship clearly. It is cumbersome and time-consuming to draw these models separately and show the existing relationships. CASE tools help with this process by assisting in building the initial (logical/conceptual) model, using it to generate a model for the next stage, and continuing the process till the last stage (physical data structure) is reached.

The diagraming or flow-charting tools don't provide this kind of extensive functionality but do have extensive libraries of predesigned templates that help in creating a flow-chart or diagram very quickly. From personal experience, diagraming tools are more useful for models like data flow diagrams or business activity models.

CASE tools

CASE tools are tools that assist in implementing the processes associated with computer-aided software engineering (CASE). They're used for designing and implementing software applications. Several factors influenced the development of CASE tools, such as CAD (computer-aided design) or "active data dictionary." Database designers noticed the ease that CAD packages provided for *drafting* (the manual process of drawing various views of machine component designs to scale) with their prebuilt templates, library of shapes, and features needed. More useful features like ease of modifications and propagating the designs to CNC machines for actual part manufacturing impressed these database designers too.

Another major influence was the data dictionary of a database. Designers experimented by extending the range of metadata held in a dictionary to include application attributes and substituting at runtime. This "active dictionary" led to model-driven engineering, but didn't have a graphical representation of any of the metadata. Once the graphical representation was added (inspired by CAD), it led to the development of earliest CASE tools.

So, how do the CASE tools help the database design process? By helping with graphical representation of the design stages and also with propagation of the designed models to later stage, right till culmination of the design process leading to a physical database structure. Because CASE tools assist with specific tasks in the software development lifecycle (SDLC), they are useful in implementing database design methodologies. As you may have noticed in Chapter 3, I used the CASE tool Erwin to design various deliverables associated with design method SSADM; such as the logical design model (LDM) or physical data model (PDM). To summarize, CASE tools can assist the design process in following ways:

- Building design layers for your application design

- Categorizing your design using subject areas

- Controlling physical display level of your models

- Forward or reverse engineering as needed

- Helping in creating reusable components for your design

- Propagating a change easily and quickly through the design stages

Building and Using Design Layers

A set of data models used for a particular purpose in the application development process constitute a design layer. Within this layer hierarchy, the first layer is often a logical data model that summarizes the business requirements (for an application). The second design layer transforms these business requirements and creates corresponding database implementation rules for a physical data model (note, a generic physical model may be created using generic ODBC as the target database). The third and final design layer represents physical implementations of the same data model for different target server platforms.

If the logical data model from the first layer is an enterprise data model, then it can be further divided into logical models corresponding to separate applications for an organization. Figure 4-1 summarizes these layers.

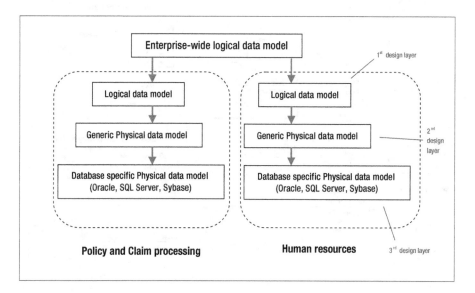

Figure 4-1. *Design layers for relational OLTP application*

The most important thing to remember about the design layer is that you must be able to link the models in different design layers and synchronize changes made in different layers (that is, make and propagate changes to other layers). A successful hierarchy is characterized by well-linked models (from different design layers) using a common model source and the ability to apply transforms across the design layer (keeping linked models in sync).

CASE tools like Erwin, ER/Studio, or Enterprise Architect provide all the features necessary to define a logical model and apply transformations to derive the generic or specific physical models from it. That way, the link is maintained through the design layer, and any modifications can be applied to the logical data model and the related physical models quickly regenerated.

Categorizing Design Using Subject Areas

Many times, when you start reviewing a large data model, it is intimidating and not very informative or intuitive. The reason is that it presents you with a large number of related entities without telling you what functionality they (or their subsets) provide. All you know is that the model belongs to a system that provides some functionality (such as accounting, human resource management, policy and claims management, and so on).

Subject areas group the entities by the subsets of functionality they provide for an information system. By classifying the entities in this manner, subject areas provide a quick subclassification of functionality and make database models easier to understand and read.

Consider the logical model for Policy and Claims processing from earlier chapters. You have seen how it looks without subject areas (Figure 3-7). With subject areas defined, you can see the difference in Figure 4-2.

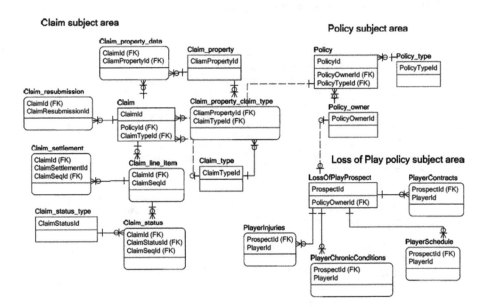

Figure 4-2. *Subject areas for a Policy and Claim processing application*

As you can see, it is much easier to get the context of the entities now, and you can probably guess what their purpose is. For example, for the Loss of Play policy subject area, it is easy to see that the entity LossOfPlayProspect is central to that policy processing, and the other entities simply provide information about the player (whose contract the prospect is trying to insure). Similar information can be derived quickly and easily from the other subject areas as well.

When subject areas are implemented using CASE tools, they can be displayed singly or as part of the main subject area. Even if you don't define specific subject areas, a main subject area is defined by default, and all entities are a part of it. When you add an entity to a specific subject area, it still remains a part of the main subject area, and any changes made to it in one subject area are automatically implemented in all the other subject areas (that the entity is a part of).

Display Level of a Model

CASE tools offer various display levels for the data models, such as the following:

- Entity (just the entities and relationships between them)

- Attribute (entities and attributes)

- Primary key (primary keys for all entities)

- Keys (primary and foreign keys for all entities)

- Definition (entity definitions and relations)

- Icon (entity and icons)

These display levels are useful in controlling the visualization depending on your need. For example, if you only want to display the entity relationships, then entity display level will suffice, or if you want to show the primary and foreign key relationships, the keys display level will be relevant (Figure 4-2 uses the keys display level). By displaying only the necessary level of detail, display levels make it easier to focus on the relevant details.

Forward and Reverse Engineering

Forward engineering involves creating physical table structures within a schema/ database for target RDBMS. You can use the design layer concept and create a generic physical model as an intermediate step if necessary. Many CASE tools can read data models prepared using diagramming tools and then forward engineer them as well.

How does a CASE tool implement this feature? Well, as a final step, a CASE tool provides data definition language (DDL) scripts using query language (that the target RDBMS supports). But before that, there are multiple options that you can select for your target scripts. The options deal with choosing the database objects and properties that you want to import, specifying whether you want to infer primary keys or relationships from indexes, setting case conversion options, generating index scripts (for implementing primary key, foreign key, and alternate key relationships), implementing referential integrity through triggers, and so forth, and can be selected easily through point-and-click menus.

Reverse engineering, as you might expect, is the reverse of forward engineering. A physical database (with objects) is a starting point. The process reads metadata for all the objects, determines the relationships, and creates a physical data model. Taking advantage of an existing database speeds the design of a new data model and the subsequent delivery of new systems. A logical data model can then be easily generated (using the physical model). DDL scripts (for database objects that need to be reverse engineered) can also be used if connecting to a database (and reading metadata) is not possible. Figure 4-3 summarizes the process.

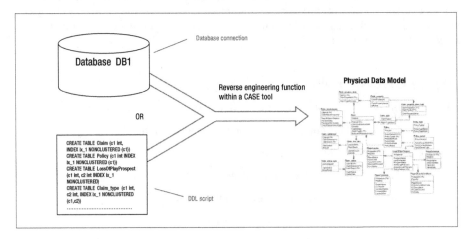

Figure 4-3. *Reverse engineering process*

It is important to make sure that referential integrity constraints are defined for the database (or scripted within DDL scripts) before trying to reverse engineer it. Otherwise, all you are going to see are the entity boxes. Of course, some relationships may still be missing from the model, but you will need to add them manually (for example, recursive relationships or supertype/subtype relationships).

Creating Reusable Components

One of the strengths of the CASE tools is the ability to create a range of components that can be easily reused. For example, domains. A *domain* is a model object that can be used to allocate attribute or column properties. Use of domains makes your model consistent because you can reuse them multiple times. Domains also make it easy to capture specific settings for your environment for quick reuse within your data models. For example, if you need to use a status attribute with a specific set of values only, you can create a domain and use it as needed.

Domains also help in reducing development and maintenance time. Any changes to a domain result in changing all the associated attributes or columns. CASE tools provide a library or dictionary that holds physical and logical domains that you create. Generally, some of the domain properties include:

- Domain name and column name

- Column datatype, default value, and valid value(s)

- Domain comment or note and column comment or name

- User-defined properties

CASE tools make it easy to reuse the entity objects and even subject areas between different models. So, you can think about them as reusable components too. Many CASE tools generate a data dictionary using entity and attribute definitions input for a model. Those definitions can also be reused (along with entities) between models and will reduce the laborious task of entering these definitions multiple times.

Propagating a Change Easily and Quickly

CASE tool features such as forward and reverse engineering, physical/logical views of a model, and quick generation of a generic physical model help in propagating any design modifications quickly to the physical data structures. This is especially important if the change is made to a key entity that is referenced by multiple entities. As you can imagine, attempts to cascade such a change manually would take time and possibility introduce error.

For example, an insurance company uses a `ClaimId` that goes up to 99,999,999. They introduce a new policy that is really popular, and now they hit the 100 million+ mark. So, `ClaimId` needs to increase in size. `ClaimId` is referenced by a large number of tables, and a change in size needs to be reflected in all those tables. CASE tools can help you quickly generate scripts that can implement this change easily and without any errors.

Diagramming Tools

The focus of a diagramming tool is to provide a large library of shapes, icons and templates that will facilitate quick drawing of a model. You can draw any model (or flow chart) that's part of the SSADM deliverables (or otherwise necessary). CASE tools don't provide flow-charting or free-form drawing functionality. For example, if you need to draw a data flow diagram, then you will need to use a diagramming tool, not a CASE tool.

Finally, diagramming tools let you insert pictures, CAD drawings, charts, clip art, or data graphics in your model. This feature can be useful where your model refers to a lot of external sources or subsystems.

The common templates/shape libraries provided by diagramming tools are as follows:

- Data flow diagram shapes

- EPC (event process) diagram shapes

- Work flow objects

- Cross-functional flowchart shapes

- BPMN basic shapes

- Gane-Sarson shapes

- Engineering (electrical/mechanical/process) shapes

- ER diagrams

- UML diagram shapes

Popular diagramming tools include Visio, Draw.IO, Gliffy, eDraw, Dynamic Draw, and others; the templates, shapes, or features they offer may differ slightly, but conceptually they are very similar.

So, the diagramming tools offer much more flexibility and speed for drawing a large variety of models, but as far as data modelling is concerned, they can't match the features provided by CASE tools. In general, diagramming tools can't:

- Reverse engineer

- Forward engineer

- Link models

- Propagate changes (from one model to another)

- Categorize using subject areas

CASE tools and diagramming tools have their own strengths, and your exact need would decide which of them suits best for your environment. Both offer a variety of modeling functions that you can leverage.

Administration and Monitoring Applications

The purpose of these tools is to assist in managing the physical database structures. Managing a database system typically involves tasks such as creating and managing databases and objects, users and roles, space usage, and backup schedules, and doing database maintenance (such as re-indexing, recreating statistics, and doing other tasks).

Monitoring a database involves setting up automated tasks for monitoring resource usage by processes, database connections, and individual users, and setting up alerts when certain threshold values are reached. In some cases, monitoring simply captures metrics of interest and stores them for a certain time period (one month, one year, and so on) for access to historical usage and, of course, auditing.

Database Administration or Management Applications

Most of the relational databases have similar structures (for obvious reasons), and that makes the task of designing a common graphical user interface for them easy. A few companies have successfully designed interfaces that work with all the leading RDBMS. Most of the database administration interfaces have the following capabilities:

- Modify database server as well as database and schema related configuration

- Add/modify/delete database objects such as tables, views, triggers, and stored procedures

- Add/modify/delete logins/users/roles and manage permissions for users/roles

- Manage disk space allocation and shrink databases to release allocated (but unused) space

- Perform database maintenance (re-indexing or building indexes) including backups

- Schedule and manage database-related tasks/jobs and document their results/status

- Manage locking/blocking/deadlocks for database server and record all the actions (for example, killed or deadlocked sessions)

- Configure SMTP or any other protocol for use by database servers to send alerts to configured email addresses or phone numbers

- Monitor replication and mirrored environments for data integrity

- Set up and configure access, security, and encryption functionality

All the leading RDBMS have their own database administration interfaces, but the problem occurs when you need to manage different RDBMS using a common interface. That's where an interface developed by a third party or a neutral vendor is useful. Companies such as Redgate or Embarcadero (DBArtisan) have developed popular tools, and companies like EMS have also developed free multi-database tools.

Monitoring Applications

Monitoring tools support a large range of functionality including monitoring performance, locking/blocking activity, database connections and security breaches, resource usage, and job outputs. They are expected to generate alerts when any (previously set up) thresholds are exceeded and also provide troubleshooting or debugging capabilities in case of any functional or performance issues. These tools establish a performance baseline, isolate performance problems, identify bottlenecks, and also provide query statistics. Here is a detailed (but generic) task list:

- Monitor inefficient or expensive (using more system resources) SQL queries and stored procedures that may cause excessive locking, blocks, or deadlocks, especially focusing on frequently executed queries. Configure thresholds for resource usage (on individual servers) for greater flexibility, making it easy to see the most expensive queries (for example, by sorting in descending order of resource usage).

- Support troubleshooting of problematic queries with query plan (sequential task listing of a query execution as planned by the query optimizer of a database server) diagnostic capabilities. View summarized performance statistics for databases and users along with individual query details such as execution plans. For example, a query may be failing due to insufficient memory, excessive number of users trying to connect to a database concurrently, or index fragmentation, and a detailed query plan may be the only way to know it.

- Avoid false alarms by setting alert thresholds based on historical statistical analysis of your server performance data. Continuous monitoring can capture and store data over a time period, making it easy to create historical data.

- Perform heuristic analysis of occurred events or behavior and derive a percentage of likelihood that an event could happen in the near future. For example, system peak usage during 9:00 a.m. to 10:00 a.m. on Monday mornings for the time entry application causes network performance issues, resulting in blocks on database server.

- Monitor operating system metrics for a more comprehensive and accurate diagnosis of performance or security issues. For example, termination of a database transaction may correspond with memory fault for a server, and it may not be possible to correlate these events unless the OS event log is monitored.

- Support setup and capture of traces (sequential listing of commands sent for execution to the database server, along with runtime parameter substitution) to files for further analysis.

- Maintain historical data of worst-performing SQL queries.

- Assist in establishing a precise link between resource contention and response time.

Most of the leading RDBMS vendors have their own monitoring and debugging tools (for example, Microsoft SQL Server has Profiler), but there are excellent third-party tools available that offer a large number of additional features and ease of use. Here are some of the leading third-party monitoring tools available currently: LogicMonitor, MyOra, Foglight, SolarWinds, Redgate SQL Monitor, Idera SQL Diagnostic Manager, and SQLSentry.

Summary

Some may question the inclusion of this small chapter. Don't we all know about CASE tools and diagramming tools? Haven't we used them enough? Probably we have—but maybe not all of these tools, or all of the features within these tools. Again, remember that the real focus is migration of RDBMS-based data to NoSQL environments.

Some of the deliverables you need to use for the data transfer may be output from the tools discussed. Understanding how these tools work will also help you understand those deliverables better.

Conversely, a few aspects of the (RDBMS to NoSQL) data transfer may require the use of advanced tools, and this chapter serves as a quick reference. It will make your task (of rapidly identifying a tool to match your requirement) much easier. I have also provided listings of the leading vendors and software packages for each of the tools, which should serve as a handy reference too. And I discussed forward and reverse engineering.

Finally, CASE tools or DBA (database administrator)/monitoring applications are rarely discussed in a vendor-neutral manner, and therefore I have covered generic features at a conceptual level to provide a better understanding. Surprisingly, you will notice that all the leading vendors provide these features (more or less), although the terminology they use may differ.

■ ■ ■

## PART II

Hadoop: A Review of the Hadoop Ecosystem, NoSQL Design Principles and Best Practices

CHAPTER 5

■ ■ ■

The Hadoop Ecosystem

Couple of years back, I was taking a train home one evening and catching up on my round up of new Hadoop tools. A co-passenger was having a covert look at my laptop, and after a while his curiosity was just piqued too much to let it go. "What area do you work in?" he enquired. I said I was an architect and focused on Big Data as well as warehousing. "Big Data!" he exclaimed. "Sounds like black magic to me." That was the common sentiment a few years back and has not changed much since.

It is often confusing and overwhelming when you start using the Hadoop ecosystem, and it takes time to know and understand each of the important (and popular) components. This chapter is designed to speed up that process with brief and concise information about important components and vendor applications that you can choose for your deployment.

The Hadoop ecosystem is the newest addition to the ever-emerging arena of data-processing technologies, and is here to stay. Just like UNIX of the 80s and 90s, it is in transition, and new products are created almost daily. It is extremely difficult to keep abreast of the new products, but is probably worth your time to have a brief look at the new products in various categories related to Hadoop and NoSQL. The products may change in near future, but this chapter aims to give you a good understanding of the front-runners and the features they offer.

The categories I have considered (for Hadoop products) are generic, such as query tools, analytical tools, search tools, messaging systems, databases, and so on. The included tools, however, offer specific functionality. I have also tried to focus on open source products (with a few priced, commercial exceptions), since they are easily accessible for experimentation and innovation. Big Data, as you know, is all about innovation. I have also included products in incubation (at Apache) and some that are not written about very much but which are useful.

I discuss the query tool Shark (Spark SQL now). You can think of Shark as Hive with Spark engine (instead of MapReduce). Kylin is contributed by eBay and is an excellent analytical tool. It helps you build cubes for data stored within HDFS. Since there are no new tools for messaging, I will briefly discuss Kafka and discuss Solr/Elastic search (as search tools) for the same reason. In-memory processing is still largely dominated by Spark, but Apache Flink is a new player in that area. Flink is a large-scale data-processing engine that offers in-memory data streaming and therefore extremely fast processing for data-intensive as well as iterative jobs.

© Bhushan Lakhe 2016
B. Lakhe, *Practical Hadoop Migration*, DOI 10.1007/978-1-4842-1287-5_5

Query Tools

A *query* tool is an interface that allows you to select or filter your data based on certain specific criteria, providing a subset of your data. It is important to create such specific subsets in the NoSQL world, because NoSQL database systems (and Hadoop) work with datasets as opposed to databases and tables. It is also important to understand the concept of datasets and how they differ from data stored in conventional relational databases. Another important thing to remember about the query tools: they don't have their own data storage. Some query tools (such as Hive) store the metadata in a repository, but not the data that's being processed by them.

Before now, the choice for such query tools was very limited, especially for ones supporting SQL interface. And MapReduce performance was a limitation. Now the next-generation products like Stinger, Impala, Presto, and Shark (Spark SQL) don't use MapReduce and claim low latency. Some of these tools use their own distributed engine for query processing (and execution), and Spark SQL uses the Spark engine. In-memory processing is a key benefit for Spark, but other in-memory solutions are also emerging. NoSQL solutions like VoltDB and SploutSQL can add performance to your Hadoop data. A popular query tool like Hive is getting a performance facelift through distributed frameworks like Spark or Apache Tez (developed by Hortonworks) to reduce latency and help with performance. What are the benefits of this approach and how does that help you? I discuss the details shortly and will start my discussion with Spark SQL.

Spark SQL

Three years back, Spark SQL started as Shark at UC Berkeley and was developed as a faster SQL alternative to the moderately performing Hive. Shark effectively challenged the doubts about inefficiency of query processing on general data-processing engines. It was the first time that an interactive SQL tool was built on top of a generic processing engine (Spark) and performed so well. The availability of a SQL engine on top of a generic processing engine offers additional benefits, such as consolidation of data access methods like batch processing, streaming, and machine learning.

Recently, Shark development was ended and folded into the Spark SQL project. Also, Hive on Spark (HIVE-7292) was introduced. Spark SQL will now provide all of Shark's features (as well as some additional ones) for existing Shark users. Therefore, Spark SQL will provide both an upgrade path from Shark 0.9 server and also new features like integration with Spark programs.

Although Spark SQL has a lot of benefits (compared to Hive), many organizations currently use Hive extensively. The Hive community proposed a new initiative that would add Spark as an alternative execution engine (instead of MapReduce) to Hive. This will make transition to Spark easier for them. This initiative is known as "Hive on Spark," or HIVE-7292.

Figure 5-1 summarizes the architectural differences between Hive, HIVE-7292, and Spark SQL.

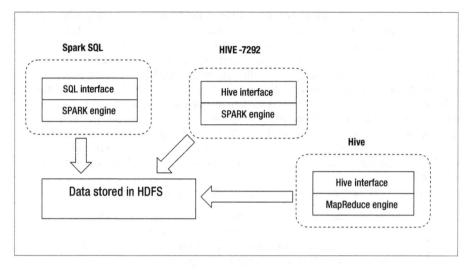

Figure 5-1. *Architectural differences between Spark SQL, Hive, and HIVE-7292*

A few years back, when the Shark project started, Hive (using MapReduce) was the only SQL interface available for Hadoop. Hive compiled SQL into MapReduce jobs and supported a variety of formats. Performance issues necessitated supplementing Hive with proprietary enterprise data warehouses (EDWs) that required rigid and lengthy ETL pipelines. The vast difference in performance questioned the query-processing capability on general data-processing engines itself and speculated whether specialized runtime engines (such as EDWs) were necessary for performance.

Shark effectively demonstrated that the performance deficiencies (which made Hive slow) were inherent to the Hive architecture and could be overcome by using Spark as a processing engine (instead of MapReduce). Also, this solution can scale as well as MapReduce. A powerful SQL query engine working with a general data-processing engine can help support various types of data access such as batch processing, streaming, or machine learning, and enables application of advanced models (to the data) easier.

To start with, Shark achieved performance improvement (over Hive) by using Spark as a physical engine for execution (as opposed to MapReduce) while still using the Hive code base. The Shark development team realized that the Hive code base was a significant overhead since it was hard to maintain and optimize. Also, performance optimizations and sophisticated analytics were almost impossible to achieve using this code base that was designed for MapReduce. Subsequently, it was decided to end development for Shark and repurpose the resources to develop a new component for Spark—Spark SQL.

Of course, the knowledge and understanding gained through Shark usage (by users) was actively applied by the development team while designing Spark SQL and thus has resulted in a more powerful SQL interface that also maintains compatibility with Shark/ Hive. Also, Spark SQL supports all existing Hive data formats, user-defined functions (UDFs), and the Hive metastore. Lastly, with features that will be introduced in the next version of Spark (1.1.0), Spark SQL will be faster (compared to Shark) by almost an order of magnitude. Thus, it will be an excellent resource to manipulate structured or semi-structured data and will support data ingestion from varied formats and sources (such as JSON, Parquet, Hive, or any other EDWs) as well as advanced analytics using sophisticated programming APIs. The long-term goal for Spark SQL is to provide an interface that supports both SQL and advanced analytics (machine learning, statistics, and so on).

To summarize, here are some of the key features of Spark SQL (latest version):

- *In-memory data processing:* Spark SQL provides the option to explicitly load data in memory for speeding up query processing. Also, it uses an efficient, compressed, column-oriented format for holding data in memory, helping to fit larger datasets.

- *Fault tolerance:* Spark SQL is well suited for short- as well as long-running queries. It can recover from mid-query faults as it uses the Spark engine for processing.

- *Data sources API:* Provides a single interface for loading and storing data. Provides prepackaged sources with the Apache Spark distribution as well as provision for integrating external (custom) data sources. Examples of built-in or prepackaged sources are JSON, JDBC, Parquet, Hive, MySQL, PostgreSQL, HDFS, and AWS S3. External sources (currently available) include CSV, Apache Avro, HBase, Cassandra, Elasticsearch, and Amazon Redshift.

- *Dataframes:* A *dataframe* is a distributed dataset organized into named columns. Logically, it is similar to a table in a relational database or a Dataframe in R/Python. Dataframes can be sourced from structured data files, Hive tables, external databases, or existing resilient distributed dataset (RDDs), an immutable distributed collection of records that can be stored in memory or on disk.

- *Catalyst (rule and cost-based optimizer):* Dataframes expose more application semantics to the core Spark engine, and therefore Spark can use Catalyst to optimize the queries.

- *Python API (PySpark):* Python is widely used with Big Data, but Python programs don't perform as well as the JVMs due to the more dynamic nature of the language. Using the new DataFrame API, Python programs can now perform as well as JVMs as the Catalyst optimizer compiles DataFrame operations into JVM bytecode.

- *Statistical and mathematical functions:* Spark SQL supports a wide range of functions such as random data generation, summary and descriptive statistics, sample covariance and correlation, cross-tabulation (a.k.a. contingency table), and mathematical functions like cos, sin, floor, ceil.

Figure 5-2 shows the Spark ecosystem and where Spark SQL fits into it.

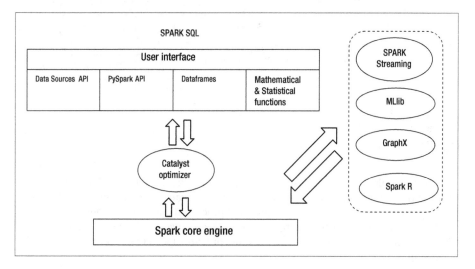

Figure 5-2. *Spark ecosystem*

Presto

Presto is a distributed SQL query engine developed by Facebook and open sourced for use by the Apache community. It is optimized for interactive queries (including complex analytic queries). You can use standard ANSI SQL syntax including aggregations, joins, and window functions.

Presto does not use MapReduce as underlying execution model. For example, Hive converts queries into a series of MapReduce tasks that execute singly in a predetermined order. Each task reads data from disk and writes intermediate output back to disk. In comparison, the Presto engine uses a custom query and execution engine that supports SQL semantics. Since all the processing is in memory and pipelined across the network between stages, unnecessary I/O (as well as associated latency) is avoided. This pipelined execution model runs stages in parallel and passes on data from one stage to the next as soon as it is available. This helps in reducing latency for many types of queries.

Figure 5-3 shows the system architecture for Presto. The client initiates a query and sends SQL to the Presto coordinator process. The coordinator parses, analyzes, and plans execution for the input query. The scheduler is responsible for coordinating the execution pipeline, assigning work to nodes based on their network proximity (the ones closest to the data would be used) and monitoring progress.

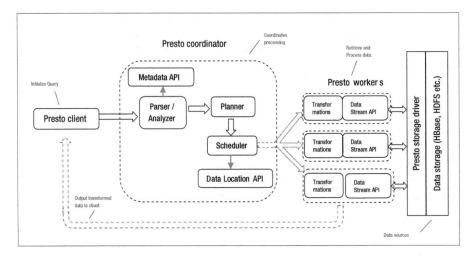

Figure 5-3. *Presto architecture*

The scheduler is also responsible for spawning worker threads (as required). These worker threads access storage (using the appropriate storage driver) and retrieve data. The client then pulls the consolidated and processed data from the output stage, which in turn pulls data from underlying intermediate stages. As discussed earlier, all this processing occurs in memory and therefore provides speed to the entire query processing.

Analytic Tools

Analytic tools are the ones that scan most (or all) of the data and perform processing that derives information or knowledge from it. Broadly, these tools can be classified in two categories. The first category is tools performing aggregations (these aggregations being very similar to what data-warehousing queries perform). Some of these tools support SQL; others do not. I will discuss an interesting product (Apache Kylin) in this subcategory.

My second category comprises tools providing the capability to perform custom algorithmic processing, including predictive and prescriptive analytics. Traditionally, these were performed using HBase or Cassandra with HDFS storage. Spark is the latest entry in this space, with better performance, but other interesting tools provide this functionality too.

Some NoSQL databases do not provide aggregation support (for example, Cassandra, HBase). Precomputing aggregates while ingesting data and storing them (for later use) is an alternative.

Finally, there are products that don't fit into one category or the other. For example, Druid (NoSQL analytic engine for aggregation) can also ingest data in real time like Storm. Druid stores the aggregates in memory (across the cluster) for faster access.

Apache Kylin

Apache Kylin is an open source distributed analytics tool developed by eBay. Kylin provides a SQL interface along with the capability to perform multidimensional analysis (OLAP) on Hadoop and supporting very large datasets. To add performance to these capabilities, Kylin prebuilds MOLAP cubes. In addition, it has distributed architecture that can benefit from MapReduce (or any other framework for processing distributed data) and also provides high concurrency. In addition to the SQL interface, Kylin also works well with other BI tools like Spotfire, Tableau, or MicroStrategy.

Following are the key features of Kylin:

- *Scalable and fast OLAP engine:* Kylin reduces query latency even for very large datasets. This is attributed to the architecture that prebuilds cubes along with calculations.

- *ANSI SQL support and interactive querying:* Since we have all used SQL for such a long time, Kylin's support for most ANSI SQL query functions is a useful feature and speeds up the development process. Interactive queries offer flexibility and speed (through prebuilt cubes).

- *MOLAP cube:* Using file storage and prebuilding calculations provide speed to a MOLAP or multidimensional cube. Besides, the traditional weakness of MOLAP (limits on data inclusion within a cube) doesn't exist for Kylin. For example, users can easily prebuild a cube in Kylin for more than 10+ billion raw data records.

- *BI tool integration:* Integration with BI tools is very important for performing advanced analytics and reporting. Kylin can be interfaced with business intelligence tools such as Tableau, Spotfire, Microstrategy, and many other third-party applications.

- *Open source ODBC driver:* Kylin's ODBC driver is developed for accessing data sources as required and thoroughly tested with the Report-writing application Tableau. The driver is open sourced to the Apache community so that it is easy to customize it for your specific use.

- *Easy and effective management:* The following features provide ease of use and management:

  - Job management and monitoring

  - Compression and encoding for reducing storage needs

  - Incremental data refresh for cubes (this allows you to process changed data only, reducing processing time)

  - Web interface for managing, building, monitoring, and querying cubes

- *Performance enhancement:* The following features provide additional performance enhancement:

  - Kyline leverages the use of the HBase coprocessor for query performance. For simple additive or aggregating operations (such as sum, count, or like), pushing the computation to the region or master server (where it can work on the data directly without network traffic overhead) can provide a substantial improvement in performance.

  - Kylin uses the "HyperLogLog" algorithm for determining distinct counts within a query. This algorithm approximates the number of distinct elements in a dataset, reducing memory consumption significantly and allowing use of very large datasets.

- *Flexible and granular security:* Kylin allows you to set up ACLs (access control lists) at the granular level of a cube or a project and also provides support for LDAP integration. This helps in integrating with corporate security easily.

- *Fault tolerance:* Kylin supports fault tolerance at the system as well as data levels:

  - *Data fault tolerance:* Cubes in Kylin can be partitioned into segments, and the advantage is that you can refresh (or rebuild) an individual segment without impacting the whole cube. So, you can have a strategy to build segments daily, weekly, or monthly as needed. Any data errors detected or changes needed can be applied to the segment of least granularity and thus provide effective fault tolerance without the need to rebuild the whole cube. Data changes that can't be accommodated by the least level of granularity will need rebuild at a higher level (for example, any data issues discovered after a week will need the weekly segments to be rebuilt). So, you need to balance the data error tolerance and query performance. Higher granularity for segments will provide a higher tolerance to data errors/changes, but will also cause more scans to execute for each query. Importantly, a cube is still available for use when some of its segments are being rebuilt.

  - *System fault tolerance:* Kylin inherits the system redundancy and fault tolerance that HDFS and HBase provide. Additionally, you can safely retry any failed build steps without any adverse effects. This ensures integrity and correctness of the final version of the build, regardless of any number of intermediate failures or retries.

Kylin Architecture

I discussed Spark SQL and Presto in the last few sections. A number of SQL-on-Hadoop tools are available. So why use Kylin? Because most of these tools need to scan the dataset partially or fully to answer your query. Not only that, any joins (within your query) may trigger data transfer across the nodes, and depending on network traffic latency, the response you receive might not be what you would like.

In contrast, Kylin precomputes aggregations for all dimensions and stores the resultant values in a cube. The process followed for building cube(s) is extensive and considers all possible combinations of dimensions, thus ensuring coverage for a larger number of queries. Also, Kylin generates pre-join HiveQL (based on metadata) for joining fact tables with dimension tables. The pre-joins and pre-aggregation results are stored in HBase. So, most of the queries are served by the MOLAP (multidimensional OLAP) cubes and are substantially fast. Queries that can't use a cube are routed to a Hive table that holds the metadata and thus execute as ROLAP (relational OLAP using star or snowflake schema). In essence, Kylin provides HOLAP (hybrid OLAP) architecture.

The next releases of Kylin are planned with Spark SQL replacing Hive (for additional speed and in-memory processing), Lambda architecture (for providing near real-time results), in-memory analytics (for performance), and capacity management. Also, there are plans to use the Spark engine.

The flow-chart in Figure 5-4 summarizes the cube build process within Kylin.

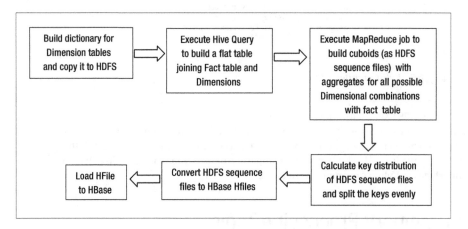

Figure 5-4. *Kylin cube build process*

Finally, let me summarize this discussion with a comprehensive Kylin architecture diagram. Figure 5-5 shows the main components of the Kylin engine: REST server, query engine, metadata manager, and job engine.

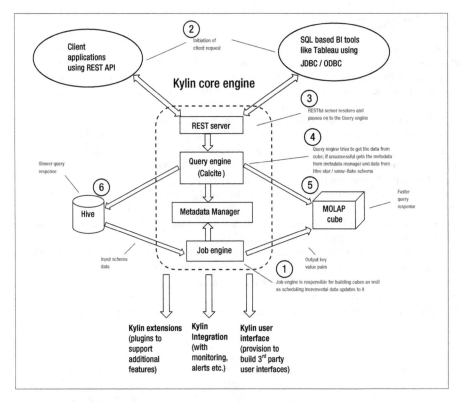

Figure 5-5. Kylin architecture

The REST server interfaces with client queries and passes them on to the query engine. If the query results can be computed using the cube data, then the results are returned almost instantly, but if they can't be computed (from the cube data), then the slower route is used, which involves using the Hive schema. You can add extensions or interfaces to Kylin core engine as needed.

In-Memory Processing Tools

For the last couple of years, memory-based processing has been dominated by Spark and Storm. Although both are extremely versatile and useful products, Apache Flink has some features that offer a definite advantage over these tested and proven products.

Flink

Flink is a large-scale data-processing engine that offers in-memory data streaming and therefore extremely fast processing for data-intensive as well as iterative jobs. How does Flink differ from Spark? Well, Spark is primarily a batch-processing framework that can closely simulate stream processing. Flink is primarily a stream-processing framework that can also perform batch processing. Spark is not a pure stream-processing engine but in fact performs fast-batch operations on small parts of incoming data or does "micro-batching." This may not be an issue for most applications, but for financial or real-time systems (where low latency is required), every millisecond is critical, and even a small performance issue can lead to severe monetary consequences.

You can also think of Flink as a replacement for Hadoop MapReduce that works in batch and streaming modes and uses directed graphs (instead of mapping and reducer jobs), thereby leveraging in-memory processing for a much better performance.

Flink has an excellent optimization engine. The Flink optimizer analyzes input code (to the cluster) and decides on the best pipeline (as it deems fit) for executing that code for a specific setup (which may be differ as per cluster hardware and number of nodes). For performance, iterative processing is performed on the same nodes (instead of the cluster running each iteration independently). Using optimizer hints, it is also possible to perform delta iterations only on parts of your dataset that may have changed.

Flink can work with YARN and also can run existing MapReduce jobs directly on its execution engine, providing an easy upgrade for organizations already using MapReduce. Finally, Flink works with on Apache Tez (only for batch processing), giving up some performance for scalability.

As for managing memory, Flink implements its own memory management inside the JVM (of DataFlow engine), thereby helping applications to scale easily and be less affected by JVM's garbage collection overhead. This also (nearly) eliminates the memory usage abnormalities (or spikes) often seen on Spark clusters. It is possible to dump a JSON representation of the pipelines Flink has constructed for your job (through a built-in HTML viewer), making debugging easy.

Fault tolerance is an important consideration for streaming applications, and Flink's fault tolerance mechanism is based on Chandy-Lamport distributed snapshots. This algorithm enables a process in a distributed system to determine the global state of the system during a computation and can be used for checkpointing. The mechanism uses small amount of system resources (thereby maintaining high throughput rates) and still provides a guaranteed level of consistency.

A lot of organizations (using Hadoop) are opting for a real-time streaming architecture (as opposed to the existing batch architecture). Static HDFS files are being supplemented with event streams, and batch workloads are being replaced with stream processors to deliver lower latency applications. The main reason for this transition is that the datasets and use cases that make up most of the workloads for Hadoop clusters are event-based (for example, event or audit logs). Another reason is that now stream processing technology is developed enough to handle more complex requirements. Finally, there are applications (like processing sensor data) that need continuous queries and can only be supported by a streaming architecture.

Usually, stream architecture consists of the following modules:

- Gathering and consolidating event streams

- Collecting, holding the streams centrally, and distributing them

- Analyzing the streams and creating derived streams

The first step is performed using applications like Flume or Sqoop, but it depends largely on the data sources. Input events may consist of data coming from (relational/ NoSQL) databases, machine-generated logs, or from sensors. This data needs to be cleaned and consolidated.

Applications like Kafka can be used for performing the second step. Kafka can collect event streams and log as well as buffer them. Kafka also offers fault tolerance (which is necessary in this case) while holding and distributing the streams.

The final step involves performing analytics on the streams. It may involve creating counters, aggregating them, consolidating streams, or creating derived data streams for further use. Apache Flink can be (and is) used to implement this step.

Flink Architecture

Remember that Flink is only a framework for distributed data analysis. At the core, Flink has a streaming iterative data flow engine. Flink uses two major APIs (the DataSet API for processing batch data and the DataStream API for processing event streams) on top of the core engine to provide the versatile functionality of processing dissimilar data with equal ease. The growing popularity of Flink has resulted in the development of domain-specific libraries and APIs built on top of these two major APIs.

Currently, the following libraries are available: Machine Learning library, a graph analysis library (Gelly), and a SQL-like API (Table). In addition, there are other projects that work on top of Flink, such as Google Cloud Dataflow and Apache MRQL. Finally, the Flink core engine can work with a variety of data-processing frameworks such as YARN/Apache Tez, can work as a standalone Flink cluster, or can be embedded in other applications. Figure 5-6 summarizes the architecture.

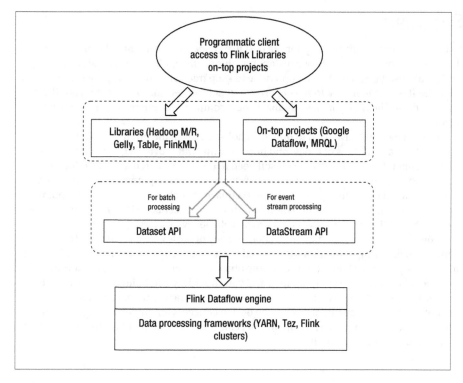

Figure 5-6. *Flink architecture*

Search and Messaging Tools

Search tools provide capability to index and search (primarily) for text data. So, they are applicable for certain types of data only. These search tools (for Hadoop) are not as flexible or extensive as the search utilities for relational databases, for obvious reasons, but they do have a place. Since a lot of NoSQL databases lack necessary secondary indexing capabilities, these products are sometimes used to augment them. Solr and Elastic Search for Hadoop are popular products in this category, and both use Lucene as the underlying indexing engine.

Messaging systems deliver messages in source-destination and publish- subscribe mode. Typically these systems work on top of real-time stream processors like Flink or Spark Streaming. Kafka is a popular messaging system (briefly discussed in the last section) that additionally allows you to have random access to your messages.

Summary

If you have worked with Hadoop for the past five years, you have probably noticed that the Hadoop world is in a state of constant transition, and applications get added (or vanish) almost daily. It is almost impossible to keep track of all the new projects, and therefore it is a difficult task to select perfectly synchronized components for your Big Data needs. By the time you have finalized, new components emerge that better suit your needs!

In this chapter, I have tried to provide a holistic view of the product categories and new products available as of today, and hopefully this will provide a good overview and a starting point for you. However, you still need to do your research and due diligence while choosing components that must satisfy your business requirements. Remember, if a new component (just introduced in the marketplace) matches your needs better but will impact your project deadlines by a month, it should be acceptable if it gives you an edge over the competition or improves your process efficiency by a large percentage.

You also need to understand that choosing any of these components involves complex engineering tradeoffs and you need to choose the option involving least amount of tradeoffs (and most benefits). Your prime objective should serve as a good starting point (for choosing main components), and you should try and build a system around it.

This chapter also serves as a transition to the Big Data world from relational technology. The later chapters discuss the design concepts for implementing Big Data solutions, and therefore the Hadoop product categories this chapter has discussed will be helpful in understanding them.

CHAPTER 6

■ ■ ■

Re-Architecting for NoSQL: Design Principles, Models and Best Practices

I was recently at a Gartner seminar about *data monetization*, delivered by Doug Laney. Doug talked about an interesting concept of assigning monetary value to the data your organization has gathered historically. He also talked about the concepts of *data bartering* and paying taxes using information instead of money (which apparently he mentioned to a couple of IRS officials and enjoyed their reactions). Doug aptly terms the economics of data as *infonomics*. Creation of a new discipline to monetize data efficiently, I feel, highlights the growing importance of data (and information) in today's world.

Now think of the underlying issue with infonomics—how do you organize, consolidate, analyze, and present large volumes of data? Since the concept involves utilizing all the data your organization has gathered over the years, data volumes will be large. Also, like anything else that needs to sold, the end product needs to be useful and presentable. A Big Data solution can be utilized successfully to organize and analyze large volumes of data. Of course, you need to re-architect your data for NoSQL usage, since relational data can't be used as-is with NoSQL databases. Certain transformations need to be applied, which I discuss in this chapter.

There are a lot of features of relational databases that you simply assume are available for any database system. For example, defining fine-grained security (or authorization) or referential integrity constraints or statistics. Also, things like concurrent updates or data type validations are handled automatically by the RDBMS. For NoSQL databases, only some of these features are available, but only with add-ons (and lots of extra work to install/configure/integrate with other components) or custom development involving time and money. For example, you have to transform your data to preserve data integrity (without availability of referential integrity) or deliver better performance without availability of advanced level of indexing or statistics. RDBMS provides all these features to you in one (relatively) easy-to-use package.

© Bhushan Lakhe 2016

B. Lakhe, *Practical Hadoop Migration*, DOI 10.1007/978-1-4842-1287-5_6

Absence of referential integrity prompts denormalization of data. That reminds us of data warehouses, and although the transformation techniques are similar, NoSQL takes it a step further by eliminating any joins altogether. As you may recall, for star schemas, a fact table needs to be joined with appropriate dimension tables for effective (and flexible) filtering of data. With NoSQL databases, even those joins are not advisable. So, joins need to be eliminated completely.

Another important thing to remember is that many of the data integrity, validation, or concurrency features were not necessary for a lot of applications, and that actually facilitated development of NoSQL databases—they trade these features for better performance and scalability.

Some thought also needs to be given to non-datacentric factors such as security (authentication/authorization) or concurrency, since these features are provided by default within a RDBMS, whereas they are not available easily for NoSQL solutions.

As a concluding thought, you must remember the functional difference in RDBMS database design and NoSQL database design. RDBMS database design is a reflection of the business functionality and processes, whereas NoSQL design essentially reflects data access pattern and facilitation of performance for it (data within NoSQL database is denormalized to facilitate quick retrieval and processing).

Design Principles for Re-Architecting Relational Applications to NoSQL Environments

NoSQL databases primarily focus on the data usage patterns and rearrange data to facilitate performance. With the HDFS storage (in some cases), scalability and fault tolerance are available by default. Because I am discussing transition, I am assuming that there is an existing RDBMS-based system that provides necessary business functionality.

Therefore, as a first step, you need to review the existing data and the processing that needs to be transitioned to NoSQL. As you are well aware, there are several types of NoSQL databases (key-value stores, columnar databases, document databases, and graph databases). Based on your data characteristics and processing requirements, you must decide what type of NoSQL database suits your needs best.

As a next step, data within the (selected) NoSQL database will need to be denormalized, aggregated, and presented to facilitate analysis and ad hoc queries. I discuss each of these aspects of transition in detail. Finally, I discuss the implementation of non-datacentric features like security or concurrency for NoSQL solutions.

Selecting an Appropriate NoSQL Database

To start with, I am assuming that you have spent some time considering whether you really need to use NoSQL in your environment and made your decision using the various factors discussed in Chapter 1. Note that Hadoop and NoSQL operate on datasets as opposed to databases and tables in a relational environment. So you can think of a NoSQL *database* as a *collection of datasets*. This section discusses the major types of NoSQL databases and their potential applications.

Key-Value Stores

These databases consist of a global collection of key-value pairs. What does a key-value pair mean in this context? Let's assume that a dataset with global sales details is accessed frequently for a marketing analytics system, and because there may be millions of sales records for popular products, retrieval takes time. It will help if this dataset is cached. So, a *key* can be defined that has this dataset as value, and then a quick data retrieval can be ensured by referring to the key.

A common problem is multiple keys pointing to the same dataset. If you can make sure that all the *values* (datasets) in your key store have unique keys, then you can successfully use it like a hash table. Key-value stores are mostly used as cache stores or key-based data. Remember, you will have issues if you try to query the same data using multiple keys.

Scaling out with key-value stores is easy and can be achieved by hashing the keys. Some key-value stores automatically do that for you. In general, key-value stores work well for applications performing lots of small reads/writes or continuous streaming because of good performance gains due to in-memory processing. Some popular key-value stores are Memcache, Redis, Aerospike, and Riak.

What kind of applications can you utilize the key-value stores for? Consider this scenario. When you browse a retail website, a random cookie value is associated with a large chunk of serialized data on the server, often created for every visitor. These cookies then hang around for weeks, taking up valuable database space. A key-value store can be used to create a key entry for a visitor with a 24-hour (or as required) expiry, thereby releasing the space automatically.

Also, consider a simple capped log implementation. You can append items to a *log* key (mapped to a file that captures log records) and retain only the last few items. You can use this to keep track of the system state without scanning through the ever-increasing amounts of logging information.

To summarize, key-value stores can be utilized for data that consists of:

- A large number of small read/write operations

- Operations on multiple data structures

- Fluid data types or requires a flexible number of columns

Finally, how can you use a key-value store for your application? Here is an example using the key-value store Memcached. A typical Memcached installation has one or more servers that cache the data (*value*) along with a unique *key* as requested by any of the clients. The key can then be used to retrieve that data quickly in the future. The cached data has expiry duration specified and is removed from cache once that duration is reached. If multiple servers are available, more data can be cached (because memory for all the servers gets added for usage).

Because Memcached calls and programming languages will change based on the API used, I will use pseudocode to demonstrate the concept. For this example, assume that the server IP is 63.1.4.52 and the port used is 2200. Then, the sequence of commands will be similar to the following:

```
# pseudocode to define new cache and server

memcacheclt = new Memcache
memcacheclt:add_server('63.1.4.52:2200')
```

Memcached can be used for reducing load on SQL databases by caching the frequently accessed data. Of course, it doesn't offer a centralized query cache (as offered by RDBMS) or use any middleware to implement caching and hence doesn't have a big problem when a cache is invalidated (possibly due to data change).

```
# Define data cache (value) and key for data within Sales table

sql = "SELECT * FROM Sales WHERE Product_id = ?"
key = 'SQL:' . Product_id . ':' . md5sum(sql)
```

If you are not familiar with md5sum, it is a program that calculates and verifies 128-bit MD5 hashes for files as well as strings. The MD5 hash (or checksum) serves as a compact digital fingerprint of a string or a file. Although an unlimited number of files (or strings) can have any given MD5 hash, it is really unlikely that any two non-identical files (or strings) will have the same MD5 hash. This helps in ensuring uniqueness of keys. Note that the underlying MD5 algorithm is no longer considered secure (although it doesn't need to be, especially for SQL strings), but because any change to a string (or file) will cause its MD5 hash to change, md5sum can be used to verify the integrity of files or strings.

```
# To start with, check if the key-value pair is defined
if (defined result = memcacheclt:get(key)) {
        return result
} else {

        # execute sql to create key-value pair
        handler = run_sql(sql, Product_id)

        # Since you get back a handler or pointer object (after
        # executing SQL), you need to convert it to an array for caching
        final_array = handler:convert_to_an_array

        # Cache it for ten minutes
        memcacheclt:set(key, final_array, 10 * 60)
        return final_array

}
```

When you cache sales rows for this product, you will see the same data for up to ten minutes. Which means it will take up to ten minutes to see any data changes that you make (unless you actively invalidate the cache by making a change to the data). Typically, you can use key-value databases for web applications and hold user profiles/preferences, session details, and shopping carts.

Document Databases

A document-oriented database stores and manages data stored as documents. A *document* can be a grouping of structured or semi-structured data. Document-oriented databases can be thought of as a subclass of the key-value stores, since the way data is stored and retrieved is similar, but the way data is processed is different. For a key-value store, the data is inherently opaque to the database; it is just value for a key. In comparison, a document-oriented system reads the internal structure of the data (or document) to extract metadata and uses it for further processing and optimization. Document-oriented databases extract type information from the data itself and group related information together for ease of use. For example, XML databases (a specific subclass) are optimized for extracting metadata from XML documents. Also, document databases are typically optimized for complex random text searches (for example, elasticsearch) as well.

With document-oriented databases, you get the flexibility of having every instance of data be different from others, and this lends valuable support for optional values as well as updates. That's why they are so popular with web applications—which change frequently, may have semi-structured data, and also need to be deployed quickly. Next, let me discuss what a document is, using an example. Consider the following text:

```
Blue striped shirt
226453
20
12345
IL (US)
```

Although it may be clear to you that this document contains the details for a clothing item, it is not clear as to what the other individual fields represent. If this information is stored in a key-value store, the semantic content (that this inventory item for a web retailer represents) may be lost and the database will have no way to optimize or index this data effectively. It may be possible to employ additional logic to separate the string into fields and assign fields to columns within a table, but it will not be a simple task. Without metadata, parsing free form data like this can be complex. Now consider the same document marked up in pseudo-XML:

```
<Item>
  <ItemName>Blue striped shirt</ItemName>
  <ItemType>Male Shirt</ItemType>
  <ItemSize>Large</ItemType>
  <ItemNumber>226453</ ItemNumber>
  <Quantity>20</Quantity>
  <WarehouseNum>12345</WarehouseNum>
  <State>IL</State>
  <Country>US</Country>
</Item>
```

So now, the document includes both data as well as metadata and that explains each of the fields. This way, it is possible to query the data like "find all the <Item>s located in <state> of 'IL'" or design index on the state field for performance. You can combine search conditions just like any other database, but the major difference is embedding of metadata within the document itself, and that eliminates the need for predefining the database fields. It also offers the flexibility of adding or removing certain fields, and thus every document in the database can have a different format. One <Item> may have <Size> while the other may have <Style> instead. That doesn't invalidate the earlier query of looking for items located in Illinois for this data.

The embedded metadata also allows the document format to be changed without affecting the existing documents. Let's say that a new <ItemPicture> field is added to the new documents. It won't affect any existing documents—they simply won't have a picture associated with them. Also, in general, any queries based on fields that are not a part of a document won't retrieve them.

Popular formats for documents include XML, YAML, JSON, and BSON. Some documents don't contain clearly defined metadata (for example, PDFs), and the database managing them may provide ways to map data using indexing or may include predefined formats based on XML such as MathML, JATS, or DocBook. In some cases, schema languages like DTD, XSD, or Relax NG are used to map documents to a more usable format. JSON is about the most popular format (used mostly for interactive web-based applications) by a number of document-oriented databases.

Documents can be stored using a unique key for reference and retrieved using it. A key can be a string, a URI, or a path. It helps to create an index on the key field for speeding up document retrieval. More indexes can be created to speed up frequent searches. Most of the popular document-oriented databases provide tools to extract and index almost all the metadata as well as the data content for documents that they manage. Queries are further supported by availability of a query language, making it easy for the users.

Document-oriented databases can be used for data that consists of the following:

- A wide variety of data types and may have a number of access patterns

- A need to build CRUD (create, read, update, delete) apps

- Data types like JSON, HTTP, REST, JavaScript, and used with web-based applications

- Processing that involves a lot of small (and possibly volatile) continuous reads and writes

- Fluid data types or requires a flexible number of columns (due to optional data)

- Large media (BLOB types) or semi-structured

Applications suited for document databases are event logging, e-commerce applications, and content management applications. Popular document-oriented database systems are MongoDB, CouchDB, and OrientDB.

Columnar Databases

A *columnar* database organizes its data in columns instead of rows. This re-orients the focus of data and helps in writing/reading data from hard disk storage more efficiently, thereby speeding up the queries performed on a dataset. A *data column* consists of name and value (and sometimes a timestamp). Each row can have a different number of columns. A row key can be used for queries, or secondary indexes (created on column values) can be used too.

For a columnar database, column values are physically grouped together as opposed to rows. Because the data is stored in record order, 5th entry for column 1 and the 5th entry for column 2 are part of the same record. This enables individual data elements (such as the following product details) to be accessed in columns as a group, instead of an individual row-by-row access.

Here is an example of a product table:

ID	ProductName	Category	Quantity	Price
1	Green Tea bags	Tea	100	3.99
2	Black Tea bags	Tea	100	2.99
3	GingerTea bags	Tea	100	4.99

For a row-oriented database, the data would be stored like: 1,Green Tea bags, Tea,100,3.99;2,Black Tea bags,Tea,100,2.99;3,Ginger Tea bags,Tea,100, 4.99;

For a column-oriented database, the data will be stored as: 1,2,3; Green Tea bags,Black Tea bags,Ginger Tea bags;Tea,Tea,Tea;100,100,100;3.99, 2.99,4.99;

But why organize the data in columns? One reason is the compression it provides for storage. As a result, columnar operations (such as MIN, MAX, SUM, COUNT, and AVG) can be performed very speedily. Also, because a columnar database is self-indexing, it can store data more efficiently (disk space–wise) compared to a relational database management system (RDBMS). Also, data compression offered by columnar databases is a big advantage. The benefits of these features can be seen for a large data volume, where data access performance is of essence. Otherwise, for smaller volumes, databases offering in-memory analytics can easily make the relative benefits of row-oriented versus column oriented databases somewhat irrelevant, due their speed—although data compression offered by columnar databases can still be useful, since memory is expensive and compression can help you fit in datasets using smaller RAM.

What kind of applications can make use of columnar databases? As stated earlier, large data volume is required to see the difference in performance. In addition, columnar databases are well suited for large amount of data aggregated in a few columns. Columnar databases do not support ACID transactions and are more useful where "eventual consistency" can be tolerated.

Another thing to remember about columnar databases is that they perform as well for applications where writes are more frequent as they do for queries. Also, these databases perform well where applications need to access only a few columns (of large numbers of rows) at once. Columnar databases can speed up your analytical queries by helping you focus on the necessary columns without reading through thousands of rows.

Finally, columnar databases can also be used for time-dependent columns (or for data that has expiry), since it is possible to set up automatic column expiry after a specific date.

Though the concept of a column store has earlier been implemented as part of relational databases, RDBMS doesn't provide the flexibility of columns differing across column family rows, which is permitted by NoSQL columnar databases (you can have varying number of columns for each row).

As is widely known, columnar databases are derived from Google's Big Table. Popular distributed scale-out columnar databases include HBase and Cassandra.

To summarize, you can use distributed scale-out columnar databases if your data:

- Needs high availability and redundancy

- Needs to span multiple data centers in different geographical locations and you need a distributed and partition-tolerant option capable of handling long latencies

- Has continuous data streams that don't need any consistency guarantees

- Has fluid data types and dynamic fields

- Has a potential for truly large volumes of data, such as hundreds of terabytes, and need aggregations on a few columns

Typically, the following kinds of applications can benefit from this kind of Big Data processing capability:

- Data analytics (user behavior, network traffic, log files)

- Bioinformatics (genetic and proteomic data)

- Stock market analysis (trade data)

- Web-scale applications (search engines)

- Social network services

Graph Databases

Graph databases have their origin in the graph theory proposed by the Swiss mathematician Leonard Paul Euler. Main components of graph databases are *nodes* and *edges* (or *relationships*). Both nodes and relationships can have properties associated with them. In addition, nodes can also be labeled with zero or more labels. Nodes represent entities that you might want to monitor (or query), and relationships are relations that exist between the nodes. Properties (or attributes) provide information about the nodes or the relationships.

For example, if "Practical Hadoop Security" were one of the nodes, one might have it tied to properties such as "book," "security reference material," or "220 pages," depending on which aspects of "Practical Hadoop Security" are relevant to a particular database.

Graph databases are often faster (compared with relational databases) for complex queries on large datasets, since they do not require expensive join operations. As they are not dependent on a static schema, they perform better for frequently changing data as well as evolving schemas. However, they can't perform as well (as relational databases) for static schemas with large numbers of data elements. Graph databases, of course, work best for graph-like queries (such as computing the shortest path between two nodes or a graph's diameter computation).

For scenarios with complex inter-related relationships (for example, queries involving multiple highways connecting cities, proteins interacting with other proteins, and employees working with other employees) between various nodes (or entities) graph databases work best. That's why graph databases are well-suited for the following types of problem domains:

- Network and IT infrastructure management

- Identity and access management

- Business process management

- Product and service recommendations

- Social networking

An important thing to remember about graph databases is that they don't work well for processing large volumes of data and therefore for applications involving large-scale graphs (such as social networks), columnar (or other suitable) databases are frequently used for storage and retrieval, while graph operations work as a top processing layer that contributes performance (for example, Titan graph database).

I'll use LinkedIn's architecture as an example. LinkedIn uses a combination of Oracle, Voldemort, Espresso, Pinot, and XML for data storage. Databases are partitioned horizontally and vertically (for performance). Due to partitioning, it is not possible to implement referential integrity or cross-domain JOINs. Also, an eventual consistency model is used and therefore data is not guaranteed to be consistent. Voldemort and Pinot are key-value stores. Espresso is LinkedIn's online, distributed, fault-tolerant NoSQL database and is used by over 30 LinkedIn applications, including member profile, InMail (the member-to-member messaging system), parts of the home page, mobile applications, and so on. Oracle is used sparingly due to its cost.

Voldemort is a simple key lookup system and is used for quickly looking up small pieces of data (such as for a user profile, data like *jobs you might be interested in, people you may know*, and so forth). Pinot is used for larger key-value lookups like historical data (*give me all the Big Data jobs from January to March*) and is scalable for storing large amounts of data.

The Cloud is a server that caches the entire LinkedIn network graph in memory (LinkedIn has developed a proprietary graph database for this purpose, which sits at the center of nearly every operation). Each instance of Cloud supports 22 million nodes and 120 million edges and needs 12 GB RAM. There were 40 Cloud instances in production by 2008 (I'm not sure how many instances there are now). The Cloud instances are updated in real time with updated data and are persisted to disk on shutdown. Having everything in RAM is a limitation, but because partitioning graphs is hard, there are no other options.

Though the Cloud caches the entire LinkedIn network, each user needs to see information relevant to him only and since computing these individual user views is expensive, LinkedIn does it only when a user connects and keeps it cached. This cached network view is not updated during the session, unless the user himself adds/removes a link (also, it's not updated if any of the user's contacts make changes).

For searches, a customized version of the Lucene search engine is used, and because cached data is searched, the results are returned really quickly. Kafka and Databus are used for data replication, and Zoie (real-time search and indexing engine that uses Lucene), Bobo (faceted search library for Lucene, *facets* being attributes of users such as industry, previous companies, patents, and so on), and SenseiDB (real-time, faceted, key-value and full-text search engine) for online searches.

Figure 6-1 shows the LinkedIn architecture as of 2012. There may have been changes to it since, but consider it as an example of using a graph database for analysis with other NoSQL databases used for storage.

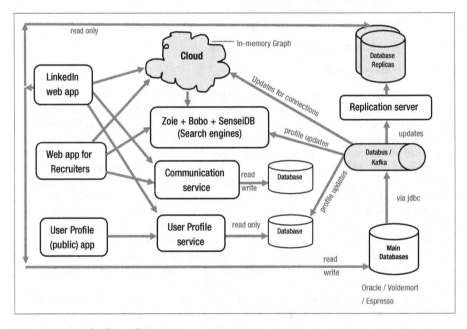

Figure 6-1. *LinkedIn architecture*

Popular graph databases are Neo4j, AllegroGraph, and InfoGrid. I will demonstrate the major concepts for graph databases through a quick example using the Neo4j database.

Graph data modeling is a process in which a user represents a specific domain through a connected graph of nodes and relationships. This graph is then used to answer questions in the form of Cypher (Neo4j query language) queries. Let me start by describing the domain (for my example) first.

Domain Description

Consider the following description of the connection between two people, James and Scott. They work for the same company. Both James and Scott have bought a set of candle-holders from Amazon.com.

We can use this statement to identify components nodes, labels, and relationships and build our model.

Nodes

Node is a primary component and can have attributes (properties), relationships (with other nodes), and labels. Typically, nodes are entities with a unique conceptual identity. In this case, the following nodes need to be defined:

- James
- Scott
- Set of candle-holders

Labels

Next, let's decide if you need to assign any labels to your nodes. A *label* is used for grouping nodes into sets and is optional. If defined, database queries can use labels instead of individual nodes, making it easier to write compact and more efficient queries. For this example, let's define two labels:

- Person (applied to nodes James and Scott)
- Object (applied to node Candle-holder set)

Relationships

The following interactions can be identified between these nodes:

- James is a colleague of Scott
- Scott is a colleague of James
- James bought a set of candle-holders
- Scott bought a set of candle-holders

Next, I'll connect the nodes together to demonstrate their interactions and complete the graph data model. Nodes labeled *Person* can be connected by the *colleague of* relationship. Nodes labeled *Object* can be connected with nodes labeled as *Person* using *has bought* relationship, as shown in Figure 6-2.

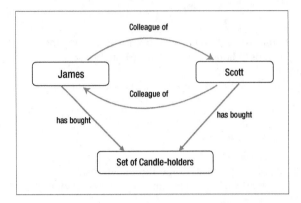

Figure 6-2. *Graph data model for Neo4j-based example*

Creating Attributes

Nodes, by themselves, don't provide any useful information and can't answer the questions that may be asked. The attributes depend on information that may be required for the nodes. For example:

- When did James and Scott become colleagues?
- What's the price for the set of candle-holders?
- From where did James and Scott buy the set of candle-holders?
- How old is James?

Addition of the following attributes help answer those questions (note that the attributes are added as key-value pairs) as shown in Figure 6-3.

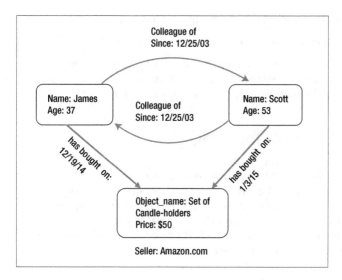

Figure 6-3. *Graph data model for Neo4j-based example (with attributes)*

Let's add the attribute data to the database using Neo4j query language Cypher:

```
// Create Entities or Nodes
CREATE (James:Person { name: "James", age: 37 })
CREATE (Scott:Person { name: "Scott", age: 53 })
CREATE (sch:Object { Object_name: "Set of candle-holders", price: "$50" })

// Create relations
CREATE (Scott)-[:COLLEAGUE_OF { since: 1072339200 }]->(James)
CREATE (James)-[:HAS_BOUGHT { on: 1418976000 }]->(sch)
CREATE (Scott)-[:HAS_BOUGHT { on: 1420272000 }]->(sch)
```

Note that the dates used (1072339200, 1418976000, and 1420272000) are epoch times (*epoch time* is seconds elapsed since January 1st, 1970, not counting leap seconds). So, if you convert *12/25/03 08:00* to epoch time, you will get 1072339200 as a result.

Finally, here's a sample query that answers "What's the price of a set of candle-holders?"

```
MATCH (sch:Object { object_name: "Set of candle-holders" })
RETURN sch.price as price
```

To summarize, graph databases can be used when the data:

- Has complex relations as in social network data
- Needs to dynamically build relations between entities that may have dynamic or changing properties

- May need complex or nested joins for the queries involved

- Belongs to location services or recommendation engines

This completes my discussion about selecting an appropriate NoSQL database solution based on your data and processing needs. Next, I discuss the changes you need to make to your data for re-architecting your application for NoSQL usage.

Concurrency and Security for NoSQL

The concepts of concurrency and security work a little differently for NoSQL environments (compared to RDBMS). Mechanisms to implement concurrency (like locking or transaction isolation levels) don't exist for most of the NoSQL databases. Security needs to be implemented using third-party solutions and is not integrated with databases. So, these features that are available by default for RDBMS need to be simulated for some NoSQL environments. This is one of the tradeoffs for better performance offered by NoSQL. I'll now discuss these concepts in detail.

Concurrency

When a user is updating data from a table within a RDBMS database, other users can't modify the same data, since it is locked (via *exclusive write lock*). Before locking data for an update, RDBMS waits to gain exclusive control of the dataset while users are reading the data with a *shared read lock*. Once there are no shared locks, the dataset is locked using an *exclusive write lock*. Concurrency is handled effectively using the database locking. RDBMS supports ACID (atomicity, consistency, isolation, and durability) transactions, that provide reliability of data.

NoSQL databases don't support ACID compliance for transactions but do have alternate strategies. *Optimistic concurrency control* (OCC) is one of them. OCC assumes that multiple transactions may complete without mutual interference. Therefore, transactions are allowed to use data resources without acquiring locks on them. However, every transaction verifies that the data used (read or written) by it is not modified by any other transaction. If conflicting modifications exist, the committing transaction rolls back. OCC can only be used in environments with low data contention, since otherwise the overhead of restarting transactions will negate the performance advantage and high throughput gained by avoiding locking.

Typically, since most NoSQL databases operate on the philosophy of "single write, multiple reads" (especially open source). They are not expecting concurrent updates and therefore are not designed to support them. By default, most of the distributed data systems support *eventual consistency*. Any system that has multiple nodes processing read requests can't contact other nodes (to verify the data that's provided) while processing a read request, if it has to deliver good performance (since verification will involve additional time). Therefore, the data provided may or may not be the latest; the best you can hope for is for nodes to synchronize and be eventually consistent. This concept is also known as BASE (basically available).

Now, if your application needs some level of concurrency control (maybe not as rigid as ACID compliance), what do you do? Here are some additional ways you can implement concurrency in your NoSQL environments:

- You can use ZooKeeper. The way Zookeeper works is by facilitating distributed locking using a quorum.

- You can use one of the well-tested algorithms for distributed consensus—for example, Paxos along with MVCC (multiversion concurrency control).

- As you have seen, locking in ACID-compliant database environments can cause readers (SELECTs) and writers (UPDATEs) to wait for each other (to complete). This situation is resolved by using MVCC. A *version* is a snapshot of data at a point-in-time. While querying a table, the readers get access to the current version of the data, and updates may happen simultaneously (in parallel). Therefore, the same query at a later point in time may use a newer version and yield different results.

- You can use the CAP model, which states that any networked shared-data system can only have two of three desirable properties: consistency (C), which means you get a single up-to-date copy of your data; high availability (A) of data (for updates); and tolerance to network partitions (P).

- Although designers still need to choose between consistency and availability when partitions are present, with the advent of contemporary networking systems, there is lot of flexibility possible for handling partitions and also recovering from them. Therefore, a modified CAP goal can be to maximize combinations of consistency and availability required for a specific application. Of course, this needs to be accompanied by plans for continuity during a partition and also for recovery later, thus overcoming perceived limitations for CAP.

Security

Security is another RDBMS feature that you never even think of as a feature. In the open source NoSQL world, there is no extensive integrated security implementation. There is no built-in authentication or authorization. There is no built-in encryption or masking either. All these features need to be implemented through separate applications or API, and you need to make sure that the applications or APIs are well integrated. Some of the NoSQL solutions available commercially (for example, MongoDB by 10Gen or Cassandra by Datastax) are including authentication, masking, and encryption features with their products, but they still lack effective means for authorization or granular security. Besides, all the commercial NoSQL products don't offer these features.

Getting back to open source products, Kerberos is widely used for authentication with a large number of open source NoSQL solutions. Kerberos is developed by MIT, is an open source application easily available, and works with a wide number of Linux flavors as well as HDFS. It also works well with Apache applications like HBase, Hive, Pig, and others. Most of the major Hadoop vendor distributions work with Kerberos, and that's why some of them are now including Kerberos with their distributions. Because Kerberos has been available for a long time, there is extensive documentation about installation, configuration, and possible issues as well as solutions.

Authorization can be performed using HDFS ACLs or using Apache Sentry (if you are using Hive). Also, there are components like Apache Knox or Apache Ranger available now to offer a comprehensive security solution. You can use Ranger (or Knox) to create access policies (for users or groups) for various Apache components like HDFS, Hive, or Hbase, which provide granular (table-level) permissions. Knox also offers LDAP integration, making it easy to integrate security for Hadoop with your corporate security. Finally, most Hadoop vendors (and some NoSQL databases) provide their own custom tools for authorization.

Data encryption is available in transit as well as *at rest* (when data is stored on a physical disk drive), using encryption and compression APIs developed by the Apache foundation. Also, there are open source encrypted file systems like eCryptfs that can be used successfully with Hadoop and NoSQL solutions. In addition, most of the major Hadoop vendors provide interfaces with third-party encryption tools.

Finally, there are excellent open source monitoring tools like Ganglia and Nagios available to monitor system resources and unauthorized access to NoSQL databases.

In conclusion, the combined strategy of implementing tools for authentication, authorization, encryption, and monitoring results in a robust security option for NoSQL databases. Open source databases mostly use open source tools, whereas NoSQL databases available commercially (paid) use their own custom tools to implement the combined security strategy.

Designing the Transition Model

The last section discussed criteria for selecting an appropriate NoSQL database. As a next step, the data (located within RDBMS) needs to be transformed for NoSQL usage. This involves denormalization and also, in some cases, conversion to star schema before denormalization. In either case, it needs to be ensured that there are no joins, no relations, and few tables as a final result.

Also, note that the process for data migration will depend on which NoSQL technology you choose. For example, the process for transitioning RDBMS data into a columnar database (such as Hbase or Cassandra) will differ from the one for key-value stores like Riak or to document stores like MongoDB. I discuss these processes in detail next.

Denormalization of Relational (OLTP) Data

Consider a scenario where OLTP (online transaction processing) relational data needs to be moved to NoSQL environment for better performance. Based on data and application, it is decided that the target NoSQL environment will be Cassandra (a columnar database). Figure 6-4 shows the logical data model for the relational database that holds the data.

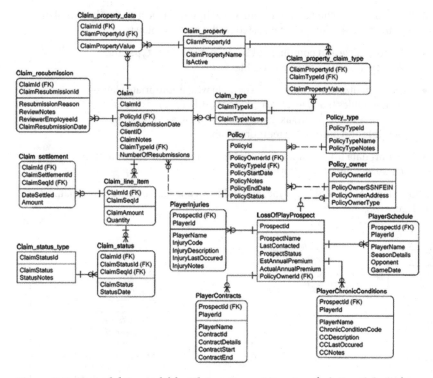

Figure 6-4. *Logical data model for Claims processing system (relational design)*

This is the same claims processing application discussed in detail in Chapter 3. Figure 6-4 shows it again for easy and quick reference. For brevity, I will only transform it partially.

Because NoSQL databases focus on queries and more frequently used datasets, imagine a scenario where the YourState insurance company (using this Claims processing system) encountered a big issue due to increased percentage of fraudulent claims often filed by unauthorized people and decided to implement a new procedure for filing claims. This procedure involved some additional processing and slowed the claim filing process, resulting in complaints by genuine policy holders with legitimate claim requests.

The CIO for YourState insurance asked his chief architect to come up with a solution, who decided to leverage the power of Big Data and NoSQL. He analyzed the situation (and reason for slow performance) as follows:

- Policy-holder verification involves joining `policy_owner` (3 million policy holders) and their policies (about 4 million rows)

- Checking claims for a policy holder involves a join with `claim` (about 20 million claims for last 2 years)

- Getting claim details involves joins with other claim related tables and further slows down the information retrieval

133

The CIO thanked the chief architect and asked him to suggest a remediation plan. Following was the remediation plan suggested by the chief architect:

- Denormalize and combine `Policy_owner`, `Policy_type`, and `Policy` tables to a temporary table

- Denormalize and combine `Claim` table with appropriate claim-related tables (such as `Claim_property`, `Claim_type`, `Claim_line_item`, and so on) as needed to eliminate as many joins as possible and output to a temporary table

- Export data from temporary tables to columnar and document databases and test performance

As a first step, `Policy`, `Policy_type`, and `Policy_owner` tables were denormalized as shown in Figure 6-5.

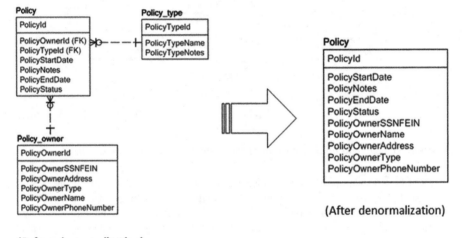

(Before denormalization)

Figure 6-5. *Denormalization of policy data*

The objective here is to reduce the number of joins, since at a high volume, there is a big performance impact on policy (and owner) information retrieval. Also, small tables like `Policy_type` can easily be combined to reduce the impact.

Also, please note that secondary indexes will need to be added for column `PolicyOwnerSSNFEIN`, `PolicyOwnerName`, and `PolicyOwnerPhoneNumber`, since most of the customers calling in (for filing claims or other claim-related services) will use one of these identifiers for locating their information. I will discuss addition of secondary indexes while implementing the final model.

As a next step, I'll denormalize claim-related data to eliminate joins and provide speed for retrieval as shown in Figure 6-6.

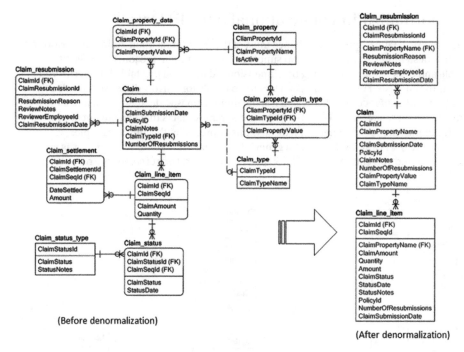

Figure 6-6. *Denormalization of claim data*

For claim data, the denormalization is a little different (compared to policy). Also, as you can see, I have kept three tables in the final count. The reason is expected processing. For claims, the primary purpose of data access by customers is to get claim details or claim status or file a new claim. In most of those situations, claim property information or claim resubmission information is not needed (except when a customer calls to resubmit a claim or needs status on resubmission), because the percentage of resubmitted claims is only 12% for YourState, and claim properties are rarely needed for customer enquiries.

Therefore, I decided to keep those entities (`claim_resubmission` and `claim`) separate from the `claim_line_item` entity, which holds details of a claim and up-to-date status. In this case, combining all the entities will simply increase record length (thereby increasing access time), and because the property or resubmission columns are not accessed frequently, will not provide a good value.

Also, in this case, secondary indexes will be required for columns `PolicyId`, `ClaimSubmissionDate`, `ClaimStatus` (for tables `Claim` and `Claim_line_item`), and for columns `ClaimResubmissionDate` and `ReviewerEmployeeId` (for table `ClaimResubmission`).

Note that I have only demonstrated the concept of denormalization for this application and the total effort (or denormalization required) may be more extensive, if you need to migrate your data to a NoSQL environment. Also, this application was OLTP, and the technique for OLAP-based data (or star schemas) is a little different.

Denormalization of Relational (OLAP) Data

In the case of OLAP applications, since most of the denormalization is already performed (while designing a star schema), you simply need to eliminate the joins (between fact table and dimensions) by adding the dimensional data to the fact table for queries you are most interested in. You may also want to do it only for narrow dimensions with a larger number of records. The reason is if the dimension is wide, then it will make the record length really large. Also, you may want to remove facts that you are not interested in (to reduce the record length). I'll discuss this approach with a quick example.

Figure 6-7 is a star schema for a generic sales analysis system. Sales_facts is a fact table, and you can see dimensions such as Customer, Location, Date, Product, and Sales_Reps.

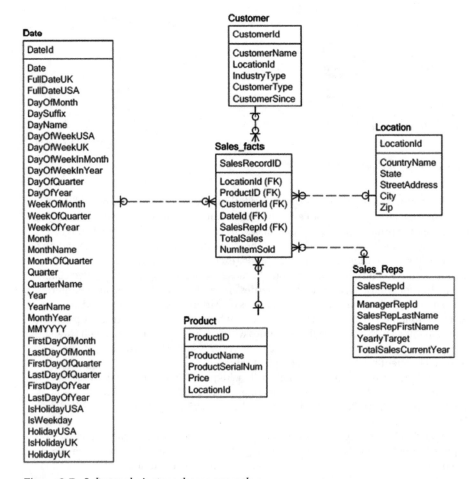

Figure 6-7. *Sales analysis star schema example*

The fact table Sales_facts only has two facts—total sales and number of items sold. This company has had a great year sales-wise, and the sales fact table has 100 million records. There are 500,000 customers who contributed to these sales along with 1,000 sales representatives, 300 locations, and 700,000 products. The sales volume poses an issue for analysis that focuses on products bought location-wise by certain type of customers, since the resulting join (100 million × 500,000 × 300) is huge. Every time there is an analytic query involving these dimensions, it takes a long time to get the results back.

Therefore, it was decided to check whether a NoSQL solution could perform better (as compared to a RDBMS-based ROLAP solution). The data architect denormalized the schema (for the type of specific analysis needed) and designed a denormalized version of the schema, as shown in Figure 6-8.

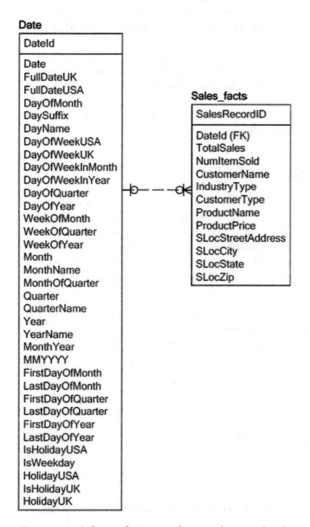

Figure 6-8. *Sales analysis star schema—denormalized*

The first step is combining the relevant part of dimension tables with the fact data (to avoid joins). Based on the performance need, it can be easily concluded that columns from dimensions `Customer`, `Location`, and `Product` need to be added to the fact table. So, you can remove the dimension `Sales_Reps` from the dataset, since it is not relevant to this requirement. Next, you can evaluate the columns in the considered dimensions and since the columns `ProductId`, `ProductSerialNum`, `LocationId` (from `Product` dimension), `CustomerId`, `LocationId`, and `CustomerSince` (from `Customer` dimension) are not relevant to this dataset, they can be removed as well.

The `Date` dimension is not combined for two reasons. First, it is small and only has 730 rows (for two years). Second, only a few queries might use it, since the analytical focus of this dataset is not time.

Last, there are only two measures or facts, and since both are relevant to the dataset, none needs to be removed. Secondary indexes will be needed for boosting performance and can be created for columns `CustomerName`, `ProductName`, `IndustryType`, `CustomerType`, `State`, `City`, and so on.

To conclude, the final denormalized models (for OLTP as well as OLAP) constitute the transitional models for NoSQL targeted re-architecture. The reason I term them as *transitional* is because they will change as per the target NoSQL solution that's planned to be used.

The next section discusses a target implementation of these transitional models using columnar databases and document databases as targets.

Implementing the Final Model

I started with design principles for re-architecting relational applications to NoSQL environments. First, I discussed how to select NoSQL technology (key-value, columnar, document, graph) based on type of your data and target application. Then I discussed implementation of concurrency and security for NoSQL environments. After that, I went over designing transition models for your relational data. As a last step, I will talk about implementing these transition models to target the NoSQL database of your choice. Broadly, there are four steps involved in the re-architecture process:

1. Evaluate and choose the type of NoSQL technology that best fits your data/application needs. Try using the chosen technology for a small project and verify features/ease of use.

2. Denormalize relational data and represent resulting model using NoSQL technology of your choice (document, key-value, column, or graph as appropriate).

3. Design/develop ETL (extract, transform, load) logic to migrate your data from relational database to NoSQL environment using tool(s) of your choice.

4. Redesign your application queries to read data from your NoSQL database .

I'll discuss implementation of a final model using a columnar NoSQL database as a target and a transition model as an input.

Columnar Database as a NoSQL Target

I have discussed the concept of columnar databases in the section "Selecting a NoSQL Database" earlier in this chapter. In this section, I will use Cassandra (a popular columnar database) as an implementation target for the transitional model designed in the last section. Some changes are needed to the model for use with Cassandra. Also, you have to make sure that the data is in format that Cassandra can read.

For example, JSON (JavaScript Object Notation) is a format that Cassandra can understand and hence will work as a notation for specifying schema. An important thing to note about schema is that Cassandra won't enforce a schema for input data (like RDBMS). If you need schema compliance, your application layer needs to handle schema enforcement.

Getting back to the JSON format, it can be used as a standard for exchanging information about specific entities between separate programs (like web browsers that can interpret JavaScript and web applications that can process the JSON format). Though JSON can be used to represent primitive data types like integers, it is more frequently used to represent complex data including key-value pairs or specifically named attributes (for example, name=Bhushan, state=IL) or arrays (for example, 12456, 636262, 863636), or even arrays of attributes ({name=Bhushan, state=IL},{name=Anish, state=IL}).

Getting back to Cassandra, two types of JSON data structures can be imported directly into Cassandra. Here's the first structure: keystore->columnfamily->rowkey->column.

```
{
  "keystore":
    {
    "columnfamily":
      {
      "rowkey":
        {
          "column name": "column value"
        }}}
```

Sometimes multiple columns need to be grouped, and therefore another layer needs to be added to accommodate multiple columns. This layer, called supercolumn, is the second type of JSON structure for Cassandra:

```
keystore->columnfamily->rowkey->supercolumn->column
```

```
{
  "keystore":
    {
    "columnfamily":
      {
      "rowkey":
        {
        "supercolumn":
          {
          "column name1": "column value",
          "column name2": "column value"
          }}}}}
```

139

For the Claims processing data model (that we built the transition model for), let me demonstrate how the `Policy` data can be structured in a keystore called `Implementation_Database`:

Policy

PolicyId
PolicyStartDate PolicyNotes PolicyEndDate PolicyStatus PolicyOwnerSSNFEIN PolicyOwnerName PolicyOwnerAddress PolicyOwnerType PolicyOwnerPhoneNumber

```
{
  "Implementation_Database":
    {
    "Policy":
      {
      "PolicyId":
        {
        "GeneralInfo":
          {
          "PolicyStartDate": "column value",
          "PolicyNotes": "column value",
          "PolicyEndDate": "column value",
          "PolicyStatus": "column value"
          }
        "OwnerInfo":
          {
          "PolicyOwnerSSNFEIN": "column value",
          "PolicyOwnerName": "column value",
          "PolicyOwnerAddress": "column value",
          "PolicyOwnerType": "column value",
          "PolicyOwnerPhoneNumber": "column value"
        }}}}}
```

Note that I have created two supercolumns: GeneralInfo and OwnerInfo. These are to classify the policy information as it exists naturally within the Claims processing database (that is, without denormalization). You can similarly represent all the denormalized tables using JSON and then think about migrating data.

Though supercolumns allow column groupings and make the schema more readable (by allowing subgroups of columns), you should note the following about the supercolumns:

- Subcolumns of a super column (for example, PolicyOwnerSSNFEIN, PolicyOwnerName, and so on for supercolumn OwnerInfo) are not indexed. Therefore, reading a subcolumn will de-serialize the rest of them and cause adverse performance impact.

- Secondary indexing doesn't work for subcolumns. Since a subcolumn is not indexed separately, when a supercolumn is loaded in memory, all of its subcolumns are loaded as well.

Similar functionality (to a supercolumn) can be achieved using a *composite* column. It's a regular column with subcolumns encoded in it. All the benefits of regular columns such as sorting and range scans are available for composite columns.

For the Policy table (or column family for Cassandra), you can represent the structure without using supercolumn, as follows:

```
{
  "Implementation_Database":
    {
    "Policy":
      {
      "PolicyId":
        {
          "PolicyStartDate": "column value",
          "PolicyNotes": "column value",
          "PolicyEndDate": "column value",
          "PolicyStatus": "column value",
          "PolicyOwnerSSNFEIN": "column value",
          "PolicyOwnerName": "column value",
          "PolicyOwnerAddress": "column value",
          "PolicyOwnerType": "column value",
          "PolicyOwnerPhoneNumber": "column value"
        }}}}
```

A sample record would look like this:

```
{
  "9876543210":
    {"PolicyStartDate": "2015-06-10","PolicyNotes": "Credit
needs to be checked","PolicyEndDate": "2016-06-10","PolicyStatus":
"Active","PolicyOwnerSSNFEIN": "234-56-7890","PolicyOwnerName": "Joe
Shmoe","PolicyOwnerAddress": "1 Oak st., Lisle, IL 60532","PolicyOwnerType":
"Individual","PolicyOwnerPhoneNumber": "6309861230"}}
```

To get back to the implementation of transition model, you can represent the denormalized claim related entities (Claim, Claim_resubmission, Claim_line_item) using the JSON notation (as an exercise).

The next task is migrating relational data to Cassandra. You need to design ETL for that purpose. This can be achieved by developing scripts using a scripting language of your choice—Java, Python, .net, and Ruby are some of the options. You can also use relational database–specific languages like Transact-SQL (or PL/SQL). Flat files following the JSON format (that matches your table or Cassandra column family structure) can be generated and loaded into the target table (column family).

As a working example, the following Transact-SQL code generates a JSON-formatted data file for Policy table (assumed to be) in a MS SQL Server database. The code is generic, and you can substitute any SQL Server table name (and primary key column name) and execute it in a database to generate a JSON data file. The only assumption is that first column is primary key; but you can easily modify it for a composite key:

```
-- declare variables
declare @i smallint, @rowkey varchar(500), @ccount smallint, @final_str
varchar(2000)
declare @cname varchar(500), @rec_str varchar(1000), @dyn_str nvarchar(500)
declare @res nvarchar(100), @parm nvarchar(200)

-- initialize them
SET @Parm = N'@res nvarchar(500) OUTPUT';
set @i = 2
select @cname = ' '
select @rec_str = ''

-- take a count of number of columns table has
select @ccount=count(*) from information_schema.COLUMNS where TABLE_NAME =
'Policy'

-- generate string for rowkey
select rowkey='{"' + convert(varchar(10),PolicyId) + '":{' from policy

-- generate string for rest of the columns
While @i <= @ccount
BEGIN

-- select each column in order
select @cname=COLUMN_NAME from information_schema.COLUMNS where TABLE_NAME =
'Policy' and ORDINAL_POSITION = @i

-- generate string to execute and get column value
select @dyn_str = 'select @res=' + @cname + ' from Policy'
EXEC sp_executesql @dyn_str, @parm, @res=@res OUTPUT;

set @i = @i+1
```

```
-- concatenate the column name and value
select @rec_str = @rec_str + '"' + @cname + '": "' + convert(varchar(100),@
res) + '",'

END

-- Output JSON for the data record after removing the trailing comma and
adding curly brackets

select substring(@rec_str,1,(LEN(@rec_str)-1)) + '}}'
```

You can generate data files similarly for all other relational tables and load the resulting JSON files in appropriate Cassandra column families. If you review the task list at the beginning of this section, you will realize that tasks 1–3 are now complete and you are ready for the final task: redesign of queries accessing your new data source. Cassandra offers a rich query language called CQL that can help you write complex queries for your application, and you can refer to the command reference at https://cassandra.apache. org/doc/cql3/CQL.html#CassandraQueryLanguageCQLv3.2.0.

Next, I discuss the same implementation using a document-oriented database as a target and use MongoDB as an example (of a document-oriented database).

Document Database as a NoSQL Target

I discuss document databases in a previous section while discussing how to select a NoSQL technology based on your data and application needs. That was more of a generic introduction. In this section, you will know more about document databases (and MongoDB specifically) and how to implement a transition model (from relational database) using them.

Let me start with the terminology differences between relational and MongoDB. A database in MongoDB has *collections* similar to tables within RDBMS database. A *collection* holds data as *documents*, which are equivalent of data rows. Just as a a data row stores data within its set of columns, a document stores data within fields and uses a JSON-like structure (called BSON) for storage. Here's how the Policy record (from the example in the previous section) will be stored in MongoDB:

```
{
"_id": ObjectId("5244bb32d8124270060001b4"),
 "PolicyStartDate": "2015-06-10","PolicyNotes": "Credit needs
to be checked","PolicyEndDate": "2016-06-10","PolicyStatus":
"Active","PolicyOwnerSSNFEIN": "234-56-7890","PolicyOwnerName": "Joe
Shmoe","PolicyOwnerAddress": "1 Oak st., Lisle, IL 60532","PolicyOwnerType":
"Individual","PolicyOwnerPhoneNumber": "6309861230"}
```

If you compare the storage format with Cassandra, you will notice that the only difference is the first "_id" field added by MongoDB that replaces the PolicyId key column in the relational Policy table. Each document in a MongoDB collection has this unique auto-generated 12-byte _id field, which serves as a primary key or rowkey for a document. Table 6-1 summarizes the term and concept differences between MongoDB and relational databases.

Table 6-1. *Term and Concept Differences Between MongoDB and Relational Databases*

Relational Term	MongoDB Term
Table	Collection
Row	Document
Column	Field
Relationships	Linked or embedded documents

For MongoDB, one interesting difference (compared to RDBMS) to note is that different documents within a collection can have different schemas or structures. Therefore, it is possible for one document to have nine fields and the other document to have ten fields. Fields can easily be added, removed, or modified without impacting read or write access to the data. Data types of the fields may differ for instances as well. So, a field can hold integer type data for one instance and may hold an array for the next.

Considering these architecture concepts, I'll move on to target model implementation for MongoDB. Document databases (unlike columnar ones) don't have columns, supercolumns, or composite columns for storage. The format is simple with a first _id field added as row key and rest of the fields following as key-value pairs separated by comma and bound by curly brackets. Subsequently, you can represent the denormalized Policy table (from earlier sections) within MongoDB, as shown in Figure 6-9.

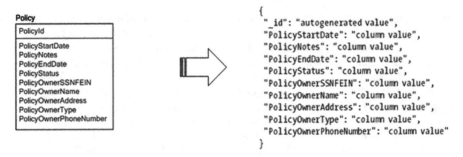

Figure 6-9. *Policy table represented as MongoDB collection*

I have already shown how the corresponding document will look like. You can represent the denormalized claim related entities (Claim, Claim_resubmission, Claim_line_item) using the BSON notation (as an exercise).

The next task is migrating relational data to MongoDB, and you need to design ETL for that purpose. This can be achieved by developing scripts using a scripting language of your choice (for example, Java, Python, .net, or Ruby), but you can also modify and reuse the Transact-SQL script developed in the last section for loading data within the Cassandra column family structure.

As a working example, the following Transact-SQL code generates a BSON-formatted data file for Policy table (assumed to be) in a MS SQL Server database. The code is generic and you can substitute any SQL Server table name (and primary key column name) and execute it in a database to generate a BSON data file. The only assumption is that first column (PolicyId) is primary key:

```
-- declare variables
declare @i smallint, @rowkey varchar(500), @ccount smallint, @final_str
varchar(2000)
declare @cname varchar(500), @rec_str varchar(1000), @dyn_str nvarchar(500)
declare @res nvarchar(100), @parm nvarchar(200)

-- initialize them
SET @Parm = N'@res nvarchar(500) OUTPUT';
set @i = 2
select @cname = ' '
select @rec_str = ''

-- take a count of number of columns table has
select @ccount=count(*) from information_schema.COLUMNS where TABLE_NAME =
'Policy'

-- Since MongoDB will generate string for '_id' column or rowkey
select rowkey='{'

-- generate string for rest of the columns
While @i <= @ccount
BEGIN

-- select each column in order
select @cname=COLUMN_NAME from information_schema.COLUMNS where TABLE_NAME =
'Policy' and ORDINAL_POSITION = @i

-- generate string to execute and get column value
select @dyn_str = 'select @res=' + @cname + ' from Policy'

EXEC sp_executesql @dyn_str, @parm, @res=@res OUTPUT;

set @i = @i+1

-- concatenate the column name and value
select @rec_str = @rec_str + '"' + @cname + '": "' + convert(varchar(100),@
res) + '",'

END
```

```
-- Output BSON for the data record after removing the trailing comma and
adding curly bracket

select substring(@rec_str,1,(LEN(@rec_str)-1)) + '}'
```

You can generate data files similarly for all other relational tables and load the resulting BSON files in appropriate MongoDB collections. Reviewing the task list at the beginning of this section will make you realize that tasks 1–3 are now complete, and you are ready for the final task—redesign of queries accessing your new data source. MongoDB offers a query language that can help you write complex queries for your application and you can refer to the command reference at `https://docs.mongodb.org/manual/reference/command/`.

Please note that the MongoDB query language syntax is quite different from SQL syntax. Here's a quick comparison of these syntaxes through a query:

```
SELECT PolicyStartDate, PolicyEndDate FROM Policy where PolicyOwnerName
='Joe Shmoe' AND PolicyStatus = 'Active'
```

MongoDB:

```
db.posts.find({user_
name:"mark",PolicyStatus:"Active"},{PolicyStartDate:1,PolicyEndDate:1})
```

Best Practices for NoSQL Re-Architecture

Relational modeling often starts with business requirements and capturing of data for business processes. In contrast, NoSQL data modeling is driven by application-specific access patterns or frequently executed queries that need to be supported. That's why NoSQL data modeling requires a better understanding of data structures and business-related processing than relational database modeling does. Here are some of the best practices that need to be followed at the design stage (while re-architecting relational data to NoSQL):

- *Denormalization:* Denormalization is duplication of same data into multiple documents (or tables) for simplifying query processing or to fit the user data into a specific target data model. Denormalization helps in reducing the joins and therefore processing complexity for a query processor in distributed systems (which NoSQL environments often are).

- *Schema fluidity:* Allows for designing entities with complex internal structures (nesting) and changing the entity structures as needed. This helps in minimization of one-to-many relationships (through nested entities) and thereby reduction in joins. This can also help in modeling of heterogeneous business entities using one collection of documents or one table. Caution should be exerted for update flows (for these entities), since embedding along with denormalization can impact updates adversely in terms of performance and consistency.

- *Application joins:* Joins are rarely supported by NoSQL databases and therefore are often eliminated at the design stage with denormalization and aggregates (embedding nested entities). However, for many-to-many relationships, linked entities are used (instead of embedded entities) and require joins. Also, when entity internals (for nested entities) are frequently modified, it is better to use linked entities rather than embedding them and then join the records at query time (as opposed to updating an embedded value).

- *Atomic aggregation:* As discussed in previous sections, NoSQL solutions don't provide ACID compliance for transactions, but support eventual consistency or in some cases application-managed MVCC. The aggregates technique for NoSQL data modelling can provide some of the ACID properties

  For relational databases, since normalized data is located in multiple entities, it requires multi-place updates. For NoSQL, by using aggregates, denormalized data is held as a single business entity (or one document, row, or key-value pair) and can be updated atomically. This doesn't provide a complete transactional solution, but if the target NoSQL database provides certain guaranties of atomicity (or locks), then atomicity can be implemented up to a degree.

- *Dimensionality reduction:* This is a technique that allows mapping of multidimensional data to a non-multidimensional model. Dimensionality reduction involves converting data of high dimensionality into data of lower dimensionality, so that each of the lower dimensions conveys much more information. Also, dimensions that can be derived from other dimensions can be eliminated. The final version of mapped non-multidimensional data is more compact and provides all the information contained in the initial multidimensional model.

As a final thought, denormalization is easier to perform for the relational data (as demonstrated in earlier section) as compared to NoSQL data, and therefore it is beneficial to denormalize the model before implementing it for a NoSQL target.

As a best practice, careful evaluation of an appropriate NoSQL solution needs to be conducted based in your data as well as application processing needs and the prior section "Selecting an Appropriate NoSQL Database" discusses the process in detail.

After the schema design stage is complete and schema is represented using the selected NoSQL solution, operational tuning also needs to be performed for the target NoSQL database. For example, secondary indexes need to be added for performance enhancement. Any additional performance tuning (specific to the target database) needs to be performed as well.

Last, there are best practices specific to NoSQL solutions (that are well documented by their vendors) that should be followed after implementing the general best practices described in this section.

Summary

NoSQL is a new player in the enterprise database area, and there are few people who have actual hands-on experience in redesigning or re-architecting relational applications to get optimal performance using the new platform and tools. The situation is also complicated by the fact that there are few tools available that allow designing for NoSQL databases. For example, you are familiar with Erwin or ER/Studio or Enterprise Architect. Can any of these tools assist you in designing your NoSQL solution or prepare a logical/physical model? The answer is no. Also, think about a scenario where your organization is using multiple NoSQL databases and needs a common interface to manage them. Is such an interface available? The answer is no.

What happens in the real world is that NoSQL design is done using relational design tools. Of course, there's nothing wrong with implementing denormalization or aggregation using relational database modeling tools. It works. Unfortunately, the same concept can't be used for managing NoSQL databases, and you are limited to using multiple interfaces if your organization employs them for various applications.

In this chapter, I have tried to provide a detailed overview of different types of NoSQL technologies and applications they can be used for. I have also discussed the generic criteria you need to consider while selecting a NoSQL technology that suits your organizational needs the best. This of course needs to be matched by a lot of reserch and consolidation effort in order to make the right decision. The whole process may seem a bit complicated, but that's how all technology transitions are. I have provided examples to help understand the concepts and hopefully they do help.

The re-architecture process for your environment may have extra steps (or fewer ones), but understanding the concepts (and steps) behind this redesign process will certainly help you transition successfully. Finally, it will help you to review the section "Deciding to Integrate, Re-Architect, or Transition" from Chapter 1 before you decide that re-architecting is the best solution for you.

## PART III

Integrating Relational Database Management Systems with the Hadoop Distributed File System

CHAPTER 7

■ ■ ■

Data Lake Integration Design Principles

I was talking with a friend at Gartner and he said that (as per the current stats), most of the data lake implementations are failures. I asked what *most* meant and he replied, "Over 95 percent." I was surprised and didn't believe him. I also joked that probably Gartner should publish a paper on causes of failures for data lake implementations, classify them, and provide percentages for each of the causes. More seriously, a lot of data lake implementations do fail or are abandoned for various reasons. In the Chicago area, I know of at least two huge corporations that abandoned such an effort and went back to their proprietary data warehouse platforms.

What is a data lake and what's the purpose of it? What are the benefits that it offers? Do the benefits justify the investment? Most importantly, what are some of the big pitfalls while implementing a data lake? In this chapter, I discuss some of the factors that you need to consider to make your data lake implementation a success.

A *data lake* is simply a massive but easily accessible and scalable data repository for storing uncategorized pools of data "as is." James Dixon, CTO of Pentaho, is credited with introducing the term *data lake* to promote a new way of organizing the Big Data that comes in from the wide range of connected devices such as sensors, smart devices, web applications, and all other devices connected to the Internet. Due to the volume and nature of data (unstructured or semi-structured), it would be impossible to process it using traditional business intelligence techniques (such as a data warehouses) and analyze it using traditional data-analysis techniques. A data lake holds the raw input data (that it receives) without any transformations and that enables the users to transform and process it in multiple ways in the future. Because the data is held in a single repository without any silos, it is easier to access, combine, and analyze. In addition, the raw data doesn't have schema attached to it. Schema or metadata is maintained separately and can be applied as needed.

So, with all the schema and accessibility restrictions removed, you can access and process any data within your corporate data lake, right? Wrong! A data lake does have security implemented just like any other application and also has mechanisms for data cleansing, profiling, metadata management, and governance. The data persisted to a data lake may be immediately or potentially of interest to an organization and therefore data-cleansing steps are implemented before storing it. Systems and processes are put in place to follow the defined principles of quality which may include de-duplication, merging/ purging, harmonizing, parsing, standardizing, and more.

© Bhushan Lakhe 2016
B. Lakhe, *Practical Hadoop Migration*, DOI 10.1007/978-1-4842-1287-5_7

The flexibility of accessing data without silos and analyzing it without having to place it into a rigid data warehouse structure is the real strength of a data lake. It is natural to compare a data lake with an established way of storing large amount of historical data—a data warehouse. I discuss how a data lake differs conceptually and structurally from a data warehouse in the next section.

Data Lake vs. Data Warehouse

Until a few years back, there was only a single option for storing, organizing, and analyzing large volumes of historical data: a data warehouse. The only sub-option was whether you endorsed the all-encompassing enterprise wide data warehouse (EDW) approach suggested by Bill Inmon or preferred the shorter, focused version of a data mart, proposed by Ralph Kimball. As you may know, conventional data warehouses are set-oriented. Set-oriented data processing is a strong point of SQL based relational databases. Also, data within warehouses is intrinsically strongly typed.

Now there is an additional option for holding (and analyzing) large volume of data: a data lake. The real question is, can a data lake replace a data warehouse or a data mart? Or can it only supplement? There is no clear answer to this question, and it largely depends on your objective (behind building a lake or a warehouse), type of data, and probable users. I cover the features, pros, and cons of both these approaches in detail.

Data Warehouse

In 1988, Barry Devlin and Paul Murphy from IBM published a paper called "An architecture for a business and information system" that introduced concept of a data warehouse. Bill Inmon published "Building the Data Warehouse" in 1992 that discussed design and implementation of an enterprise wide data warehouse, and in 1996, Ralph Kimball introduced dimensional modeling and data marts in his book *The Data Warehouse Toolkit*.

So, data warehouses have been around for more than 25 years and are an established methodology for data consolidation, organization, and processing. There have been a number of modifications and enhancements for designing and implementing warehouses. Also, there are a large number of tools available for implementing warehouses. There are advanced structures such as cubes that can help enhance performance for retrieval of analyzed and summarized data, by performing the necessary calculations and aggregations in advance.

A data warehouse reorganizes transactional data by "subject areas" or functional divisions as opposed to storage in "normalized" data tables. Consolidating the measures or "facts" required from a functional area, data is then organized in fact tables (that contain all the facts or measures) and dimension tables that provide information about the facts. The resulting schema is called a star schema, with a fact table at the center surrounded by supporting dimensions. Sometimes, if the dimensional data has hierarchy, the multiple levels of dimensional data are maintained resulting in a snowflake schema instead of a star schema. A transactional database (for an application) may result in multiple functional or subject areas and also may contain multiple fact tables depending on the measures users are interested in. Figure 7-1 shows a simple star schema, and Figure 7-2 shows a possible snowflake version of it.

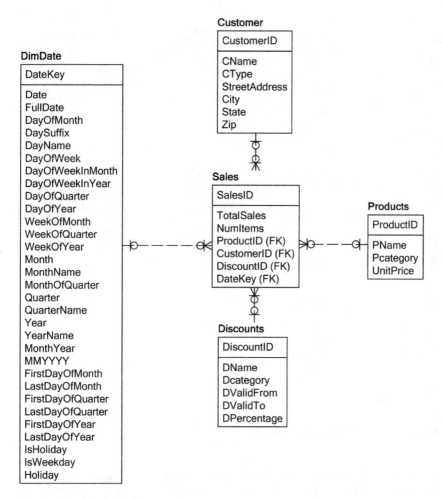

Figure 7-1. *Example of a star schema*

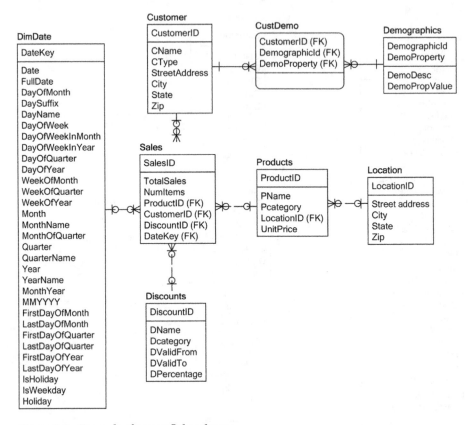

Figure 7-2. *Example of a snowflake schema*

So, as you can observe for this simple sales management system, the fact table Sales holds the measures of interest (here, TotalSales and NumItems) at the lowest possible granularity (such as daily sales, weekly sales, or monthly sales) and dimension tables provide details of the measures and also can be used as attributes to filter out data as required. For example, total sales for February, total sales for a product or a customer for February, and so on.

The snowflake version of the schema has a couple of additional tables that specify additional relationships of the dimensional tables. It is of course possible to denormalize those dimension tables and get all the data within a single table, but that would reduce the readability of the schema, and it would be harder to understand the way data is organized for those dimensions. Besides, the dimensional tables are fairly small (compared to fact tables) and therefore the joins to retrieve data from them wouldn't be costly.

Structures such as cubes perform aggregations in advance and store them at various granularities (aggregates by time or by geographical region or demographics). That way, any queries that need specific aggregated data can retrieve that data almost instantaneously. Even if the data is not pre-aggregated, the star schema reduces joins and helps perform the aggregations fairly quickly. Data warehouse implementations by major vendors have a wide range of tools (such as indexing, caching, and so forth) to facilitate retrieval and aggregations at lightning speed. These of course are the benefits of storing your data in a warehouse.

A big limitation of data warehouses is that they store data from various sources in a specific static structure—fact table(s) and supporting dimensions. The defined measures and dimensions drive the type of analysis that is possible on that data. This severely restricts the possible insights that can be gained from your data and restricts the scope (of possible output from your warehouse) to canned reports, pre-defined dashboards (with limited user interaction), and at the most parameterized reporting capability. If the users need any additional insights, they need to build ad hoc queries (again limited by measures from the fact table) that may not perform well (especially for large datasets).

For example, consider the already mentioned sales management system and assume that you want to correlate sales of specific items with seasons or type of business your customer has or size of your customer's company. Because dimensions with any of the required information don't exist, it's not possible to establish any of those correlations. Moreover, a warehouse doesn't exactly facilitate the process of correlating data or discovering patterns in your data.

Combining data from multiple warehouses (mapping to various applications) would involve huge joins between multiple fact tables and may not be practical. Also, since warehouses don't have distributed architecture, the data retrieval may be further impeded by lack of parallelism and speed of disk drives used by the involved warehouses. Finally, the stringent structure of a warehouse may not be able to accommodate unstructured or semi-structured data, unless the data is severely transformed to fit into it.

Here are the pros of a warehouse:

- Data is organized in static structures that facilitate speedy retrieval of data for predefined processing.

- Data retrieval can be further facilitated by vendor BI (business intelligence) features such as cubes, indexing, or caching mechanisms.

- It's possible to perform complex aggregations or calculations in advance and store the results for fast response.

And now the cons:

- A data warehouse stores data in a specific static structure that drives the type of possible analysis. This severely restricts the possible insights that can be gained from your data.

- Combining data from multiple warehouses (mapping to various applications) would be almost impossible due to:

  - Huge joins between multiple fact tables

  - Lack of distributed architecture (and subsequently parallelism)

  - Heavy dependence on the speed of disk drives used (due to lack of other supporting mechanisms like parallelism)

- The static structure of a warehouse may not be able to accommodate unstructured or semi-structured data unless the data is severely transformed to fit into it.

155

Data Lake

A data lake can remedy the issues discussed in the preceding section. I will review the architectural differences that a data lake has (compared to a data warehouse).

Conceptually, data from the various applications (that a corporation has) is ingested into a lake without any transformations applied to it and is stored "as-is." However, practically, such data is not very useful and therefore some data cleansing (such as removing duplicates or blanks, conforming to date formats, and so on) is applied to this data along with metadata generation and cataloguing. HDFS is a popular destination for this data due to the low hardware cost, redundancy, and distributed architecture that allows parallelism for data access (read or write) and also allows expansion "on-the-fly" or without making your system unavailable to users. Additionally, HDFS supports MapReduce or YARN for distributed processing, further enhancing the performance.

In order to provide flexibility for your queries, a data lake maintains the metadata separately. So you are not limited by static structures while querying your data or extracting your own insights. This is sometimes called *schema on read*, since a schema can be specified for your data while reading it (as opposed to first defining the static schema and then inserting data into it).

Because data is not accumulated in huge fact tables, joins may not be as expensive or slow for data held within a lake. Besides, there are no silos created by individual applications, and data access is only limited by a user's role within an organization (and authorization to access certain data).

Finally, an HDFS-based data lake can easily accommodate unstructured or semi-structured data held in JSON, Parquet, ORC, or any other file formats. For HDFS, it doesn't make any difference what format is used for storing data. Data blocks are distributed over available DataNodes and replicated for redundancy. So, combining unstructured or semi-structured data with structured data is quite possible, although transforming and linking such data may need complex transformations and extensive programming effort.

If a data lake offers all these advantages over a data warehouse, why aren't all warehouses migrated to lakes? Well, data lakes can't be used for every data consolidation and analysis scenario. Extensive programming is required to simulate simple features that are available by default within warehouses. While working with relational databases or vendor-supported database and warehouse systems, you don't need to write programs or functions for every small feature that you need. For example, databases have triggers for referential integrity. Also, you can just define primary or foreign keys and be sure that your data is clean and well referenced. If you need to simulate these features or referential integrity within your data lake, you will need complex logic (supplemented by extensive programming) for any data modifications.

Lastly, HDFS doesn't perform well for small volumes or a large number of small files. So, if your data volume is smaller than a couple of terabytes and/or contains a large number of small data files, then overhead of distributed processing (for MapReduce or YARN) impacts performance badly, and the result is poorly performing system. In such cases, it is not recommended to use HDFS or a HDFS based data lake.

To summarize, here are the pros of data lake:

- Not restricted by a static schema. Can use a "schema on read."

- Data is not accumulated in huge fact tables; joins may not be as expensive or slow for data held within a lake.

- A data lake can easily accommodate unstructured or semi-structured data held in JSON, Parquet, ORC, or any other file formats.

- HDFS-based data lake offers advantages such as low hardware cost, redundancy, and distributed architecture that allows parallelism for data access (read or write).

- Additional space can be allocated to a data lake on-the-fly or without making system unavailable to the users. Also, HDFS supports MapReduce or YARN for distributed processing, further enhancing the performance.

And now for the cons:

- Data lakes don't perform well for volumes less than a couple of terabytes or for a large number of small data files. This is due to the inherent architectural issues of HDFS for small data volumes or large number of small files.

- No way to implement referential integrity or data inter-relationships within a data lake.

- Most of the features available within relational databases or data warehouses need to be implemented programmatically.

- Advanced structures such as cubes or caching mechanisms are not available for performance enhancement.

To summarize, you need to use a data lake or a data warehouse based on your objective (type of analysis you need), data volume, and type of data (structured/semi-structured/unstructured).

Concept of a Data Lake

The world around us is changing constantly and so are the data sources. Around six to eight years back, the only sources of data were user input for applications (that a company used) or data/logs generated programmatically. All these sources generated structured data that followed specific rules, and data management was simple. A data warehouse was the only option for consolidating, managing, and analyzing large amount of structured data.

Today, that's not true anymore. The extensive use of social media, professional networks, and other web applications generate massive amounts of semi-structured and unstructured data that's very beneficial to analyze. Also, sensors for a large variety of machines generate huge quantities of data that must be analyzed. Conventional data warehouses are not capable of performing this task. Subsequently, you need to look for new options or platforms that can assist in processing this data—and fast.

Data lakes are categorized based on their intended purpose:

1. *Data reservoirs*: Reservoirs are simply a governed accumulation of data in HDFS that's cleansed and subjected to profiling rules.

157

2. *Exploratory lakes*: Exploratory lakes are a collection of application data ingested in HDFS with nominal cleansing and with transformations or formating applied or merging (from multiple sources) done as needed.

3. *Analytical lakes*: Analytical lakes ingest data within HDFS and feed it to their analytical models for advanced analysis such as predictive analysis or prescriptive analysis. This data (or a part of it) can also act as a staging area for a data mart or enterprise data warehouse (EDW).

Let me now discuss each of these types in detail, with examples.

Data Reservoirs

Many times, the data gathered by an organization does not need to be used immediately. It may simply be held for future usage. A good example is log data from various applications or auditing. That doesn't need to be used immediately, but if and when there is a performance problem or a security breach, you need those log files. Depending on the number of applications your organization has or criticality of those applications, you may have a large number of files that possibly need to be sorted, correlated, and processed for information. HDFS offers a good storage platform for this type of data. Note that there is no need to attach a schema to this data. Depending on the need, a subset can be extracted quickly for troubleshooting.

Also, there are situations where large amount of historical data is accumulated over time in a data lake but no analysis is defined, since it is not currently needed. All these situations result in a data reservoir, which is really a governed data lake with security, data cleansing, and data profiling defined, but without any analytics. Another common role for a data reservoir may be to act as a data distribution *broker* (between different systems that it interfaces with). Because the latest values from original data sources are continuously entering the data reservoir, a selected subset of those values can be distributed to other systems. These subsets of values can also be accessed (as required) through real-time interfaces, providing the latest set of data as needed.

Data from multiple applications is held within a data reservoir without silos and is available to users depending on their role within an organization. In addition, data governance as well as indexing (or cataloging for fast retrieval) is performed on the data. Data here is organized and ready for analysis, but no analysis is defined. A reservoir may consist of data from isolated data marts (data pre-analyzed in the data mart), but no analysis may have been defined on that data in the reservoir. A data reservoir may contain data from unstructured or semi-structured sources that is indexed or tagged as applicable.

After it is established that data from a particular data source is required to be a part of the data reservoir, it is ingested into the data reservoir. The ingestion process usually includes an initial copy of data into one or more of the data reservoir repositories, followed by defining a process of performing incremental updates (to the data) as it changes in the original sources.

Finally, even though the data reservoir appears to be a collection of data sources, it really needs to have a complex set of components for actively governing, protecting, and managing the data. The internals of the data reservoir consist of a number of subsystems, covered in the following subsections.

Data Reservoir Repositories

Data repositories are at the core of a data reservoir. Data within these repositories is shared and used by all the users within an organization who functionally need to have access to it. Each of these repositories corresponds to an application or functionality within an organization. Data within these repositories is maintained and refreshed per the organizational policy. For example, if the functional need for an application may necessitate maintaining data for the last five years for analysis, the corresponding data reservoir repository needs to be configured to hold data for the last five years and overwrite any older data.

Each of the repositories may have different archival and refresh rules, depending on the application it corresponds to. The administrator for a data reservoir needs to understand and configure the repositories as required. Each repository either offers unique information or provides a unique perspective for a dataset. If a new application is added (for an organization), it may result in a new data repository being added to your reservoir, and removal of an application may similarly prompt removal of a repository from your data reservoir. Since some of the applications may have data duplication, that may carry over to the repositories and subsequently, the same kind of data may be shared by multiple repositories.

Data Reservoir Services

Data reservoir services manage the data stored within various repositories. This involves refreshing the data (within repositories) as per business rules, keeping shared data (within multiple repositories) synchronized, providing feeds of transformed data as required, removing obsolete data as necessary, and providing an interface to the user community to access data within a repository. An index or a catalog is used to help users locate the data they need as well as verify that it is exactly what they need for their analysis.

Another important function performed by these services is access control. These services control and provide user access for the data reservoir repositories based on preconfigured roles. Sometimes authentication and any granular permissions that are required authorization, as well as masking (of personally identifiable information, or PII), are managed by specialized governance services (covered in the next section).

Governance Engine

Sometimes the governance tasks are performed by specialist middleware. These tasks include access control, auditing, monitoring, data cleansing and profiling, data transformations, and workflow management. There are separate services performing these tasks, and are all part of the middleware. Some organizations prefer to use separate solutions to perform these tasks.

Security requirements can originate from various sources. The following are the types of key security threats you need to guard against:

- Deliberate (theft, denial of service, corruption, or removal of information)

- Accidental

- Failures

In addition, legal, statutory, regulatory, and contractual requirements (as well as business requirements and objectives) drive your security configuration. Authentication is the first step in establishing effective security.

Authentication

Kerberos is one of the most popular options used with Hadoop for authentication. Developed by MIT, Kerberos has been around since the 1980s. The current version was designed in 1993 and is freely available as an open source download. Kerberos is most commonly used for securing Hadoop clusters and providing secure user authentication. Kerberos offers a single sign-on approach. A client needs to provide a password only once per session and then can transparently access all the authorized services. Kerberos also is compatible with many widely used systems, such as Microsoft's Active Directory.

A client requests access to a Kerberos-enabled service using Kerberos client libraries. The Kerberos client contacts the Kerberos Distribution Center (KDC—the central Kerberos server that hosts the credential database) and requests access. If the provided credentials (login/password) are valid, KDC provides requested access. KDC uses an internal database for storing credentials, along with two main components, the authentication server and ticket granting server. (Check out Chapter 4 in my book *Practical Hadoop Security* (Apress, 2014). See www.apress.com/9781430265443.)

Most Hadoop vendors provide Kerberos with their Hadoop distributions, along with detailed instructions for configuring it. You can also refer to the Kerberos installation guide at http://web.mit.edu/kerberos/krb5-1.6/krb5-1.6/doc/krb5-install.html for installation and configuration.

Authorization

The users and groups set up through Kerberos can help you manage permissions at the file level for Hadoop. However, if you need more granular permissions or need to create roles that group permissions (for ease of use and quickly assigning a set of permissions for group of files), you need to use tools for authorization control.

Popular open source tools include HDFS ACLs and Apache Sentry. Of course, most Hadoop vendors provide their own tools for authorization. For example, Hortonworks provides its versions of Apache Ranger and Apache Knox (both developed by Hortonworks and committed to Apache foundation). Cloudera provides its version of Apache Sentry (developed by Cloudera and committed to Apache foundation).

As per the HDFS permission model, for any file access request, HDFS enforces permissions for the most specific user class applicable. For example, if the requester is a file owner, then owner class permissions are checked. If the requester is a member of group owning the file, then group class permissions are checked. If the requester is not a file owner or member of the file-owner's group, then "others" class permissions are checked. This permission model works well for most situations, but not all.

For instance, if the sales team, the manager of the IT department, and the finance controller are responsible for managing the sale prices for a sales management system and need write permission to the Purchase_price file, the existing groups (for access control) would not be sufficient to implement these security requirements, because all these personnel belong to different departments (and possibly HDFS groups). You could create a new owner group called Price_modifiers, but keeping the group's membership up-to-date could be problematic as personnel changes, resulting in wrong or inadequate permissions due to manual errors or oversights.

Used for restricting access to data, ACLs provide a very good alternative in such situations where your permission needs are complex and specific. Because HDFS uses the same (POSIX-based) permission model as Linux, HDFS ACLs are modeled after POSIX ACLs that have been used by UNIX and Linux for a long time. ACLs are available in Apache Hadoop 2.4.0 as well as all the other major vendor distributions. You can use the HDFS ACLs to define file permissions for specific users or groups in addition to the file's owner and group. ACL usage for a file does result in additional memory usage for NameNode, however, so your best practice is to reserve ACLs for exceptional circumstances and use individual and group ownerships for regular security implementation.

Refer to Chapter 5 in my book *Practical Hadoop Security* (Apress, 2014). See www.apress.com/9781430265443 for details on how HDFS ACLs work and for detailed examples for setup and use.

PII Masking

In addition to authentication and authorization, PII masking is mandated by compliance regulations for financial, insurance, medical, and a few other industries. Given the volume and complexity of the data, it is best not to attempt masking manually. If data within your organization is governed by any federal regulations, you may want to choose a solution from the large number of priced solutions available that can discover and mask sensitive PII data for your dataset. If your data reservoir contains any PII data, it is a good idea to evaluate a solution that meets the needs of your environment and deploy it as one of the services for data governance.

The way these masking solutions work is that they encrypt or scramble the sensitive data, and only authorized users (who have the decrypting or unscrambling key) can view it. There are options to maintain these keys at the session level or transaction level as need be. The client interfaces can also use a certificate for decrypting—to avoid entering a key every time there's a need to access the encrypted data.

Encryption

Encryption of sensitive data and restricting access to it are important functions of data security services. Data masking supplements encryption, but it doesn't eliminate the need for it. If data needs to be encrypted, there are two types of encryption that need to be considered:

- *Encryption at rest*: Involves encrypting data that's stored on a disk drive (or multiple disk drives)

- *Encryption in transit*: Involves encrypting data in transit (that is, while data is communicated between a server and a client or between different components of a system)

Encryption at Rest

A data reservoir is implemented using a HDFS cluster. For a HDFS cluster, data *at rest* is the data distributed to all the DataNodes. If your data is sensitive, or if encryption is necessary for compliance with legal regulations like the insurance industry's HIPAA or the financial industry's SOX, you need to use this type of encryption.

Although no Hadoop distribution currently provides encryption at rest, major vendors such as Cloudera and Hortonworks offer solutions developed by third-party vendors. For example, Cloudera uses zNcrypt (earlier from Gazzang but now acquired by Cloudera) to provide encryption at rest for files and data blocks. Amazon Web Services (AWS) offers encryption at rest with its Elastic MapReduce web service and S3 storage. All these solutions are proprietary or limit you to a particular distribution of Hadoop.

For an open source solution to encrypt Hadoop data at rest, you can use the functionality provided by Project Rhino. In 2013, Intel started an open source project to improve the security capabilities of Hadoop and the Hadoop ecosystem by contributing code to Apache. This code is not yet implemented in the Apache Foundation's Hadoop distribution, but it contains functionality that includes distributed key management and the capability to do encryption at rest.

Specifically, the Intel distribution used cryptography codecs to implement encryption and offered file-level encryption that could be used with Hive or HBase. It used symmetric as well as asymmetric keys in conjunction with Java keystores. You can refer to the following JIRA articles for Apache foundation:

> *Hadoop HDFS/HDFS-6134 (Transparent data at rest encryption)*: Because of privacy and security regulations for many industries, sensitive data at rest must be in encrypted form. For example, the healthcare industry (HIPAA regulations), the card payment industry (PCI DSS regulations), and the US government (FISMA regulations).
>
> This JIRA aims to provide a mechanism to encrypt HDFS data at rest that can be used transparently by any application accessing HDFS via the Hadoop Filesystem Java API, Hadoop libhdfs C library, or the WebHDFS REST API. The resulting implementation should be able to be used in compliance with different regulation requirements.

Hadoop Common/HADOOP-10150 (Hadoop cryptographic file system): There is an increasing need for securing data when Hadoop customers use various upper layer applications, such as MapReduce, Hive, Pig, HBase, and so on.

HADOOP CFS (HADOOP Cryptographic File System) is used to secure data, based on the HADOOP "FilterFileSystem" decorating DFS or other file systems, and transparent to upper layer applications. It's configurable, scalable, and fast.

Encryption in Transit

It is very important to secure inter-process communication for Hadoop. Just using an authentication mechanism (like Kerberos) is not enough. You also have to secure all the means of communication Hadoop uses to transfer data between its daemons as well as communication between clients and the Hadoop cluster. You can achieve this by having the right communication protocols encrypted.

Inter-node communication in Hadoop uses the remote procedure call (RPC), TCP/IP, and HTTP protocols. Specifically, RPC is used for communication between NameNode, JobTracker, DataNodes, and Hadoop clients. Also, the actual reading and writing of file data between clients and DataNodes uses the TCP/IP protocol, which is not secured by default, leaving the communication open to attacks. Lastly, the HTTP protocol is used for communication by web consoles, for communication between NameNode/ Secondary NameNode, and also for MapReduce shuffle data transfers. This HTTP communication is also open to attacks unless secured.

To encrypt TCP/IP communication, for example, an SASL wrapper is required on top of the Hadoop data transfer protocol to ensure secured data transfer between the Hadoop client and DataNode. The current version of Hadoop allows network encryption (in conjunction with Kerberos) by setting explicit values in configuration files `core-site.xml` and `hdfs-site.xml`. To secure inter-process communications between Hadoop daemons, which use the RPC protocol, you need to use the SASL framework.

See Chapter 4 in my book *Practical Hadoop Security* (Apress, 2014) and `www.apress.com/9781430265443` for more on how encryption in transit can be configured for your Hadoop cluster.

Data Quality Services

Data cleansing and profiling are the major components of Data Quality services. Typically, the data cleansing process starts by performing statistical analysis on tables, rows, and columns. Next step is categorizing and evaluating data against business rules. Last step is validating data against patterns such as phone numbers, zip codes, or credit card number formats.

Data profiling results show where data quality is lacking, requiring data cleansing services (for resolving the inconsistencies). I discuss both these components in detail.

Data Cleansing

Typically, data cleansing is performed in four stages:

- *Mapping stage*: A data source (to be cleansed) is mapped to appropriate reference domain(s) from a repository (also called knowledge base).

- *Automated cleansing stage*: Changes (based on the knowledge base) are proposed for the data to be cleansed. Sometimes some of these changes are made without manual interaction.

- *Interactive cleansing stage*: Data stewards can review the proposed data changes and accept or reject them.

- *Export stage*: Lets you export the cleansed data with changes applied.

Those stages work well for single domains, but what happens for a source *composite* domain (a domain consisting of two or more single domains) that maps to a data field that consists of multiple related terms? The multiple fields (for example, last name, first name, and so on) can be mapped to individual domains in the composite domain that's used as a reference for data cleansing. Another approach is to have logic built in to the mapping service that will resolve the multiple fields and map them serially with the composite domain used as reference.

Matching

As part of the mapping process, you need to create matching rules as part of your matching policy. You can create a matching policy with the following:

- Create a mapping process that identifies the data source and map (single or composite) domains to columns

- Create a matching policy process that contains one or more matching rules and test each of matching rules separately

- Create a matching results process that runs all the matching rules together and, if satisfied, adds the policy to the knowledge base

For the individual matching rules, you can specify whether you need a 100% match with the reference value or if a partial match will qualify as well. You can have multiple matching rules as part of a matching policy, but not multiple policies. Also, you can tweak individual matching rules and add or remove them based on input data.

For example, an organization decided to merge duplicate records for all their customers when it discovered that its customers used different formats while specifying their names (while buying from its retail website), and that resulted in the multiple customer IDs assigned to the same customer. Here are the rules they set up for merging:

1. *Detect if name order is switched*: Detect whether name orders are switched for first and last names (such as matching "John Dave" to "Dave John" for attributes first and last name.

2. *Match names and initials*: Match initials with names (match "M" with "Mark") for attributes first name and middle names.

3. *Match partial names*: Match substrings for names (match "Mitch" to "Mitchell" or "Beth" to "Elizabeth") for attributes first name and middle names.

4. *Match using phonetics*: Match using Soundex or Double Metaphone algorithm (match "Smith" to "Smyth" or "Jon" to "John") for attributes first, middle, and last names.

5. *Match compound names*: Match compound names (match "De Villiers" to "Devilliers" or "VanDamme" to "Van Damme") for attributes last names.

6. *Detect missing hyphen*: Detect whether hyphens are missing for attribute last name (match "Hillary Rodham Clinton" to "Hillary Rodham-Clinton").

Data Profiling

Data profiling is a process of analyzing data for a data source and displaying the statistics. Profiling can be used to measure data quality and has two major goals: to facilitate the data quality processes for supporting your choices and to assess how effective those processes are. To summarize, data profiling performs the following types of tasks:

- *Creation of statistical profile*: Involves generating statistics (such as counts, percentage of data) for blank field values, null values, duplicates, unique data values, most and least frequently occurring data values, and so on.

- *Textual analysis*: Involves developing profiles for text fields, which include minimum/maximum/average length, repetitiveness of data values

- *Numeric analysis*: Involves analysis of numeric fields and calculation of arithmetic means, ranges, quartile distributions (usually first and third quartile), standard deviation, and variances

- *Pattern-based analysis*: Involves assessment of data for conformance with commonly used patterns such as email addresses, credit card numbers, postal codes, or specialized patterns like SKU or serial numbers

Data profiling provides the following benefits:

- Helps identify data quality issues and provides insight into the quality of source data

- Assesses the effectiveness of data quality processing, data cleansing, and matching

- Can generate notifications for significant statistics or events that may require action; usually, condition that occurred and recommended action (for remedying that condition) are notified

To summarize, the discussed services are necessary to add and maintain quality for your data. Figure 7-3 shows a graphical view of a proposed data reservoir with all the necessary services.

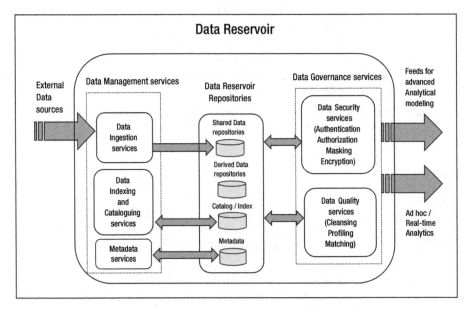

Figure 7-3. *Data reservoir with all necessary services*

Here's the sequence of operations generally performed on data ingested within a data reservoir:

- Data load or ingestion (required)

- Data cleansing and profiling (required)

- Indexing or cataloguing (required)

- The description of the data source may include details like:

  - Name of the data source (short and long description)

  - Data type stored within the data source and details of its classification

  - Data structure (for structured data) and possible data column information for semi-structured or unstructured data sources

  - Data location (in terms of its physical location and also the electronic address)

- This description of a data source can help someone looking for data to discover and assess the appropriate data sources.

- Relationship discovery (optional) can help to create a better understanding of the data

- Tagging (optional) can help add attributes to your data and retrieve quickly based on them

- Data governance (including security configuration)

Factors for a Successful Implementation

- A well-defined objective and design

- An extensive and well-defined governance process (including security)

- Well-designed data repositories

Exploratory Lakes

Exploratory lakes can be built using a similar process to that of building a data reservoir, with the main difference being lack of services for data management as well as data governance. Also, the shared data repositories may need to transform or be reformatted as a result of the data exploration activities, and data from multiple sources may need to be combined. Exploratory lakes may have some basic data cleansing done (for example, duplicate or blank removal), but data profiling, stringent access control, or metadata extraction (or assignment) is not performed for exploratory lakes. The reason is that exploration activities focus on patterns within your data and gaining insights rather than getting your data perfect for consumption by warehouses or for visualizations. That's why you can't use your data reservoir for exploratory activities and vice versa.

Typically, organizations that employ specialized data scientists, business analysts, or statisticians may have them perform custom analytical queries to gain new insights from data stored in a data lake. These exploratory efforts may not involve IT and may be followed by visualizations (presented to higher management) in order to verify the relevance and utility of the analytics performed. Due to the way data is held in a data lake, it is possible to perform quick iterations of these analytics to the satisfaction of decision makers.

Generically, data exploration is a process of experimenting with and visualizing your data to discover and understand the patterns and trends in that data. It may involve reformatting your data or applying transformations or may also need you to combine values from multiple data sources. That's why it's better to make a copy of your data (only the parts you are exploring, since the total data in your lake may run into multiple terabytes) while performing exploratory analytics and not modify your real data—unless you (and your management) are sure that you will be implementing the changes permanently.

A preferable method is to copy all the required repositories (required ones only!) to a development or work area, perform data transformations for your explorations on those repositories, and once you are sure what explorations are being implemented, apply transformations (corresponding to those explorations only) to the data repositories in your data lake.

Sometimes data exploration may result in new analytics models, business rules, or possibly derived repositories. The deployment of these changes may also result in changes to the systems that interface with any of these repositories. So, you need to make sure that the changes you make to your exploratory data lake are implemented for all the related systems.

Data Validation for Exploratory Analysis

It is always a good idea to make sure that the data you are analyzing is valid. Here are some steps you can perform prior to exploratory data analysis:

1. *Decide on questions of interest*: Questions help in focusing on knowledge or insights that you may seek from your data. They also provide direction to the limitless possibilities your explorations may head toward. You have to (of course) start with the most important question: *Do I have all the relevant data to answer these questions?* In particular, a pointed question can help eliminate variables (or data) that are not immediately relevant and may serve as a *dimension-reduction tool* (a tool to reduce redundant information).

   For example, if your dataset is health insurance claim data, then the question *What's the percentage of claims filed by unmarried males?* eliminates all the insured population that's not unmarried and male.

2. *Load necessary data*: You need to load all the necessary repositories in a work area and review the data. You may need to perform data cleansing and profiling on that data and transform/combine it as need indicates. Sometimes, if your dataset is too large, you may want to copy a data sample (or multiple samples) from it to save space and valuable resources for analysis.

3. *Determine data structure*: Next, you need to determine the structure of your data. That is, identify the data types for data fields (or columns) and also determine what information they hold, within the data rows for each of the repositories that you need to analyze. Unless you know what information each of the data fields holds, you can't possibly perform any analysis. You may need to use the data catalog as well as metadata for this purpose (as a starting point). As with any exploratory analysis, you may modify or add metadata at the end of your data explorations.

For example, the data row "Bhushan Lakhe~1 Oak st.~Chicago~ IL~60605" in one of the repositories may not mean anything unless accompanied by structure information that tells you that "~" is a field delimiter (or separator) and the fields are name, address line1, city, state, and zip (in that order).

4. *Perform basic inspection and statistical review*: You might want to start by making sure that your dataset looks complete and if time-bound, contains the timestamps corresponding to start and end date ranges. Next, you may want to check basic statistics for any numerical fields such as mean, variance, range, 1st and 3rd quartile values, or nulls. For large datasets, these steps will be performed on the sample data set that you have chosen.

5. *Validate with at least one external data source*: You need to make sure that the data you are analyzing is not corrupted or incomplete or having any data type mismatch issues. A good way to start is with record count. You then compare the record count with the source system (where data was ingested from). To eliminate data type mismatch possibilities, visual inspection is a good start. As a next step, you may want to compute descriptive statistics such as mean or variances and compare with the source system.

Once the data you are trying to analyze is validated, you can start your exploratory analysis.

Exploratory Analysis Through Visualizations

When you are exploring your data, using visualizations (such as plots) can quickly provide key information about your data, such as basic properties (such as minimum, maximum, or median), or help you find patterns in your data (values reduce with elapsed time, data values follow a distribution such as Poisson or chi-square, and so forth). This is important in the initial stages of data analysis, since it gives you a quick start and a definite direction to follow for your data explorations. Ultimately, as you progress with your analysis, visualizations can be helpful in determining possible modeling strategies. Also, post-analysis, graphics can be used to cross-check an analysis if your results are unexpected. Finally, visualization is a powerful tool to communicate your results or findings to others (especially non-technical or management stakeholders).

Exploratory graphs serve the purpose of quickly checking your data with the objective of developing a good personal understanding of the data and deciding on immediate goals for analyzing it. That's why finer details like axis labels, legends, or descriptive text are not necessary for exploratory graphs. However, multiple colors or plot symbol sizes are necessary to use for conveying various dimensions of information.

R is a programming language popularly used for statistical computing and graphics and is currently supported by the R Foundation for Statistical Computing at www.r-project.org. The R language is also used for developing statistical software and performing data analysis. Major relational and NoSQL databases have now provided support and interfaces with R. Microsoft is the latest to support R processing and visualizations for MS SQL Server 2014.

Written by Ross Ihaka and Robert Gentleman (at the University of Auckland, New Zealand), R is enhanced and supported currently by the R Development Core Team. R is a GNU project and is freely available under the GNU General Public License. Also, precompiled binary versions are available for various operating systems. R uses a command-line interface, but R Studio provides a graphical front end and is very popular.

R provides simple and easy-to-use command-line functions for accessing data stored in a relational or NoSQL database. The functions read.table() and read.csv() can be used for reading tabular data in an R dataframe (in-memory data matrix or table). Note that read.table() should be used for files with any character as delimiter, whereas read.csv() is meant to be used for comma-separated (CSV) files only (with comma as a delimiter). The function readLines() can be used for reading lines of a text file and processing them. So, for example, the following command line will load data from a file Mydata.dat that has first line as headers and ~ as a delimiter into a dataframe called MyDf (> is R's command line prompt):

```
> MyDf <- read.table("Mydata.dat", header=T, sep="~");
```

For large datasets, you can limit the rows using the nrows option. For example, this command will only load the first 100 lines from file Mydata.dat:

```
> MyDf <- read.table("Mydata.dat", header=T, sep="~", nrows = 100);
```

R also provides an easy way to access data from any database that supports ODBC connection through a package called RODBC. You can install and use it as follows:

```
> install.packages("RODBC")
> library(RODBC)
```

So, if you have your data stored in a Microsoft SQL Server database MyDB, and one of the tables is MyTable, then you can load it in a dataframe MySQLDf as follows. Note that when you are connecting to the database, you need to open a connection to the database using the command odbcConnect(), and after you have completed your database operations, you need to close the connection using the command odbcClose(). In the following, MyODBDC is the name of the ODBC user data source:

```
> DBHandle <- odbcConnect("MyODBC")
> MySQLDf <- sqlFetch(DBHandle, "MyTable")
> odbcClose(DBHandle)
```

Sometimes, you may have a huge data table and want to load only the top 100 rows or use a query to load data in a dataframe. The following command loads the top 100 rows from table MyTable in a dataframe:

```
> MySQLDf <- sqlQuery(DBHandle, 'select top 100 * from MyTable')
```

If you have multiple databases on your server and don't want to create ODBC connections for each of them, you can use a construct like the following:

```
> DBHandle <- odbcDriverConnect('driver={SQL Server}; server=MySQLhost;
database=MyDB; trusted_connection=true')
```

This quick tutorial of R is by no means exhaustive and is only meant to give you some idea as to how your data can be loaded in a dataframe in R. Refer to the R manual or a good R book (such as *R Programming for Data Science* by Roger Peng (Lean Publishing, 2016) for more. Check out https://leanpub.com/rprogramming if you want to gain a better understanding of R. I will use R for demonstrating statistical computations as well as graphic visualizations.

Here are some ways of summarizing one-dimensional data effectively:

- *Five-number summary:* You can use this summary to quickly get the distribution for your data and it consists of the minimum, 25th percentile, median, 75th percentile, and maximum for the input data set. The R function fivenum() can be used on the command line as follows (> is R's command line prompt, and any text after # is considered a comment:

```
> x <- c(1,3,5,7,9,2,4,5) # input dataset
> fivenum(x) # compute five number summary
[1] 1.0 2.5 4.5 6.0 9.0
```

 So, for this dataset (which is monthly profit for a company in millions of dollars for the last eight months in the state of Illinois), 1.0 is minimum, 2.5 is the 25th percentile, 4.5 is the median, 6.0 is the 75th percentile, and 9.0 is the maximum.

- *Boxplots:* Boxplots are mostly used when you need to visualize distribution of a single variable and provide a visual representation for the five-number summary along with additional information (such as outliers). *Outliers* are values that are more than 1.5 IQRs (IQR is the difference in values of the 25th and 75th percentile) above or below the 25th or 75th percentile. So, for this example, any values less than –2.75 or greater than 11.25 will be outliers. Outliers (when valid values) signify unusual data values that may have a specific reason for occurrence and need to be investigated separately. Outliers also impact the five-number summary unfavorably (due to the presence of values outside the normal value range for a variable).

Getting back to boxplots, they can be drawn in R using the boxplot() function (see Figure 7-4):

```
> boxplot(x) # draw a boxplot of dataset x
```

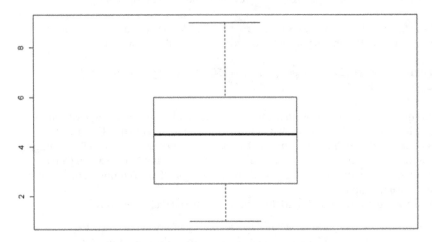

Figure 7-4. *Boxplot for a dataset*

Bar plot: You can use bar plots (see Figure 7-5) for visualizing your data when it is grouped and you want to quickly compare data across the groupings. Considering the example (showing profit for a company for the last two months) again, you can use a bar plot to compare profits by week. So, each of the weekly profit entries can be thought of as a "group." You can, of course, create groupings as sums, counts, or any other aggregate functions and use the resulting dataset as input for barplot function. A barplot can be drawn in R using the barplot() function:

```
>barplot(x, main="Weekly Profits in US Million Dollars", xlab="Week
(starting least recent)", ylim=c(0,10), ylab="Profits (US Million
dollars)",names.arg = c(1,2,3,4,5,6,7,8))
```

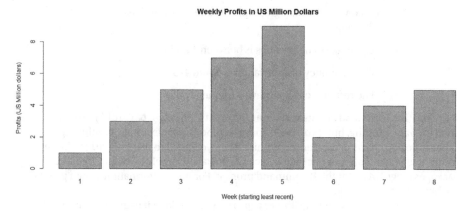

Figure 7-5. *Barplot for a dataset*

Since the height of the bar is proportional to the data value of a grouping (in this case, weekly profits), it is easy to compare the values (visually) across groups.

- *Histograms:* You can use histograms where you need to show the complete distribution of the data, as opposed to the five data points shown by the boxplots. Histograms help you check the pattern(s) within your data for any symmetry, multi-modality, or conformance to any of the standard distributions (such as normal or chi-square). The hist() function within R can draw a histogram for your dataset (see Figure 7-6).

```
> hist(x, breaks=8, xlim=c(1,10), main="Histogram for weekly profits",
xlab="Weekly profits (Million US dollars", col = "grey")
```

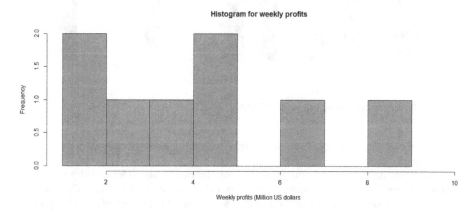

Figure 7-6. *Histogram for a dataset*

You can review the histogram quickly and easily understand the following:

- The range of data values is between 1 and 9

- The frequency of data values 1–2 and 4–5 is 2

- The rest of the values have a frequency of 1

The `Plot` command and its variations (`boxplot()`, `hist()`, `barplot()`) are good for basic plotting, but if you need complex plotting (for example, combining or superimposing charts or advanced graphics) then you need to use the `ggplot2` library within R. It is available as a package and can be installed simply by typing `install.packages("ggplot2")` at the R command prompt. For more information, about `ggplot`, see `http://ggplot2.org`.

Once you have installed the library `ggplot2`, you can load it using the command `library(ggplot2)` at the R command prompt. The command `qplot()` can be then used to create complex plots. For example, the histogram from the last example can be created as the following, using `qplot()` as shown in Figure 7-7:

```
> qplot(x, geom="histogram", xlab="Profit (Million US dollars)",
ylab="Frequency",bins=20)
```

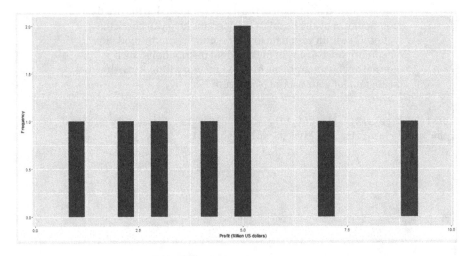

Figure 7-7. *Histogram using the ggplot2 library*

As you can see, the graphics are nicer and have a more professional look. I use `ggplot2` more extensively in the next section.

So, to summarize, the preceding plots are popular visualizations for one-dimensional data or a dataset for a single variable. If your dataset (for a single variable) is really large with millions of rows, you can sample your dataset and use the same plotting techniques. Note that R uses a lot of memory, and you need to calculate the memory usage proactively (before you analyze a dataset in R). Failure to do so may result in a crash.

While you are exploring and analyzing your data, you will need to investigate data in two dimensions and beyond. There are a number of additional techniques used for that purpose (I discuss them next):

- *Multiple or overlayed plots*: You can draw (or overlay) multiple boxplots or histograms within the same plot, and this can help you identify the relationship between two variables more easily (especially when the variables belong to the same category). For example, the weekly profits (from the dataset used earlier) for the last two months are for state of Illinois. The profits (for the same period) for the state of Indiana are as follows: (0, 1, 1, 2, 5, 1, 2, 8). If the profits for Illinois are called IlliProf and profits for Indiana are called IndiProf, you can overlay the boxplots (using qplot() command from ggplot2 library) as follows (the result is shown in Figure 7-8):

```
> qplot(ind, values, data=stack(data.frame(IlliProf,IndiProf)),
geom="boxplot") + theme(axis.text=element_text(size=16,face="bold"),axis.
title=element_text(size=12))
```

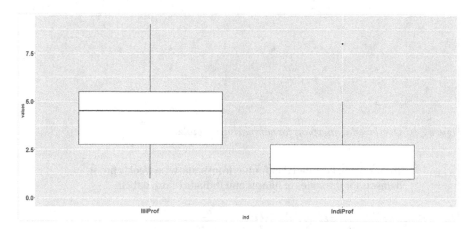

Figure 7-8. *Multiple boxplots for comparing variables*

You can, of course, overlay more boxplots (corresponding to additional variables) by adding them to the data.frame function. The theme() function is used to override the properties of the default theme (for example, text size for axis labels). Refer to http://docs.ggplot2.org/current/theme.html for details of the theme function.

- *Scatterplots:* Typically, you can use scatterplots for visualizing two (or more) continuous or quantitative variables. Continuous variables can be measured using a scale and have a numerical value. In general, a continuous variable is measured, not counted. For example, *Length* (measured in inches or centimeters), *Height, Weight, Temperature, Time, Distance.* In some cases, variables may need to be transformed (such as computing log or square root) for effective visualization. You can visually compare the profit values for the states of Illinois and Indiana through a scatterplot, as shown in Figure 7-9. I have used different shapes for datasets dat1 and dat2.

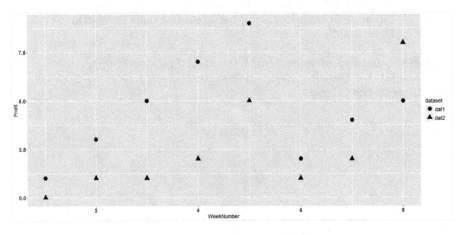

Figure 7-9. *Overlayed scatterplots for comparing variables*

To start with, I created dataframes from state-wise weekly profit datasets for the states of Illinois and Indiana (dat1, dat2):

```
>dat1 <- data.frame(c(1,2,3,4,5,6,7,8),IlliProf)
>dat2 <- data.frame(c(1,2,3,4,5,6,7,8),IndiProf)
```

Next, I unified the column names for these datasets to facilitate use of the rbind command (which combines dataframes by rows) and combined the dataframes:

```
> colnames(dat1) <- c("WeekNumber", "Profit")
> colnames(dat2) <- c("WeekNumber", "Profit")
> dat <- rbind(dat1, dat2)
```

Finally, I created labels for use by shape aesthetics and used ggplot to create the overlayed scatterplot using the combined dataframe created in the last step (the result is shown in Figure 7-9):

```
> dat$dataset <- factor(c(rep("dat1", dim(dat1)[1]), rep("dat2", dim(dat2)[1])))
> ggplot(dat, aes(x=WeekNumber, y=Profit, shape=dataset)) + geom_
point(size=5) + theme(axis.text=element_text(size=14,face="bold"), axis.
title=element_text(size=14), legend.text=element_text(size=14), legend.
title=element_text(size=14))
```

Note the different shapes of the two datasets (circle and triangle)
that make it easy to differentiate and compare the values. Colors
or sizes can also be used for the same purpose. Also, note the
use of theme() function to change the axis text/title and legend
text/title. You can adjust the text sizes for various components
of a plot using this function or join the data points via a line for
facilitating understanding of any correlations.

Correlation

Correlation results from a relationship or dependence of one variable on another and
can also be determined statistically for two datasets. R offers a function called cor() for
this purpose. A *correlation coefficient* describes the amount by which two data variables
vary together. You just need to use the two numeric variables you want to examine as
the arguments to the cor() function. For example, if you want to check how the weekly
profits for state of Illinois correlate with the ones for state of Indiana, you can use the
following R command:

```
> cor(IlliProf, IndiProf, method="spearman")
[1] 0.7656655
```

The closer the value to 1, the stronger the correlation. For the cor() function, the
method parameter refers to the type of correlation coefficient to be computed, and
the possible values are "pearson" (default), "kendall", or "spearman" (named after
the British statisticians who created those coefficients). Also, a negative correlation is
possible between two variables when they vary in opposite directions. Finally, as a more
practical application, you can calculate the correlation among multiple variables at once,
just as you can plot the relations among multiple variables.

So, for example, if you have a dataframe that has sales details for a cosmetics retailer,
and the retailer's management needs to know which geographical locations are selling
a particular item more (so that they can introduce more items from that category in that
store), they can create multiple attributes for each of their locations (such as location
within a mall or strip mall, located near a major clothing retailer, located in area with
certain demographic, and so on) and check which attribute is most closely related with
the sale of an item. That can give them a good idea about what category of items may
be sold at a location depending on the value of its attributes. If you assume that the
dataframe is called dfSales, then the following R command can be used for determining
the correlation (assuming there are five attribute values represented numerically)
between various attributes and sales:

```
>with(dfSales, cor(Attr1, Attr2, Attr3, Attr4, Attr5, Sales))
```

For huge data frames, you can use subsets based on the values of any of the columns or date. So, for the preceding dataframe, if there are millions of records for each location, and if attr2 holds the zip, you can save the subset as a new dataframe and analyze the sales for zip code 60561 as follows:

```
>dfSales60561 <- subset(dfSales, Attr == 60561)
>with(dfSales, cor(Attr1, Attr2, Attr3, Attr4, Attr5, Sales))
```

If you need to analyze sales for zip 60561 after January 1, 2016, and before February 1, 2016, you can use the following command and use the resulting subset with the with() command:

```
>dfSales60561Jan16 <- subset(dfSales60561, date >= as.Date("2016-01-01") &
date < as.Date("2016-02-01"))
```

Lastly, you can visually determine whether a correlation exists between two variables by inspecting the pattern of data values. A similar or same pattern indicates a possible correlation. I have used the cor() function to determine whether there is a possible correlation between weekly profits for the states of Illinois and Indiana. Let me overlay these datasets using a line plot on the same plot (as shown in Figure 7-10):

```
> ggplot(dat, aes(x=WeekNumber, y=Profit, linetype=dataset))+geom_
line(size=1) + theme(axis.text=element_text(size=14,face="bold"),axis.
title=element_text(size=14), legend.text=element_text(size=14),legend.
title=element_text(size=14))
```

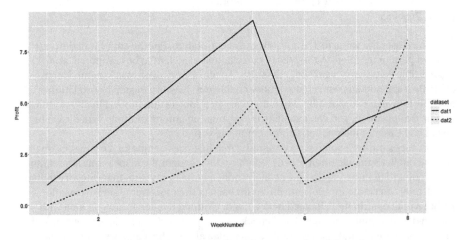

Figure 7-10. *Determining correlation visually using an overlayed line plot*

As you may observe, the command used to generate this overlayed line plot is almost same as the one used to generate the overlayed scatterplot, with two differences:

- Within aes(), line type is used to differentiate (instead of shape) between datasets (linetype=dataset instead of shape=dataset).

- The function geom_line() is used instead of geom_point().

As far as the visual inspection is concerned, you can conclude that the data patterns are similar, but not very similar. So, a correlation might exist, but not a very strong correlation (and that is supported by the result from cor() function being 0.7).

Clustering

The last technique used for exploratory analysis is *clustering*, or *cluster analysis*, a popular technique for visualizing multidimensional data. Clustering easy to use and can serve as a really quick way to understand a multidimensional dataset. Clustering involves organizing data values (that are close) together and classifying them as distinct groups. I will discuss two types of clustering:

- Hierarchical clustering

- K-means clustering

Hierarchical Clustering

Hierarchical clustering aims to organize your data into a hierarchy. There are two approaches to achieve this objective: *agglomerative* or "bottom up" and *divisive* or "top down."

The *agglomerative* approach starts by assuming individual data points as *clusters*, and then you start gathering them together into small clusters, which are grouped as part of bigger clusters. Bigger clusters are grouped together recursively until you have one big, massive cluster. To summarize, here are the steps followed:

1. Locate the two closest data points in your dataset

2. Group them together and call them a cluster

3. Use your cluster, find a new data point, and repeat

The divisive approach is exactly the opposite. You start with all your data points as part of one big cluster, and the cluster is split recursively as you move down to form a hierarchy (of smaller clusters).

Both these methodologies need you to measure the distance between two points and also require you to have an approach for merging two data points to create a new *cluster*. Therefore, it is important to use a distance metric that works best for your data—otherwise, your clusters won't be valid and you won't get any useful information from them. The following are commonly used distance metrics:

- *Euclidean distance:* This is the "straight-line" distance between two points.

- *Manhattan distance:* Between two points, this is the sum of the absolute differences of their Cartesian coordinates. It is also known as *city block distance,* since you need to think how many "city blocks" do you need to travel to get from point A to point B (on a grid or lattice of city blocks).

When you are merging clusters, how should you measure the distance from a data point to a merged cluster of points or between two merged clusters? One approach (called *complete*) is to use maximun distance between the two groups—that is, find two points within these groups that are furthest apart and use that as the distance between the groups. Another approach is *average merging,* which computes the average of the coordinate values in each group and uses that as the distance between the two clusters. *Complete merging* is the default method used by the hclust() function in R. For details of the hclust() function in R see https://stat.ethz.ch/R-manual/R-devel/library/stats/html/hclust.html.

There's not necessarily a correct merging approach that will work for any given application, so you need to choose a merging approach that works best for your data. Usually a lot of experimentation and exploration is needed to extract meaningful patterns and clusters from your data.

K-means Clustering

The K-means clustering approach has the objective of finding the *centroids* (or *multidimensional center point*) of a fixed number of clusters within your multidimensional data. As with hierarchical clustering, this algorithm is also iterative. The level of difficulty is high because you need to locate the *centroids* in a high-dimensional space, and that's why you need an algorithm that's capable of making these computations.

K-means clustering uses a partitioning approach, and data is partitioned into a number of groups at each iteration of this algorithm. This algorithm requires you to pre-specify the number of estimated clusters. Even though you may not know in advance, you should guess and run the algorithm. You can, of course, change the number of clusters and run the algorithm again to see if anything changes. Following are the steps:

1. Specify the number of clusters (>= 2)

2. Specify a random set of points as the centroids of these clusters

3. Assign data points to their closest centroid (and thereby a cluster)

4. Calculate centroid positions again and iterate

This approach also requires a defined *distance metric* (in addition to the fixed number of clusters and initial guess for cluster centroids), and the same distance metrics (as used for hierarchical clustering) can be used. Unfortunately, there's no defined method for determining the initial centroid configuration, and many algorithms simply select data points randomly (from your dataset) as the initial centroids. The K-means algorithm produces a final estimate of cluster centroids (their coordinates).

Factors for a Successful Implementation

- A well-defined objective for data exploration and a detailed plan

- Availability of qualified data scientists to design data exploration as per objective

- Availability of expert data visalization professionals to quickly create visualization for data insights developed by data scientists

To summarize, I have discussed popular techniques for data exploration (and analysis) for data held in a lake. The next section covers techniques for using your data lake as an analytical lake:

Analytical Lakes

Some organizations have a stable and established process to use data held in a lake. Instead of just holding the data (in a lake) or performing exploratory analysis to disccover new insights from their data, they use the data (from their lake) to feed their analytical models for advanced analysis, such as predictive analysis (what may happen) or prescriptive analysis (what should we do about it). A data lake (or a part of it) can also act as a staging area for a data mart or EDW.

In addition, real-time processing (and analytics) can also be performed within an analytical lake environment. In fact, real-time processing is gaining increasing popularity for newly designed architecures. Good examples are application of learning algorithms for decision making or providing fast insights. Credit card companies use real-time analytics to detect unusual card activity (for example, card used in China for a US-based customer).

An insurance company in South Africa used learning algorithms and predictive models with their claim data for detecting fraudulent claims and came up with startling insights, like claims filed between 10:00 p.m. and 5:00 a.m. were largely fraudulent. Most of the genuine ones were filed between 9:00 a.m. and 11:00 a.m.!

This section briefly discusses all these techniques.

Using Data for Analytical Models

Predictive models are used more frequently (as compared to prescriptive models), so I will discusss usage of data (from a lake) with predictive models. The main objective of a *predictive* model (sometimes also called *machine learning* or *pattern recognition*) is to generate the most accurate estimates of quantities or events associated with the input data.

R uses two main conventions for specifying models:

- Formula interface

- Non-formula (or "matrix") interface

The formula interface uses syntax like this: `outcome ~ var1 + var2 + ....` where var1, var2, (and so on) are explicitly listed predictors for the outcome. Consider the following formula that would predict the grading of a diamond using four characteristics:

```
modelFunction(grading ~ CtWeight + Cut + Color + Clarity, data = DiamondGrading)
```

The formula interface has pros and cons. For example, transformations can be specified inline. But unfortunately, R does not efficiently store the formula information, and thus datasets containing a large number of predictors may unnecessarily slow the computations.

The non–formula interface uses a matrix or dataframe to specify the predictors for the model, and the outcome is assigned to a vector object. For example:

```
modelFunction(a = GradePredictors, b = grading)
```

Predictive modeling in R usually follows a similar workflow:

- Create model using the basic function: `fit <- abc(trainingData, outcome)`

- Cross-check the model properties using visualizations (print, plot) or commands (summary) or any other methods

- Use the predict method to predict outcomes for new data sets: `predict(fit, newData)`.

Since the various modeling packages are developed in isolation (with each other), there are inconsistencies in the way these models are specified or predictions are made. For example, many models use a single method for model specification (such as formula or matrix only).

Model Building Steps

Common steps used for building a model are:

- Estimation of model parameters (predictors, outcomes, and so forth)

- Determination of tuning parameters values (that can't be calculated directly from the data) for validation

- Determining the performance of the final model (that will generalize to any new data)

How can you use your data to find an optimal model? Usually data is split into *training* and *test* data sets:

- *Training data set:* Used to estimate model parameters and also to pick the values of the parameter(s) that determine complexity for the model.

- *Test or validation data set:* Can be used to validate the model efficacy. Of course, you should not use this data for training.

Be careful while determining the split between your training and testing data. If you use too much data for training, that will prevent you from getting a good assessment of predictive performance. You may end up with a model that fits the training data very well but does not generalize (know as *overfitting*). On the other hand, if you use too much data for testing, there won't be enough data to get a good assessment of model parameters. Even though the best (statistical) course of action would be to use all the available data for model building and use statistical methods to get good estimates of error, many users of these models prefer to have an unused (by training) dataset for validating and evaluating performance.

There are a few different ways to do the split (between training and testing data), such as the following:

- Simple random sampling (R function `sample()` can be used to create a random data sample)

- Stratified sampling (based on the outcome)

- Using date or methods that focus on the distribution of the predictors

Once you have a set of predictions (using a model), various metrics can be used to evaluate performance:

- For regression models, R2 is very popular.

- The root mean square error is a common metric for understanding the performance.

- Spearman's correlation can be used for models that are used to rank samples (`cor(, method = "spearman")`).

You have to make sure to use separate datasets for training the model and testing for valid estimates (using your model).

Using Data as a Staging Area for EDW or Data Mart

This refers to the possible use of your data lake as an operational data store (ODS). Since your data lake consists of data from various online transation processing (OLTP) as well as online analytical processing (OLAP) applications, it may be possible to build an ODS by cleaning, transforming, and holding the data in temporary or transitional structures that map to your EDW or any of your existing data marts. This, of course can only use structured data from your lake. Designing ODS is a complex topic and beyond the scope of this chapter (and the book). Check out Chapter 3 of Bill Inmon's book *Building the Data Warehouse* (Wiley, 2008) for futher details. Here's a link to the book: http://www.wiley.com/WileyCDA/WileyTitle/productCd-0764599445.html.

Real-Time Processing and Analytics

Real-time processing for data in a data lake can conceptually have processing similar to Lambda architecture. The differences:

- There will only be two layers: batch and real-time (instead of batch, presentation, and speed).

- The batch layer will move all the data for an application (for which real-time processing is needed) to lake one-time only—no need to redo this processing.

- Real-time data update will be performed using data streaming through Spark streaming, Amazon Kinesis, or a similar solution.

I discuss batch processing in great detail in Chapter 9. I will discuss data streaming briefly in the next section.

Event Stream Processing

Originally, ESP started as custom data flow–centric processing to detect specific conditions and act on them (for example, fraud for financial systems) and is a technology to enable detection, consumption, and processing of high-volume, high-speed events in near real-time to support analysis.

Typically, ESP is comprised of:

- Application server that captures and processes high-speed events (transactions) based on specific logic

- Development environment for processing/transforming OLTP data

- Components including engine, GUI development tools, connectors (to get data feeds from various sources), visualization interface, and data storage structures

- Usually separate languages for coding (or development) and querying

ESP is used to support real-time, on-the-fly analytics to identify time-critical business situations using:

- High-speed querying of data in event streams and applying mathematical algorithms

- Application of complex logic to data streams

Figure 7-11 shows an example of ESP for a hospital management system that should help clarify the ESP concepts.

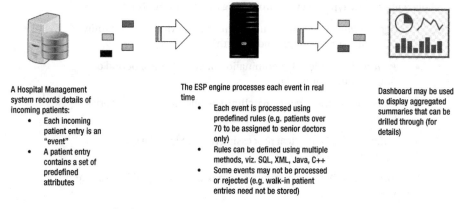

A Hospital Management system records details of incoming patients:
- Each incoming patient entry is an "event"
- A patient entry contains a set of predefined attributes

The ESP engine processes each event in real time
- Each event is processed using predefined rules (e.g. patients over 70 to be assigned to senior doctors only)
- Rules can be defined using multiple methods, viz. SQL, XML, Java, C++
- Some events may not be processed or rejected (e.g. walk-in patient entries need not be stored)

Dashboard may be used to display aggregated summaries that can be drilled through (for details)

Figure 7-11. *Example of ESP*

The main components of an event stream processor are: data transfer engine (responsible for capturing event data from a source using connectors or interfaces developed using lower level languages like Java or C++), memory structure (for holding event data in memory and passing on to execution engine for further processing), and execution engine (that executes logic for transforming event data). Figure 7-12 shows where these components fit in the architecture.

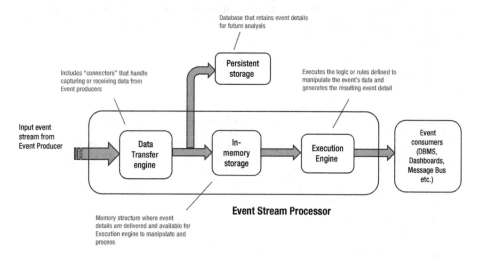

Figure 7-12. *ESP internals*

Following are the types of event processing that's commonly performed:

- *Aggregation*: Aggregate values within a time window or quantity of events (sum, average, and so forth)

- *Pattern detect*: Identify combination of events over a period of time (minutes/hour/day)

- *Filtering*: Remove events matching specific values or categories/ types

- *Calculations*: Numerical processing (using SQL-like query language or Java)

- *Thresholds*: Define a minimum or maximum acceptable attribute value for an event

- *Transform/Convert*: Apply data transformation processing, convert data types, data values, and so on

- *Derive*: Estimate or deduce data values using statistical or predictive models

Complex Event Processing

Event *cloud* or *complex event processing* involves processing a series of related events together to identify patterns and correlations. For example, as seen in Figure 7-13, my BMW displays a warning message to brake slow if the temperature is below 32 degrees, the air pressure in tires is low, and it's snowing.

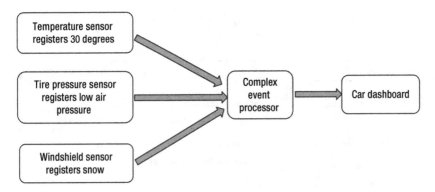

Figure 7-13. *Example of complex event processing*

Apache Foundation offers excellent open source options for ESP, such as Samza, Spark, Storm, and Flafka (Flume + Kafka). Here are the leading ESP (priced) product vendors:

- *DataTorrent*: RTS

- *Informatica*: RulePoint

- *IBM*: InfoSphere Streams, Operational Decision Manager

- *Microsoft*: Stream Insight

- *SAP/SAS*: Event Stream Processor

- *Tibco*: BusinessEvents, Streambase

There are a lot of real-world applications of ESP. Here are a few common ones:

- Managing traffic on streets, or traffic control

- Processing brain neuron signals using a Hadoop computing cluster

- Fraud detection and prevention using correlations, causation, and predictive modeling for insurance companies

- Advertisement-targeting platforms are using Hadoop to capture and analyze click stream, transaction, video, and social media data

- Managing content, posts, images, and videos on social media platforms

- Financial agencies are using Big Data Hadoop to reduce risk, analyze fraud patterns, identify rogue traders, more precisely target their marketing campaigns based on customer segmentation, and improve customer satisfaction

- Processing unstructured data like sensor output from medical devices, doctor's notes, lab results, imaging reports, medical correspondence, and clinical data

Factors for a Successful Implementation

- A detailed plan for one of the following objectives:
  - Design for interfacing with existing EDW

  - Designing predictive, regression, propensity, or presecriptive models and feeding data to these models

  - Ingesting real-time streaming data and processing it for analytics

- Availabiity of qualified analytics professionals to design analytic models or descriptive analyrics as needed

- Availability of qualified ETL professionals for developing interfaces for data ingestion and transformations as needed

Summary

Over the last few years, *data lake* has turned into a buzzword that management (who decides to invest in a lake) and implementors (architects, developers, users) too often implement before thinking it through. That's why most implementations fail. Data lakes are not about using economic storage through Hadoop clusters for archival and are not even about the data storage without silos or distributed processing. Data lakes are about turning your data into information, knowledge, and wisdom. If you can generate one useful insight per application from your lake, then I would consider your data lake implementation a huge success.

Data lakes provide you the freedom to explore your data without any unwanted consequences, and without the inhibitions of a static schema or a rigid data structure. You also have the freedom of saving any new schema insights as new metadata. So you are only limited by your creativity. These are all the pros, or good parts.

The cons or bad parts deal with all the non-lake activities that you need to perform, such as defining security, governance, data cleansing/profiling, and master data management, because a data lake doesn't mean that anyone from your organization can access any data as they like. Structured and non-structured data need to be processed separately. Besides, applications that use the same data with dissimilar units of measurement (maybe due to country-wise differences regarding usage or non-usage of the metric system) are still going to cause you issues if you need to analyze their data together—unless you spend time harmonizing the units. Real-time streaming or stream analytics are still going to be difficult to configure and use.

To summarize, data lakes are not going to provide answers or insights for all your applicational needs. They are just the beginning of a new paradigm in data processing, not the end. A tool is only as good as the use you make of it. The real data insights have to come from you—data lakes just offer a medium for you to visualize them and then present them to rest of the world.

CHAPTER 8

■ ■ ■

Implementing SQOOP and Flume-based Data Transfers

About five years back, when the Apache Hadoop ecosystem was ready for its data processing challenges, it introduced its own tools for data ingestion, including Sqoop and Flume. These tools were initially unfamiliar, as was rest of the Hadoop ecosystem. I was assisting an IBM client (a big health insurance company) with its data warehousing needs, and its RDBMS-based solution was not performing well. The company also had a lot of historical data on mainframes, and the big volume of that data (about 10 TB) was an issue. Though Hadoop was new, I convinced the client of the need for a ten-node Hadoop pilot and used Sqoop to pull the data into HDFS (Hadoop Distributed File System). We had tried with 2 TB only, but the response time was about 1/50th of the mainframe response time, even with old hardware and slow disks. This encouraged us (as well as the client) and finally we deployed the solution for production usage.

A large number of organizations are offloading the extract-transform-load (ETF) jobs to Hadoop. There are a number of reasons for this. Optimal usage of processing resources (because ETL processing is offloaded to a commodity-hardware–based Hadoop cluster), optimal usage of disk space (again, Hadoop cluster uses budget-friendly disk drives) for transitional storage, performance (due to distributed processing), and redundancy (data blocks are replicated on a Hadoop cluster) are the major ones.

Now, as the Hadoop ecosystem has matured, more tools are available for data transfer. Also, Hadoop started as a batch-processing solution, but currently with the advent of tools like Spark, Storm, Apex, and Kafka for streaming, Hadoop is also being used as a real-time analytic solution. Subsequently, tools for ingestion of events or streaming data are added to the Hadoop ecosystem.

One important consideration is the type of source data you have (structured, semi-structured, unstructured, or a mix) and what your objective is (for transforming it). Your ETL tools need to have connectivity to source as well as target systems. Another consideration is use of graphical tools for data pipelining (or defining stages of transformations from source to target) that reduce the development time or command-line tools as well as lower level programming language–based tools that offer greater flexibility. Of course, code development will take a longer time with such usage, but if you have complex transformation needs, then there is no easy option.

© Bhushan Lakhe 2016
B. Lakhe, *Practical Hadoop Migration*, DOI 10.1007/978-1-4842-1287-5_8

Finally, most of the Hadoop distribution vendors have added their own proprietary tools for data ingestion. For example, Microsoft provides Azure Data Factory for ingesting data into in its HD Insight platform (a Windows-based adaptation of the Hortonworks Hadoop distribution). Though most of these tools provide a graphical interface, substantial development time is involved in creating jobs for data ingestion.

So, how do you decide what's the best tool for your environment? Let me discuss some parameters to consider.

Deciding on an ETL Tool

If you decide to integrate your RDBMS-based application with Hadoop, then you are planning to use Hadoop as your enterprise data hub. Once the data is in HDFS, then you perform aggregation and analytics (asynchronously as batch or streaming as a real-time system). Therefore, you will need to design ETL for moving data in and out of Hadoop. Sqoop and Flume are popular tools for this purpose and can be used to populate HDFS and refresh it periodically as batch processing. If you need to ingest data in real time, then you need to use a tool such as Kafka, Flink, or Spark Streaming for ingesting streaming data (and storing it using an appropriate target). This section discusses how.

Sqoop vs. Flume

Let me start with Flume. It's really a framework for collecting and integrating data within Hadoop. Flume uses processes called *agents* to collect and store the data. These agents can read data from a variety of sources, like web servers, application servers, system logs, or even mobile devices and write output to HDFS. For high volumes of data, you can configure multiple Flume agents and implement horizontal scaling.

Sqoop is more of a connectivity tool or utility for moving data between structured data stores (such as relational databases and data warehouses) and Hadoop. Sqoop is designed for an efficient transfer of bulk data and supports all the leading relational databases like Oracle, Microsoft SQL Server, DB2, and others. Also, since Sqoop is based on a *connector architecture,* it supports the use of third-party plugins or connectors to provide connectivity to new external systems. Sqoop provides performance by transferring data in parallel.

So, the typical use cases for Flume are log consolidation (for example, consolidating audit logs from all the NameNodes for an organization), or capturing and filtering tweets, or capturing clickstream data for customer product searches (for a web retailer). Because Flume architecture is event-driven, it finds use in scenarios where you have certain events to capture (and store) either on a continuous basis or within a predefined time window.

Sqoop usage focuses on moving large volumes of data between RDBMS (or a data warehouse) and Hadoop. Sqoop doesn't deal with event streams. It's more about a predefined transfer of data using connectors capable of reading data from specific sources and writing it to specific targets. Hadoop is not always the target. Sometimes, data processed by Hadoop needs to be transferred back to an RDBMS or a data warehouse.

To summarize, Sqoop is used for ad hoc or scheduled data transfer between structured sources and HDFS. Table 8-1 summarizes the differences between these tools.

Table 8-1. *Feature Comparison for Sqoop and Flume*

Sqoop	Flume
Sqoop is mostly used for data transfer from (and to) structured data sources such as RDBMS.	Flume is used for moving bulk streaming data into HDFS.
Sqoop has a connector-based architecture. A *connector* is code that is capable of connecting to the respective data source and fetching the data to be written to HDFS, or vice versa.	Flume has an agent-based architecture. An *agent* is code or program that fetches streaming data from the source.
HDFS is a either source or destination for data using Sqoop.	Flume writes data to various channels, and HDFS may be one of the channels (or destinations).
Data loads for Sqoop are not event driven.	Flume can have data loads that are event driven.
Typical use cases for Sqoop involve data transfer from (or to) RDBMS, like Oracle, SQL Server, MySQL, or document databases like MongoDB, CouchDB, or warehouses like Teradata, or columnar databases like HBase or Cassandra.	Typical use cases for Flume are load of streaming data such as tweets generated on Twitter, clickstream data from web applications, or log files from a web server.

Processing Streaming Data

Chapter 7 discusses event stream processing concepts. This section compares the open source Apache tools available for processing streaming data. At the forefront is Spark Streaming. The other options are Samza, Storm, and Flafka (Flume + Kafka). There are, of course, solutions from all the major vendors, such as RTS from DataTorrent, RulePoint from Informatica, InfoSphere Streams from IBM, and Stream Insight from Microsoft. I will not be discussing these solutions. I'll start with Spark.

Spark and Spark Streaming

Spark is a popular distributed computing engine that provides a variety of tools such as Spark SQL (query tool), Spark Streaming (event stream processing), MLib (machine learning), GraphX (graphics libraries), and Spark R (R functions for analytics). Spark Streaming is an extension of core Spark API that enables scalable, high-throughput, fault-tolerant stream processing of live data streams. Data can be ingested (into Spark) from sources like Kafka, Flume, Twitter, and Amazon Kinesis and can be processed using complex algorithms expressed with high-level functions like map (transform), reduce (aggregate), and join (combine data streams). Processed data can be pushed out to HDFS, databases, or live dashboards, or you can also apply Spark's machine learning or graph-processing algorithms on data streams.

Spark uses the concept of resilient distributed datasets (RDDs). These are collections of objects spread across a cluster and persistent in memory. They are built quickly through parallel transformations and are resilient (as the name suggests), which means they are rebuilt automatically on failure. Transformations such as filtering, union, join, and group by, or actions such as sum, count, for each, and more can be performed on RDDs.

Spark Streaming doesn't process streams one at a time, but divides them in small batches of time intervals before processing them. This process is called *micro-batching*. The Spark abstraction for a continuous stream of data is DStream (for discretized stream), which is really a micro-batch or sequence of RDDs (as shown in Figure 8-1). Spark Streaming offers support for merging historical data with streaming data.

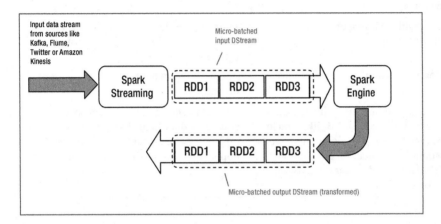

Figure 8-1. *Spark Streaming processing*

You can write Spark Streaming programs using Scala, Java, or Python by referencing appropriate DStreams and applying functions to them. You can use functions like map (process each element of DStream through a function), union (return a new DStream that contains the union of the elements in the source DStream and other Dstream), count (return a count of elements in each RDD of the source Dstream), reduce (return a new DStream by aggregating the elements in each RDD of the source Dstream), and so on.

DStreams can also be used as input for MLib, Spark SQL, or GraphX (for further processing and analysis). Every input DStream (except file stream) is associated with a receiver (Scala doc, Java doc) object, which receives the data from a source and stores it in Spark's memory for processing. You can receive multiple streams of data in parallel in your streaming application by creating multiple input Dstreams, associated with multiple receivers.

Storm

Using Storm, you can design a directed graph of real-time computation (called a *topology*) and execute it on a Hadoop cluster where the master node will distribute the code among worker nodes to execute it. Storm defines spouts, or data streams comprised of immutable sets of key-value pairs called tuples. A *tuple* or a data row (a collection of elements in ordered sequence) is a basic unit of abstraction for Storm), and *bolts* (processes that transform input streams using functions, filters, aggregations, and joins) transform those streams. Bolts can (optionally) pass data to other bolts down the processing pipeline.

Since Storm processes a single event at a time (as opposed to micro-batching), it has really low latency and can be used for real-time analytics, ML, budgeting, and more. However, it has no concept of look back aggregations. Also, using Storm, it is not easy to combine batch processing with streaming data.

For stream processing, tuples are either randomly distributed across all the tasks running a bolt, or specific fields from all the tuples are grouped and routed to the same task. Tasks are threads executed by worker processes or JVMs, as shown in Figure 8-2.

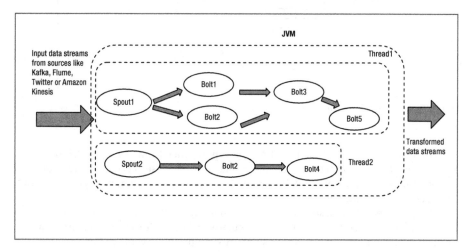

Figure 8-2. *Storm streaming*

Trident is a high-level abstraction processing library that works with the core storm API and is often used to add functionality and reliability. This library offers a range of functions for joins, aggregations, grouping, and more. More importantly, it enables Storm to use the "exactly once" delivery pattern (which means that a data packet is delivered only once without any loss or duplicates) and adds reliability to its delivery.

Samza

Originally developed at LinkedIn, Samza is a distributed stream processing framework. A data *stream* is divided in a number of *partitions* (ordered sequence of messages). A job processes stream(s) and is divided in a number of tasks. Each task processes data from partitions from the input stream(s) and processes messages within a partition sequentially. Figure 8-3 shows job processing within Samza.

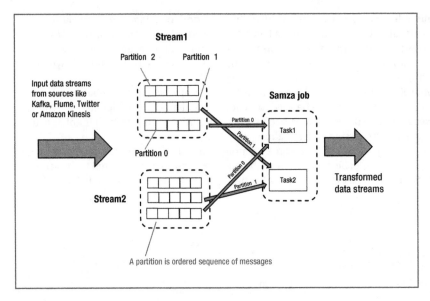

Figure 8-3. *Samza job processing*

For Samza, processing (and coordination) is performed by the Samza API, but the execution and streaming layers are pluggable. So, you can select solutions that are appropriate for your environment. By default, YARN is used as execution layer, and Kafka is used as the streaming layer.

Having reviewed these stream processing solutions briefly, where do you use any of these solutions? Figure 8-4 has a detailed comparison. You can review the features that are of interest to you and decide on the solution appropriate for your environment.

	Spark Streaming	Storm	Samza
Processing	Micro-batch	Stream	Stream
Latency	Second	Sub-Second	Sub-Second
Delivery model	Exactly-Once	At Least Once (Exactly-Once with Trident)	At Least Once
Language support	Scala, Python, R, Java	Ruby, Python, Javascript, Perl	Scala, Java
Throughput	100K+ records per node per second	10K+ records per node per second	100K+ records per node per second
State Management	Maintains State (persistent to storage)	Doesn't maintain State (unless Trident is used)	Maintains State (via embedded key value store)
Re-processing (Kappa architecture	Yes	No	Yes

Figure 8-4. *Feature comparison between Spark, Storm, and Samza*

For example, if you have a retail banking environment and you are using a stream processing solution for fraud detection, a sub-second response is important for you, and Storm or Samza would be better options for you. If, however, you are interested in implementing Kappa architecture for your data lake, then you would be using Spark Streaming or Samza. If you have data scientists who are well versed in R, then Spark Streaming would be of interest.

Using SQOOP for Data Transfer

Sqoop is a data-transfer tool based on *connector architecture*. What this means is that it supports third-party plugins or *connectors* that provide connectivity to relational or NoSQL database systems. Being a part of the Hadoop ecosystem, it has *read* and *write* capabilities to HDFS.

Even though most of the current database management systems (DBMS) support SQL as a query language, there are differences between various DBMS with respect to SQL dialect (to some extent). These differences pose challenges for data transfer across the systems. Sqoop *connectors* help overcome these challenges effectively and make the data transfer (between database systems) easy and fast.

The range of Sqoop's connectors includes popular RDBMS such as MySQL, PostgreSQL, Oracle, SQL Server, and DB2. Sqoop also provides a generic JDBC connector that can be used to connect to any database that supports Java's JDBC protocol. Lastly, Sqoop's optimized MySQL and PostgreSQL connectors (which use database-specific APIs) perform bulk transfers efficiently. Figure 8-5 shows the details of Sqoop architecture.

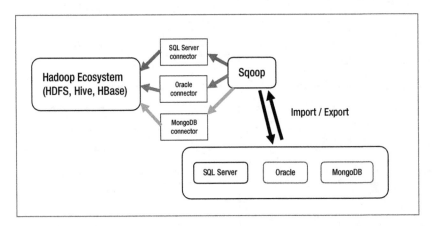

Figure 8-5. *Sqoop architecture*

If you need to use Sqoop for data import/export, download, install, and configure it (see `http://mirrors.ibiblio.org/apache/sqoop/1.4.6/`). More details are at `https://sqoop.apache.org/docs/1.99.1/Installation.html`. Note that the download links refer to Sqoop version 1.4.6—use the latest version). After that, you can download and install connectors for the data sources you want to use.

For example, if you want to import data from MySQL to HDFS, you will need to download the MySQL connector first (`http://ftp.ntu.edu.tw/MySQL/Downloads/Connector-J/`), unzip the archive `mysql-connector-java-5.1.36.tar.gz` to extract the jar file, and finally move `mysql-connector-java-5.1.36-bin.jar` to the `/usr/lib/sqoop/lib` directory (again, the links refer to the existing version and might change for a later version). The following commands can be used for the purpose (# is the Linux command prompt):

```
# tar -zxf mysql-connector-java-5.1.36.tar.gz
# cd mysql-connector-java-5.1.36
# mv mysql-connector-java-5.1.36-bin.jar /usr/lib/sqoop/lib
```

After that, you can use the connector for import/export. For example, the next command imports a table called `MyTbl` from MySQL database server to the HDFS directory `MyData`:

```
$ sqoop import \
--connect jdbc:mysql://localhost/userdb \
--username root \
--table MyTbl \
--m 1 \
--target-dir /MyData
```

Now, the preceding command will get the data for the whole table from MySQL. But what if you only need data for the last day? Or the last week? Sqoop offers incremental load of data using values for any of the columns within the data table. So, if the table MyTbl has a date column with timestamp or last modified date (modified_date), you can use that to get data for the last day as follows (assuming you are doing the incremental load on 2/29/16 and want to load the data for 2/28/16):

```
$ sqoop import
--connect jdbc:mysql://localhost/userdb \
--username Myusr \
--password Mypwd \
--table MyTbl \
--m 1 \
--target-dir /MyData/incremental_table
--check-column modified_date
--incremental lastmodified
--last-value 2016-01-27
```

However, note that the preceding command will fetch all the rows for table MyTbl that were added (or modified) starting 2/28/16 00:01. So, if your application allows for updates or modifications to the existing records, this command will get the updated rows for you as well. What if you just need the newly added rows?

Sqoop provides another mode for incremental load, called append (instead of lastmodified), that will only get you the newly appended records (for a table). You can't use a timestamp or last modified date for this mode (for obvious reasons). You will need to use an ID column that has increasing values, and you need to know the largest value loaded by the last incremental load. For example, if MyTbl has a MyId column that holds the self-incrementing ID, and you determine that the last incremental load loaded maximum ID value of 9834, then the following command will fetch all the records that were added after that load:

```
$ sqoop import
--connect jdbc:mysql://localhost/userdb \
--username Myusr \
--password Mypwd \
--table MyTbl \
--m 1 \
--target-dir /MyData/incremental_table
--check-column modified_date
--incremental append
--last-value 9834
```

To summarize, Sqoop supports two types of incremental imports, append and lastmodified, and can be used in conjunction with the --incremental argument to specify the incremental import you need to perform. You can use append mode if you are importing rows for a table where new rows are added with increasing row ID values. Then you can specify the row ID column with the --check-column option and import rows where the check column has a value greater than the one specified with --last-value.

Alternatively, you can use the `lastmodified` mode if your table doesn't have a row ID column with increasing value but contains a last-modified column. In that case, you can use the last-modified column with `--check-column` option and import rows where the check column has a value greater than the timestamp (or date) specified with `--last-value`.

For production usage, you will need to create a script that first determines the `--last-value` for the previous incremental load and then substitutes that value within your Sqoop command to fetch the records you need. You can then schedule this script as a job for incremental load.

See the Sqoop user manual for command-line options you can use with Sqoop: `https://sqoop.apache.org/docs/1.4.6/SqoopUserGuide.html#_incremental_imports`.

Finally, I will mention an additional way to load data incrementally. You can leverage the query parameter and use a SQL `select` statement to limit the import to new or changed records only as follows:

```
$ sqoop import
--connect jdbc:mysql://localhost/userdb \
--username Myusr \
--password Mypwd \
--table MyTbl \
--m 1 \
--target-dir /MyData/incremental_table
--query 'select * from MyTbl where modified_date > 2016-01-27'
```

You can structure the query to match your incremental load needs or the structure of your source data table. The advantage with using the query option is that you can have better control over the data that needs to be imported, and you can specify multiple conditions to filter your data more effectively.

Using Flume for Data Transfer

The strengths of Flume (as a data-transfer mechanism) are in the capabilities of processing streaming data and consolidating data from multiple sources. That's the reason Flume is used for event and audit log consolidations. Also, Flume works well with Log4j-based logging that's very popular for Hadoop installations. Browsing through various Hadoop logs while troubleshooting a job or investigating a security breach can be difficult and may introduce a manual error. Defining a Flume agent (with related configuration) may initially take time, but you only need to do it once. Subsequent modifications to the agent are easier and quicker, and most importantly, the process of consolidating logs (for an issue) becomes easier and faster.

In some cases, the volume of log data may be massive, and a well-defined Flume agent can filter necessary data without any manual intervention. Flume is reliable, scalable, and easy to customize. Flume also supports dynamic configuration and contextual routing.

Flume Architecture

Flume architecture revolves around generation of an *event* (atomic data unit transported by Flume) by a *client* and its processing by an *agent*. Here are definitions of key terms:

Client: An entity that produces events and makes them available to one or more Agents for processing.

Event: Atomic unit of data transported by Flume from its point of origin (source) to its final destination (sink). Event is a byte array with (or without) header(s).

Source(s): Event data receptor(s). Sources receive the data generated by an event (or from a channel) and output it to one or many channels. For example, Syslog can be used as a source.

Channel: Temporary data pipe. A channel is a temporary holding area for an event after it is received from a source and being output to a sink. Memory (RAM) or a file can be used as a channel.

Sink: Data destination. A sink is used as destination for event data. One of the most popular sinks is HDFS, that is, logs or other events are stored within HDFS as files.

Interceptor: Inspects, transforms, or filters events as needed. For example, a `timestamp` interceptor adds a timestamp header for an event, or a `regex_filter` interceptor filters out events per the specified regular expression.

Channel selector: Process of writing an event to one or more configured channels based on a header. An event can be *replicated* (written to all the channels) or *multiplexed* (directed to different channels based on a header such as port). For example, and event received on port 12345 goes to channel1, if received on port 54321 goes to channel2, and so on.

Sink processor: Process of writing to a sink (from defined sink group) based on load balancing or failover strategy (as chosen).

Agent: A process or a Java Virtual Machine (JVM) that runs the dataflow to transport events from a source to a sink, utilizing other components like interceptors (for filtering events) or channels (for temporary storage). Flume deploys as one or more agents as required.

Figure 8-6 shows how these Flume components fit in the overall architecture. The next section discusses each of the these Flume components briefly.

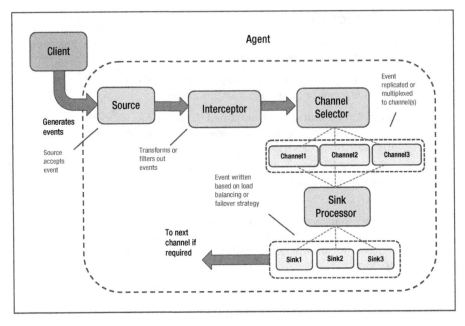

***Figure 8-6.** Flume architecture with major components*

Understanding and Using Flume Components

The last section reviewed definitions for the major Flume components. We also saw where each of those components fit in the overall Flume architecture. Now it's time to discuss two of the most important components in detail.

Source

A *source* is a flume component that receives event data from a client and places it on one or more channels (remember, a source needs at least one channel to function). Popular sources include Syslog, Netcat, Exec, and others.

The Exec source runs a command outside Flume and turns the output into a Flume event. To use the Exec source, I will define a source s1 and set all its relevant properties in the Flume agent configuration file (called `flume.conf` and located in `/etc/flume/conf`). I'll start with the type property and set it to exec:

```
s_agent.sources=s1
s_agent.sources.s1.type=exec
```

All sources in Flume are required to specify the list of channels to write events to using the channels (plural) property. We will use a single channel here:

```
s_agent.sources.s1.channels=c1
```

The only other required parameter is the command property, which tells Flume what command to pass to the operating system. For instance, we can use the following command that prints newly added lines from HDFS audit log:

```
s_agent.sources.s1.command= tail -f hdfs-audit.log
```

Note that the -f (or follow) option of Linux tail command appends data, as the file grows. By default, the input file (here hdfs-audit.log) is checked for growth every second, but you can change that time interval if you want. There are other properties you can define for Exec source, and you can refer to properties for different Flume sources at: https://flume.apache.org/FlumeUserGuide.html#flume-sources.

To conclude, this is how we can configure a single source s1 for an agent named s_agent. The source, an exec source, will extract relevant rows for a job from the HDFS audit log file hdfs-audit.log. All events will be written to the c1 channel.

Sink

A *sink* is a flume component that removes events from a channel and transmits them to their next destination (which might be a source). This transfer is transactional, that is, agents use transactional exchange to guarantee delivery across destinations—data is not removed from a channel unless the data transfer to next destination is successful. Sinks require exactly one channel to function. Here are the different types of sinks:

- Terminal sinks that deposit events to their final destination (for example, HDFS, HBase)
- Auto-consuming sinks (such as Null sink)
- IPC sink for agent-to-agent communication (for example, Avro, Thrift)

If your requirements can't be met by any of these sinks, you can write a custom sink for your purposes by extending the org.apache.flume.sink.Abstractsink class.

HDFS is a popular sink used with Flume. An HDFS sink can be used to open a file in HDFS, write streaming data into it, and close it after the data stream has ended or stopped. To use the HDFS sink, you need to set the type parameter on your named sink to hdfs:

```
s_agent.sinks.sink1.type=hdfs
```

This defines a HDFS sink named sink1 for the agent named s_agent. There are some additional required parameters you need to specify, starting with a path in HDFS where you want to write the data:

```
s_agent.sinks.sink1.hdfs.path=/usr/flume/mydata
```

I have used an absolute path without a server name, but you can use an absolute path with a server name (hdfs://namenode/usr/flume/mydata) or a relative path (mydata) as you may need. The last mandatory parameter (channel) for the HDFS sink (or any sink) specifies the name of the channel that it will be reading from:

```
s_agent.sinks.sink1.channel=ch1
```

This tells the sink1 sink to read events from the ch1 channel. For a complete listing of sink properties, please refer to https://flume.apache.org/FlumeUserGuide.html#flume-sinks.

Implementing Log Consolidation Using Flume

Earlier in this section, I discussed Flume architecture and also discussed sources and sinks briefly. That will help you understand how Flume can be used for data transfer. To enhance that understanding and illustrate how you can perform aggregation and consolidation using Flume, I will now talk about a brief working example. Since Flume is used extensively for consolidating audit and other Hadoop component logs, I will use that as an example.

My objective for this example is to set up agents on each of my source servers and set up an agent on my target server (within my Hadoop cluster) used for collecting or consolidating logs. Subsequently, I will demonstrate setup of a source server (since that setup can be replicated for as many sources as you need) and the target server, each of which with its own configuration file. I have installed Flume on all my source servers and my Hadoop cluster. Here's the source agent configuration file with key entries specified:

```
## SOURCE AGENT ##
## configuration file location:  /etc/flume/conf/flume-src.conf
## START Agent: /etc/flume/bin/flume-ng agent -c conf -f conf/flume-src.conf
-n s_agent

## exec-source
s_agent.sources = MyServer
s_agent.sources.apache_server.type = exec
s_agent.sources.apache_server.command = tail -f /etc/httpd/logs/access_log
s_agent.sources.apache_server.batchSize = 1
s_agent.sources.apache_server.channels = memoryChannel
s_agent.sources.apache_server.interceptors = itime

## timestamp-interceptor
s_agent.sources.apache_server.interceptors.itime.type = timestamp

## memory-channel
s_agent.channels = memoryChannel
s_agent.channels.memoryChannel.type = memory
s_agent.channels.memoryChannel.capacity = 100
```

```
## Send to Flume Collector
## avro-sink
s_agent.sinks = avro_sink
s_agent.sinks.avro_sink.type = avro
s_agent.sinks.avro_sink.channel = memoryChannel
s_agent.sinks.avro_sink.hostname = 10.243.169.122
s_agent.sinks.avro_sink.port = 4545
```

As you can observe from this configuration, the source server is called MyServer. The command used for data capture is the Linux tail command. Log entries are held in memory (channel memoryChannel) instead of a file. Interceptors are used for filtering, and here, the interceptor itime uses timestamp to determine which entries are new. The source agent then sends the log entries to a corresponding Flume agent for collection (located on my Hadoop cluster—the IP address corresponds to my network's external IP address). The target server has a corresponding configuration file set up as the following:

```
## TARGET AGENT ##
## configuration file location:  /etc/flume/conf/flume-col.conf
## START Agent: flume-ng agent -c conf -f /etc/flume/conf/flume-col.conf -n target

## avro-source
target.sources = AvroIn
target.sources.AvroIn.type = avro
target.sources.AvroIn.bind = 0.0.0.0
target.sources.AvroIn.port = 4545
target.sources.AvroIn.channels = mc1

## Channels ##
## Source writes to a channel for one sink
target.channels = mc1

## memory-channel
target.channels.mc1.type = memory
target.channels.mc1.capacity = 500

## Sinks ##
target.sinks = LogConsolidator

## Write to HDFS
## hdfs-sink
target.sinks.LogConsolidator.type = hdfs
target.sinks.LogConsolidator.channel = mc1
target.sinks.LogConsolidator.hdfs.path = /user/flume/MyData/%{log_type}/%y%m%d
target.sinks.LogConsolidator.hdfs.fileType = DataStream
target.sinks.LogConsolidator.hdfs.writeFormat = Text
target.sinks.LogConsolidator.hdfs.rollSize = 0
target.sinks.LogConsolidator.hdfs.rollCount = 10000
target.sinks.LogConsolidator.hdfs.rollInterval = 600
```

Note that Apache AVRO is the file format that's being used for transmitting the data, and Flume is listening on port 4545 (since the source agent is sending data to port 4545). The sink collector channel mc1 writes file entries to HDFS. The maximum number of events (log entries in this case) Flume will store in this channel (log entry persistence) is 500. What this means is that if the target server crashes and more than 500 log transactions are queued, only 500 transactions will be saved—unless you can clear the channel (by writing the transactions to HDFS). This limit can be increased (by changing the value for parameter `target.channels.mc1.capacity`), if you have enough memory or disk space available.

As a last step, I need to start Flume agents on source servers as well as my target Hadoop cluster. On source servers:

```
$ /etc/flume/bin/flume-ng agent -c conf -f conf/flume-src.conf -n s_agent
```

And on my target Hadoop cluster:

```
$ /etc/flume/bin/flume-ng agent -c conf -f /etc/flume/conf/flume-col.conf -n target
```

You can add more sources and install Flume agents to send the files to your target cluster. Flume doesn't perform any transformations, but you can use Linux shell utilities or programming languages like Python or Scala to apply transformations to source data as you need.

Summary

The Hadoop world and the Big Data arena are in a very dynamic period, and new Apache components (as well as priced solutions) are added almost weekly. Many of these solutions focus on analytics. Some talk about real-time analytics, others provide textual and sentiment analysis. There are analytics solutions that even analyze social media data in other languages (like Chinese or German or Spanish). Then there are data-discovery solutions that categorize and mask sensitive data or create metadata for your data. There are, however, no additions to the Apache repertoire for ETL processing. There are a few priced solutions available, but they don't add enough value to spend money and time (for retraining your resources).

Streaming analytics is gaining a lot of popularity, and Kafka, Storm, Spark, and Samza are used extensively. That's the reason I have discussed them briefly, but there is still a huge dependence on Sqoop and Flume for ETL. The newer versions of these components are adding useful features, and it would be good to see them performing some real transformations in addition to data import or export. Meanwhile, due to the maturity of these components, large amounts of prebuilt solutions are available, and new plug-in connectors for Sqoop are added regularly.

It will help you to do some web research for your ETL requirements, if you plan to use Flume, Sqoop, or even Kafka, Spark, and Storm.

Of course, you need to be careful and not get carried away by the Spark-mania since Spark is developed using Scala and there are a lot of issues that users are discovering with time. Also, to put things in perspective, Scala has 0.5% market saturation (about as much as Lisp), compared to 21.5% for Java. In fact, with the introduction of native functional programming constructs for Java (with release 1.8), there are no advantages for using Scala. Add a huge number of transitive dependencies that Spark (and Scala) introduce (compared to other alternatives), and it's not an attractive proposition anymore. Since developers need to master all these dependencies to gain a good working understanding of Spark, there are very few true experts available in the market. Spark Python is also a popular option now (since it's as fast as Scala), and more data scientists are comfortable using it.

So, what are the alternatives? Apache Ignite, Apache Drill, Apache Kylin, Apache Geode, and Apache Beam are all good alternatives. If you are interested in processing streming data, you should review these components.

PART IV

■ ■ ■

Transitioning from Relational to NoSQL Design Models

CHAPTER 9

■ ■ ■

Lambda Architecture for Real-time Hadoop Applications

Some time back, I was at IBM Global Services interviewing candidates for a DBA position. I asked candidates about the paramount task they would perform as a DBA at a client site. I expected production backups as an answer, and only one out of six candidates answered correctly. A simple task and yet overlooked by most. Curiously, absence of a well-defined process for backing up data is what ultimately led Nathan Marz to one of the most talked about architectures for Big Data. By his own admission (in his book *Big Data: Principles and Best Practices of Scalable Realtime Data Systems* (Manning, 2015), Nathan overlooked backing up data before performing routine maintenance work and, since the maintenance involved deleting data, set the project back several weeks by accidentally deleting some important data. That experience apparently shaped his views about how a system should be architected. It made him realize that the new architecture should not only be tolerant to machine failure, but to human mistakes as well.

The Lambda architecture (which Nathan designed) focuses on immutable data and batch computations, as opposed to incremental computation. The basic premise of Lambda is that incremental computations and updates add complexity to processing and thereby impact performance. The architecture can be simplified and made more efficient by avoiding (or at least reducing) incremental updates. Data immutability is provided by building a batch layer (without modifying the master dataset) that caters to user queries and data needs. There is also a serving layer to bring additional efficiency to data distribution.

The final layer (speed layer) is the only one that performs incremental computations to get the latest modifications to the data after the batch layer was computed. This way, the volume of data that's involved in incremental computation is low and the overall performance impact minimal. Query responses are computed using a combined data set (a union of data from the batch layer and the speed layer).

© Bhushan Lakhe 2016
B. Lakhe, *Practical Hadoop Migration*, DOI 10.1007/978-1-4842-1287-5_9

You can see that this architecture simplifies a number of tasks. Adding new features is easy because it may involve adding processing (queries) or at the most new views (enhancement to the batch layer). Recovery from human mistakes is easily possible because you can rebuild views from batch layer or speed layer as required. Performance optimization can be achieved easily as well, by tuning the batch layer or indexing views as necessary. Finally, this architecture is generic enough to be applied to any data-processing environment.

This is just a brief introduction to Lambda, but you can see how useful this architecture can be for designing real-time or near real-time systems using NoSQL databases. Add the well-known benefits of Hadoop (fault tolerance, distributed computing, low cost, performance, scalability) to this solution, and you can use this architecture to design an efficient, cost-effective, and high-performance real-time system.

The Lambda architecture has the following objectives:

- Processing should leave (base) data unchanged and build an access layer (tuned for user queries) enabling easy recovery from human errors.

- Processing should be performed asynchronously, ahead of time (of data access) and in a batch mode,

- Incremental computations should be reduced to a minimum (or if possible eliminated).

Now let's discuss the layers of Lambda architecture in detail and also how you can build a good real-time system using it.

Defining and Using the Lambda Layers

In the previous section, I discussed the origin and philosophy behind Lambda architecture. I also briefly mentioned the layers or components of Lambda and their purpose. In this section, I discuss these in detail and also explain how they can be implemented for real-world scenarios.

These layers are logical, or at a conceptual level. When implementing them, the NoSQL databases you need to use are physical and have their own shortcomings—if used in isolation. It is good to understand their strengths (and weaknesses) while using them for your implementation. For example, a columnar database like Cassandra can offer a high throughput but offers a very limited data model (compared to RDBMS). So, there is work involved in adapting your relational schema to it. I discuss this transition in Chapter 8, and as you have seen, you need to complete several tasks for a successful transition.

Another thing to note is the mutability of datasets associated with any NoSQL databases when used in isolation. However, when these NoSQL databases are used as a part of Lambda architecture, the total solution easily overcomes mutability and is human fault tolerant. Let's see how that happens. I'll start with the first layer—the batch layer.

Batch Layer

Latency is a common issue encountered while dealing with huge datasets. Distributed processing mechanisms like MapReduce or YARN may try to minimize it, but considering the use of these huge datasets for analytics and the complex processing involved, the total time used for the processing is not acceptable most of the time. As a result, either the processing needs to be divided in smaller units (which may not be possible every time) or possible user queries are limited in their scope. Lambda architecture tries to remedy this situation by performing precomputations on the data (termed *master data*), based on anticipated queries. The technique involves building views (and indexing them) that may possibly support most of the user queries or read access to data. Since these views are computed from large datasets, they take time to build and therefore this operation is performed asynchronously or in *batch mode*. These preemptive views form the *batch layer* or first layer of Lambda architecture.

I will discuss how these views are built using the master data, but first I'll talk about designing and creating the master data set (that you need to use for your batch layer).

Designing Your Master Data

Considering all possible scenarios, either you may need to re-architect (or migrate) an existing RDBMS-based application to NoSQL (in case near real-time queries are required) or you may be designing a brand new NoSQL-based system with a need for near real-time queries. Steps to follow are similar and start with the logical model discussed in Chapters 2 and 3.

It may seem odd to construct a logical data model for NoSQL implementation, but as explained in Chapter 3, there are several compelling reasons for it. Absence of modeling tools and techniques for NoSQL modeling is a major reason. Another reason is that the procedure for analyzing a business process and establishing a model for capturing data (generated by it) remains almost the same. What changes is the final representation of the model and the way you store it. Nathan Marz proposes a "fact-based" model for holding the master dataset.

Fact-Based Model

To start with, let's define *data* as information that can't be derived from any other information. For the fact-based model, data is deconstructed in fundamental units called *facts*. Fact data is *immutable* or not updatable. So, any updates to data result in addition of a new data row (or unit) that's differentiated using a timestamp. This is to ensure that information (or history, in conventional terms) is not lost. Data immutability has two important advantages:

- *Human-fault tolerance*: With a mutable data model, any faulty or undesired data modifications can overwrite good data permanently and can't be recovered. With an immutable model, bad data can simply be deleted without any adverse effects.

- *Simplicity*: Mutable data models need the data to be indexed for speedy retrieval and updates. With an immutable data model, indexing is not needed since you simply append new data to your master dataset. This simplifies storing master data.

So, how are "facts" generated from data and how are they made immutable? Let me discuss this concept using an example. `DataScourerNinjas.com` has a very interesting business model. It procures and tracks information about thousands of corporations and sells it to companies developing software. The information is useful for software manufacturers in targeting these corporations for specific software that they develop. Figure 9-1 gives a peek into the type of data DataScourerNinjas gathers:

Corporation	Business category	Business details	IT strength	Customer support strength	Yearly revenue	Profit last year	Payroll software or vendor	Helpdesk software or vendor
Toyota motors	Automobile	Sedans, SUVs, Minivans	5000	2000	$70 Billion	$3 Billion	ADP	Zendesk
Accenture	Consulting	Management and Technical consulting	3000	500	$32 Billion	$3 Billion	Custom	Salesforce
General Electric	Energy	Electrical distribution, Electric motors	10,000	2000	$148 Billion	$15 Billion	ADP	SAP – CRM

Figure 9-1. *Potential corporate software sales targets (mutable information)*

Consider a situation where a data issue is detected with one of the entries, `Profit last year`, (for all corporations) and all entries for another corporation. The data is not reliable and needs to be collected again (partially or completely). Or, consider a scenario where the values need to be recorded for a corporation for last six months (since that's when it "qualified" for DataScourerNinjas to track information for it). Following are the issues with this data in these situations:

- It's not possible to know that data is collected in parts at different times.

- It's not possible to know what the past or historical values were (since part of data is overwritten).

This is an example of mutable schema. When data changes, it overwrites the existing data. Also, since parts of data might be more dynamic (changing often) than others, ideally it should be possible to maintain history of all the parts of data separately. This is not possible with mutable schema. So, how can the preceding design issues be resolved? Lambda has a possible solution: fact-based schema. How can the preceding mutable schema be represented as an immutable fact-based schema? Look at Figure 9-2.

CorpBusDetails

Corporation	Business category	Business details	Timestamp
Toyota motors	Automobile	Sedans, SUVs, Minivans	8/1/2015 09:30:13
Accenture	Consulting	Management and Technical consulting	9/2 /2015 10:00:23
General Electric	Energy	Electrical distribution, Electric motors	9/13/2015 10:05:11

CorpITDetails

Corporation	IT strength	CollegeGrads	Timestamp
Toyota motors	5000	3500	8/1/2015 09:30:13
Accenture	3000	2900	9/2 /2015 10:00:23
General Electric	10,000	6000	9/13/2015 10:05:11

CorpCustSupDetails

Corporation	Cust Support strength	Males	Timestamp
Toyota motors	2000	1500	8/1/2015 09:30:13
Accenture	1000	600	9/2 /2015 10:00:23
General Electric	2000	1700	9/13/2015 10:05:11

CorpHelpDeskDetails

Corporation	Helpdesk software or vendor	Timestamp
Toyota motors	Zendesk	8/1/2015 09:30:13
Accenture	Salesforce	9/2/2015 10:00:23
General Electric	SAP – CRM	9/13/2015 10:05:11

CorpFinDetails

Corporation	Profit last year	Yearly revenue	Timestamp
Toyota motors	$4 Billion	$70 Billion	1/1/2015 00:00:01
Accenture	$3 Billion	$32 Billion	1/1/2015 00:00:01
General Electric	$15 Billion	$148 Billion	1/1/2015 00:00:01
Toyota motors	$3 Billion	$50 Billion	1/1/2014 00:00:01
Accenture	$2 Billion	$22 Billion	1/1/2014 00:00:01
General Electric	$10 Billion	$138 Billion	1/1/2014 00:00:01

CorpPayrollDetails

Corporation	Payroll software or vendor	Timestamp
Toyota motors	ADP	8/1/2015 09:30:13
Accenture	Custom	9/2/2015 10:00:23
General Electric	ADP	9/13/2015 10:05:11

Figure 9-2. *Fact-based immutable schema*

The idea really is very simple. First, separate the "facts" that can change independently (of each other) and then track them (separately). Consider the example just given. For a corporation, strength of customer support can increase temporarily if there is an issue that draws a lot of customer reaction. But that may not impact the payroll software that they use or the strength of their IT. So, it's important to separate these facts and maintain a separate history. How do you achieve immutability? Every time there is a change in value, a new row is added along with the timestamp (corresponding to the date/time when the value change occurred). The values may change at different times, but there is a way to know when each of these changes occurred.

You may observe that the column Corporation is included in all the datasets. The reason is that it is used an identifier to uniquely identify the data (across the facts). In this case, it identifies the corporation the data refers to. However, it is not a unique identifier, since the new records that are added will only have the timestamp different. So, the unique identifier will be Corporation *and* Timestamp. Let's look at how this model can be used to support facts about the information tracking system I am using as an example (Figure 9-3).

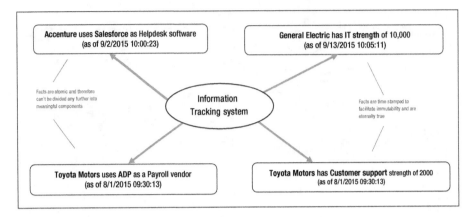

Figure 9-3. *Facts represented by immutable tracking system schema*

Consider this fact: *Accenture uses Salesforce as help desk software as of 9/2/2015 10:00:23*. It is eternally true and is immutable—since a new fact will be added with a corresponding timestamp (in the future), leaving this fact untouched (or unmodified).

Unlike a relational database, where you need to worry about the underlying relations, interconnectivity of data, and update performance, you can keep on adding millions of facts—all time stamped for effective batch processing without worrying about any updates. Also, because there is no incremental processing involved, you don't need to worry about performance. In the next section, I discuss how this fact-based model is used for batch processing.

Applying a Fact-based Model to Relational Applications

Although Lambda defines *fact* as a fundamental unit of data, in the case of real-world systems with structured data, a fact can be an atomic unit of data constituted by a specific group of columns and can be identified using a unique identifier (primary key), since the non-key columns are only dependent on the key columns for identification. So, in relational terms, a *fact* can be a table in the third normal form. (I am sure Nathan didn't have this interpretation in his mind while designing Lambda, but it's surely interesting to see how it can be applied to relational systems, albeit with some modifications.)

Consider a simplistic sales management system. A retailer sells a number of products and registers the sales in a table, shown in Figure 9-4. The sales data is denormalized and "facts" (product, customer, and location metadata in this case) are mutable. Why is this data mutable? Well, think of a situation where customer JCPenney decides to move to another location or the retailer decides to stock the item Men's Striped Cotton shirt at a different warehouse. First, it will be difficult (and slow) to update all the rows with appropriate metadata. Second, information or history will be lost after the updates, since there is no way to specify the date/time of modification.

SalesID	SalesDate	TotalSales	Product	Ptype	PLocation	PPrice	Customer Name	Customer Address	Customer Type
102525525	8/1/2015 09:30:13	$3,450	Men's Striped Cotton shirt (large)	Men's cotton garment	1234 Lemont road Darien IL 60561	$23	JCPenney	1 Oak St. Darien IL 60561	Corporate
126262666	9/2 /2015 10:00:23	$7,740	Men's Denim shorts (Medium)	Men's denim garment	1649 Halstead St. Chicago, IL 60604	$18	Kohls	21 Maple St. Naperville IL 60563	Corporate
137737373	9/1 3/2015 10:05:11	$9,966	Women's solid cotton skirt (black)	Women's cotton garment	1234 Lemont road Darien IL 60561	$33	Kohls	21 Maple St. Naperville IL 60563	Corporate
146366467	10/1 6/2015 11:29:16	$3,120	Gray Woolen scarf	Women's woolen accessory	1234 Lemont road Darien IL 60561	$10	Old Navy	54 Argyle St. Westmont IL 60559	Corporate
136669735	10/1 3/2015 12:09:18	$9,656	Women's woolen skirt (polka dots)	Women's woolen garment	1649 Halstead St. Chicago, IL 60604	$34	Old Navy	54 Argyle St. Westmont IL 60559	Corporate
136566656	10/20/2015 14:06:41	$2,160	Men's gloves (Black leather)	Men's leather accessory	1649 Halstead St. Chicago, IL 60604	$20	JCPenney	1 Oak St. Darien IL 60561	Corporate

Figure 9-4. *Denormalized mutable sales schema*

Can this data be represented using a fact-based model (especially considering the modified definition of a fact)?

Follow these steps to convert this schema to an *immutable* fact-based schema:

- Extract atomic logical groupings
- Add timestamp to each grouping

As you can observe in Figure 9-5, I have added identifiers for each of the tables, and the sales table doesn't contain any metadata any more. Metadata is moved to separate tables, but to make it immutable, you need to add a timestamp column. Then each row will reflect the values as of a specific date/time, and information will not be lost. The immutable data will now look as shown in Figure 9-5.

Sales

SalesID	SalesDate	Total Sales	Product ID	Customer ID
102525525	8/1/2015 09:30:13	$3,450	1	1
126262666	9/2/2015 10:00:23	$7,740	2	2
137737373	9/13/2015 10:05:11	$9,966	3	2
146366467	10/16/2015 11:29:16	$3,120	4	3
13666973 5	10/13/2015 12:09:18	$9,656	5	3
136566656	10/20/2015 14:06:41	$2,160	6	1

Location

Location ID	Street Address	City	State	Zip	LTime stamp
1	1234 Lemont road	Darien	IL	60561	8/1/2015 09:30:13
2	1649 Halstead St.	Chicago	IL	60604	9/2/2015 10:00:23

Product

Product ID	PName	PCategory	Location ID	Unit Price	PTimestamp
1	Men's Striped Cotton shirt (large)	Men's cotton garment	1	$23	8/1/2015 09:30:13
2	Men's Denim shorts (Medium)	Men's denim garment	2	$18	9/2/2015 10:00:23
3	Women's solid cotton shirt (black)	Women's cotton garment	1	$33	9/13/2015 10:05:11
4	Gray Woolen scarf	Women's woolen accessory	1	$10	10/16/2015 11:29:16
5	Women's woolen skirt (polka dots)	Women's woolen garment	2	$34	10/13/2015 12:09:18
6	Men's gloves (Black leather)	Men's leather accessory	2	$20	10/20/2015 14:06:41

Customer

Customer ID	CName	CType	CStreet Address	CCity	CState	CZip	CTimestamp
1	JCPenney	Corporate	1 Oak St.	Darien	IL	60561	8/1/2015 09:30:13
2	Kohls	Corporate	21 Maple St.	Naperville	IL	60563	9/2/2015 10:00:23
3	Old Navy	Corporate	54 Argyle St.	Westmont	IL	60559	10/13/2015 12:09:18

Figure 9-5. *Immutable version of sales schema*

Another issue to consider is uniqueness of data. Because it's possible to generate a new row for any changes to a data row, the unique identifiers (ID columns such as CustomerID, LocationID, and others that I defined) will not be unique unless supplemented by a timestamp. Lambda recommends adding a timestamp column for every fact, and for our example, a fact is identified by each of the data tables. Complete change history is available with this approach as well, since we assume that a new row will be added if any of the column values change.

Immutability of this schema also makes it *eternally true*. In fact, any data row provides the version of truth for the contained information as of the date/time of the associated timestamp. I'll now demonstrate how this model can be used to support facts about the sales management system that I am using as an example.

Figure 9-6 shows examples of facts about the sales management system and also demonstrates two important properties of facts: *atomicity* and *eternal truth*.

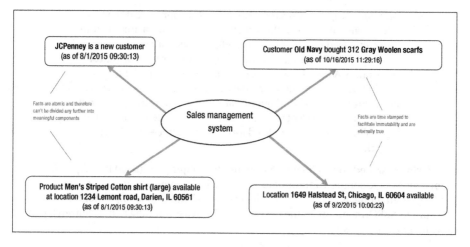

Figure 9-6. *Facts represented by immutable sales schema*

Facts are *atomic* because it's not possible to divide them further into meaningful components. For example, the fact that JC Penney is a customer (since it bought items) can't be divided further, since parts of that fact won't be meaningful in the context of sales management system (or even otherwise). An important consequence of being atomic is non-redundancy of information across distinct facts. The timestamp provides a time context since a fact becomes true (or starts existing) at a particular time and then remains *true eternally* after that. Both these properties make the fact-based model a simple and expressive one for your dataset.

Last, an important point to note about this example of a sales management system is that it uses a complex fact as opposed to a columnar fact suggested by Lambda architecture. A *columnar* fact (adding a timestamp to maintain the change history of a column) may be suitable in the context of a system with few data components, but it would be impossible to implement for complex relational applications, and my focus is implementation of Lambda architecture to re-architect relational systems or design complex systems with a large number of data components.

If you are familiar with data warehouse systems, you may also draw similarities with type 2 dimensions that maintain history for an attribute or column. To summarize, the fact-based schema offers the following benefits:

- *Time-specific queries*: Data can be queried for any time-specific historical values that are supported by your dataset. For example, if you need to know total sales for Kohl's between September 1, 2015, to October 30, 2015, or products available as of September 15, 2015, then it is easily possible and supported.

- *Human-fault tolerance*: This is achieved by simply removing or deleting erroneous facts. Valid facts are unaffected.

- *Advantages of normalized and denormalized forms*: This key
  advantage is because of the structure of the Lambda architecture.
  The fact-based model is normalized and used for data storage.
  Data updates are handled by inserting new rows with the latest
  timestamp. As you know, queries don't perform well for a
  normalized model. Therefore, data storage and query-processing
  layers are separated, and queries are supported by denormalized
  views, built as a part of the batch layer. So, you keep your data in
  normalized and denormalized forms and can receive the benefits
  of both.

Having designed your schema, you can use techniques discussed in Chapter 8 to
adapt it for NoSQL solution appropriate for your environment and use it for data storage.
The fact-based model is a conceptual or logical model and can be implemented using an
appropriate NoSQL solution. In the next section, I discuss building denormalized batch
views for query processing.

Building Batch Views

The purpose for building batch views is to facilitate performance for user access (such
as queries, reporting, and so on). Any user interaction with a huge dataset (mostly the
case where NoSQL is used) needs a large amount of resources, can still not perform well
(slow), and may even fail due to lack of resources. If joins and aggregations are performed
in advance and stored as data objects, any queries that use these data objects (instead of a
master dataset) might perform better. The precomputed data can be indexed to speed up
reads and random seeks (which Hadoop and NoSQL are not very good at). This concept
is very similar to the RDBMS *materialized views* that can be indexed. These precomputed
views or *batch views* constitute the batch layer for Lambda architecture.

Designing Batch Views for Your Fact-based Model

While designing a batch view, you need to focus on your prime objective: any queries that
need to be executed against your master dataset should now execute through a function
on the (newly designed) batch view instead of the whole dataset. That way, the indexed
batch view can facilitate a quick retrieval of values you need. You can create multiple
batch views for your dataset to cover all the functionality required by your application.
Although, the more batch views you create, the longer it will take to rebuild your batch
layer. So, you have to maintain a balance (between number of views and available
processing time) and decide on an optimal number of views to match your processing
power, priorities (in terms of query frequencies), and processing time for rebuild.

One important point to note is that parallelism for data retrieval and processing is
always guaranteed if you use a Hadoop-based NoSQL solution (due to the distributed
nature of Hadoop). There are, of course, other benefits of using HDFS for storing your
master dataset as well as the batch views.

I'm going to look at how batch views can be built for applications we designed fact-based models for (in the previous section): the information tracking system and the sales management system. The information tracking system is designed by DataScourerNinjas and used by their potential customers, who are software companies that design and sell software offering specific functionality (payroll, customer relationship management, and so on).

From their experience, most of the software companies look for potential customers who have been profitable for last five years and have a large customer support staff (at least average of 1,000) for last five years. Some of the companies look for short-term profitability of the last three years but insist on dealing with companies that have IT full of college graduates (at least 60%) for the last three years. Also, since these software products are specific to an industry, it is important to focus on companies in a specific business category. Considering these factors, they designed the following batch views:

- Companies profitable for last five years (included columns: Corporation, Profit last year)

- Companies that have an average customer support staff of 1,000 (or more) for the last five years

- Companies that have IT with at least 60% of college graduates (on average) for the last three years

One more thing to consider while designing batch views is their size. In some cases, if your dataset is really huge, the batch views will be huge as well and you may need to think about breaking them up further. For example, consider the information tracking system under discussion. Assume that there is a huge boom that results in thousands of new companies, and DataScourerNinjas is successful in getting data for them. If you have your batch views by month, the volumes may still be large for quick processing of queries, and you may want to redesign your batch layer with views by a week or even a day. That will increase your (total) processing time (since you will only process weekly or daily, as opposed to a month), but will help with performance and also reduce size (as well as processing) for your speed layer.

Implementing Batch Views

A few things to consider about the batch view designed in the last section. This view can easily be implemented using HDFS for storage, and any of the available NoSQL solutions such as HBase, Cassandra, or MongoDB. Alternatively, you can leave the data in HDFS and use Hive for metadata management and MySQL for holding the metadata. Nathan suggests that you write your own functions and abstractions using Java or any other language of your choice, because using packaged NoSQL solutions adds complexity and can affect performance.

I will use Hive for demonstrating the concept (of designing and building batch views), for several reasons. Writing code for MapReduce has its own limitations, keeping in mind the various distributed engines that are available on a regular basis (at least in the recent past). Besides, I don't expect everyone using this book to be adept at Java or C# programming. And this chapter is more about understanding the concept of Lambda architecture rather than writing code that you can use in a production environment.

Also, for appending vertical or time-based data, Nathan has developed a Java-based application called Pail. You can think of Pail as a container for HDFS. The Thrift (the interface that Nathan uses for serialization) schema creates Java objects. These Thrift Java objects are serialized and deserialized by implementing the PailStructure interface and also useful in implementing vertical partitioning. These are advanced topics that use Java programming—therefore, I have preferred a more generic approach (that may be easier to understand to a wider audience) involving using Hive partitions (daily, weekly, or monthly as your application may warrant) to append new data. I have used Hive partitions to demonstrate the concept of how new data can be managed for your master dataset and processed in the batch views that are created.

You can assume that a memory-based database solution is used (such as VoltDB, Apache Geode, or Ampool) by the web interface to hold the data for a day and then is transferred nightly to HDFS. So, I will create the four Hive tables that will hold the master data for this system. This is a first step required for implementing the batch views discussed earlier. I have also used a timestamp for partitioning the tables.

If you need to perform transactions or need ACID support, you need to perform some configuration changes for Hive before you create the new tables. As you may be aware, CRUD (create, read, update, delete) operations are supported in Hive from 0.14 onwards. To enable support for CRUD operations, make sure your hive-site.xml file has the following parameters configured:

```
hive.support.concurrency - true
hive.enforce.bucketing - true
hive.exec.dynamic.partition.mode - nonstrict
hive.txn.manager -org.apache.hadoop.hive.ql.lockmgr.DbTxnManager
hive.compactor.initiator.on - true
hive.compactor.worker.threads - 1
```

Restart Hive after implementing these configuration changes. Additionally, a ZooKeeper instance must be up and running when using ZooKeeper Hive lock manager. Refer to the following links for additional setup details:

```
http://zookeeper.apache.org/doc/r3.1.2/recipes.html#sc_recipes_Locks
https://cwiki.apache.org/confluence/display/Hive/Hive+Transactions#HiveTrans
actions-LockManager
```

Remember, transactions are supported on objects stored using the ORC file format only. Lastly, you will need to enable support for ACID properties while creating a table and specify bucketing or key columns (which, by the way, can't be updated). So, your create table statements will need to have the following construct:

```
clustered by <key column(s)> into <number of buckets> stored as orc
TBLPROPERTIES ('transactional'='true')
```

I am not using transactional support for my example, and therefore, here's the code to create these Hive tables:

```
CREATE TABLE CorpBusDetails(
Corporation STRING,
BusCategory STRING,
BusDetails STRING
)
PARTITIONED BY (AsOf TIMESTAMP)
ROW FORMAT DELIMITED FIELDS TERMINATED BY "\;";

CREATE TABLE CorpCustSupDetails(
Corporation STRING,
CustSuppStrength INT,
Males INT)
PARTITIONED BY (AsOf TIMESTAMP)
ROW FORMAT DELIMITED FIELDS TERMINATED BY "\;";

CREATE TABLE CorpITDetails(
Corporation STRING,
ITStrength INT,
ColGrads INT)
PARTITIONED BY (AsOf TIMESTAMP)
ROW FORMAT DELIMITED FIELDS TERMINATED BY "\;";

CREATE TABLE CorpFinDetails(
Corporation STRING,
YrlyRevenue BIGINT,
ProfLastYear BIGINT)
PARTITIONED BY (AsOf TIMESTAMP)
ROW FORMAT DELIMITED FIELDS TERMINATED BY "\;";
```

Note that these tables are stored as files within HDFS, and Hive just holds the metadata in order to manage data modifications (and manipulation via queries) more effectively. So, how will new data be added on a daily basis? Using dynamic partitions. You will need to enable dynamic partitioning for your Hive installation and adjust a few configuration parameters. Read the details at https://cwiki.apache.org/confluence/display/Hive/LanguageManual+DML#LanguageManualDML-DynamicPartitionInserts.

Any new data can be appended by creating a staging table (pointing at the file holding new data) and adding the new partition to a table, as follows:

```
CREATE EXTERNAL TABLE CorpBusDetails_stg(
Corporation STRING,
BusCategory STRING,
BusDetails STRING,
AsOf TIMESTAMP
) ROW FORMAT DELIMITED FIELDS TERMINATED BY "\;"
LOCATION "/TrackingInfo/CorpBusDetails/staging";

FROM CorpBusDetails_stg INSERT OVERWRITE TABLE CorpBusDetails PARTITION
(AsOf) SELECT Corporation,BusCategory,BusDetails,AsOf;
```

You will notice that the staging table has an additional column and points to a staging directory (holding the new data) for table CorpBusDetails. The same principle can be applied for adding new data to tables CorpCustSupDetails and CorpProfitDetails. Also, the process of copying new data file to the appropriate staging directory, creating staging table, and adding the new partition to base table can be automated and scheduled.

The next step is creating the batch views. I will first create a table called BatchProcHist to maintain history of batch views created:

```
CREATE TABLE BatchProcHist(
ViewName STRING,
CreatedAt timestamp)
ROW FORMAT DELIMITED FIELDS TERMINATED BY "\;";
```

Next, I will create the first view: *Companies profitable for last 5 years*. The easiest way to determine this is to add the profits for last five years and make sure it's a positive integer. Here's how you can quickly calculate that using a temporary table:

```
Create table Profitemp1 as Select ProfLastYear, AsOf, Corporation from
CorpProfitDetails where year(AsOf) <= year(from_unixtime(unix_timestamp()))
and year(AsOf) >= (year(from_unixtime(unix_timestamp())) - 5)

Create table ProfLFiveView as select Corporation, sum(ProfLastYear) as
ProfLastFive from Profitemp1 group by Corporation having sum(ProfLastYear) > 0

INSERT INTO TABLE BatchProcHist
  VALUES ('ProfLFiveView', from_unixtime(unix_timestamp()));
```

As you must have observed, I also wrote a history record to table BatchProcHist after I created the first batch view.

The second view involves calculating an average (*Companies that have average customer support staff equal to or more than 1,000 for the last five years*). Because you will need to calculate the up-to-date average for the speed layer, you will need to store the count of records used for calculating that average as well:

```
Create table CustSuptemp1 as Select CustSuppStrength, AsOf, Corporation from
CorpCustSupDetails where year(AsOf) <= year(from_unixtime(unix_timestamp()))
and year(AsOf) >= (year(from_unixtime(unix_timestamp())) - 5)
```

```
Create table AveCS1000View as select Corporation, sum(CustSuppStrength)
as TotalCustSup, count(CustSuppStrength) as CountCustSup,
(sum(CustSuppStrength) / count(CustSuppStrength)) as AveLastFive from
CustSuptemp1 group by Corporation having (AveLastFive >= 1000)
```

```
INSERT INTO TABLE BatchProcHist
  VALUES ('AveCS1000View', from_unixtime(unix_timestamp());
```

The temporary tables (Profitemp1, Profitemp2, and CustSuptemp1) can be dropped at this point. They will be created the next time these batch views are rebuilt.

You can build the last batch view (as an exercise), and additional views can be built similarly as per functionality that's required to be supported. As a last step, secondary indexes need to be created to facilitate speedy retrieval, but that's done in the serving layer. Just as an example, for the first batch view designed, the following secondary indexes will help performance:

- Corporation

- ProfLastFive, Corporation

Remember that creating secondary indexes involves processing time and disk space. So, you need to be careful while designing these indexes and optimize their usage. Also, because indexing the views is a very important step (from performance, disk space, and processing time perspectives), it will need to be performed by someone with a good understanding of your data as well as functional needs (analytics and frequently executed queries). If your indexes do not coincide with your queries, you will experience performance issues and also waste valuable system resources (and time) building them.

One important point to note about the batch views is the size and changeability of your dataset. If your dataset is enormous or really dynamic, the resulting batch views may be huge or may be missing a lot of new data, and you may have to perform processing in smaller batches. For example, consider the tracking system example. Assume there is a sudden boom in the market and a lot of new companies are getting added to the repertoire of DataScourerNinjas on a weekly basis. If you rebuild your batch views every month, a lot of new data may have been added in that period that's not a part of the batch views (it will be available through speed layer for your queries, but may reduce the efficiency and speed of the speed layer due to larger volume of records). Therefore, you may want to rebuild batch views every week instead of every month. This will also keep your speed layer small and better managed.

For enormous datasets, you may want to split batch views by week (instead of month) too, since that will reduce your processing resources and time per view (since you will only process a week as opposed to a month), but may complicate your retrieval strategy (since you will need to determine the correct view to query and multiple views if the duration spans across weeks).

Last, the obvious question you may have with this approach is about the time or latency for creating such batch views. Since these views are created from the whole master dataset, clearly they will use a large amount of system resources, and still the computing may not complete within the available maintenance window. Even if it does, they may not have all the data collected by your system, since data might get added while (or after) these views are computed, and your query results might be outdated by many hours. How can Lambda provide near real-time results? The answer lies in the next layers of Lambda and the way they overcome the data latency issue.

Serving Layer

The serving layer "serves" the batch views or provides fast access with minimum latency. Therefore, the serving layer needs to be a specialized distributed database that can host the batch views and support good performance for random as well as sequential data access. The serving layer also needs to be capable of quickly swapping a batch view with a newer version when it is rebuilt by the batch layer, so that user queries can return up-to-date results. So, it needs to support batch updates.

The important thing to remember here is that the serving layer swaps the new batch view *rebuilt* by the batch layer—not processed incrementally. Lambda architecture doesn't perform any incremental processing in the batch or serving layer. There are several issues with incremental processing. Any incremental processing involves updates, inserts, and deletes. All these operations involve random writes, since a database needs to manage space. For example, if a key column gets updated, the record needs to move to a different page and will involve removal of record from a page and insertion on another page. The first operation will leave unused space on a page and the second will need the database server to look for unused space. Wherever enough space is available, the record will be inserted (of course following some kind of insertion algorithm) randomly. Similarly when records are deleted, space is available on a page that can be used.

So, incremental processing creates pockets of unused space and therefore a a need for online compaction to effectively manage space. This processing consumes valuable system resources that can otherwise be used for other purposes. Another complexity added by incremental processing is the need to write atomically and also synchronize reads and writes so that half-written values are never read. This of course needs to be implemented through *isolation levels* and ACID transactions and adds a lot of complexity to processing.

Therefore, if incremental processing is not expected, your database server won't suffer from the operational burden of managing *online compaction* or ACID compliance. To summarize, the following features are expected from the serving layer:

- Ability to host batch views, optimizing latency and throughput

- No need to support random writes but ability to replace batch views as batch updates

- Error tolerance (since views can be quickly redeployed from the batch layer)

- Robustness, predictability, and ease of configuration (as well as operation)

- Indexing capability for fast retrieval

One last point to remember about the serving layer is that there is no single distributed database that can be recommended or used. You need to consider the nature of your data before deciding on the serving layer, since each distributed (or NoSQL) database has its own strengths and you need to make sure that it matches your data.

ElephantDB

Nathan proposes use of ElephantDB; a database that serves or deploys key-value data from Hadoop for fast and efficient access. ElephantDB has two major components:

- Library used by MapReduce jobs for creating an indexed key-value dataset, stored on a distributed file system

- Daemon or background process that can provide a read-only, random access subset of a deployed dataset

A cluster of servers that serves a full dataset is called a *ring*. ElephantDB server doesn't support random writes and uses a Thrift interface, making it possible for most of the languages to easily read from it.

ElephantDB is not very easy to interface with Hive, and using it requires advanced programming knowledge. Besides, there are limitations using indexing in ElephantDB, and it doesn't provide a SQL interface for querying. Subsequently, I will use SploutSQL as serving layer since SploutSQL doesn't need any programming to deploy or server Hive objects and also provides SQL as query language, making querying easier and eliminating time in learning a new query language.

Splout SQL

Splout SQL is a read-only database and that simplifies its architecture. Here are the salient features (of its architecture):

- Splout can be installed on a set of commodity hardware machines to form a cluster. Every machine (or node) runs a DNode service and optionally a QNode service (there must be at least one QNode service for a cluster).

- QNodes interface with users via REST API and serve user queries or receive deploy requests.

- QNodes communicate with appropriate DNode(s) for serving a query, and the DNode(s) respond back with necessary data set.

- Splout leverages a Hadoop cluster for indexing (as well as balancing using pre-sampling) the data, and resultant files are retrieved by the DNodes as part of a data deploy request. You can sort your data before insertion for contiguity and to minimizing disk seeks.

- Data is partitioned (as per your need) and distributed across nodes. Also, queries are restricted to a single partition and therefore are fast.

- Generation and deployment of data can be simultaneous and don't impact each other.

- High availability and scalability is inherited through the use of Hadoop.

- Data is deployed as a *Tablespace,* which is a group of tables with a common partitioning schema.

- For easier management, Tablespaces are versioned, and multiple Tablespaces can be deployed simultaneously.

- Splout can import data directly from Hive, cascading, or Pig.

- QNodes and DNodes are implemented as Java services.

- Splout uses Pangool for low-level Java Hadoop development and generates SQLite files used by DNodes for serving data.

Figure 9-7 summarizes the Splout processing and interfaces.

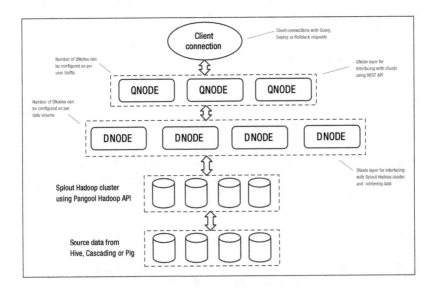

Figure 9-7. *Splout SQL processing and interfaces*

To use Splout SQL, you will need to install it. See the instructions at `http://sploutsql.com/gettingstarted.html`. You need to configure Splout after installation and specify location of jar files as well as your Hadoop installation. After that, you can start the QNode and DNode services on Splout cluster nodes. If you are importing data from Hive (as in the example I have used), add Hive `conf/` and `lib/` folders to the `HADOOP_CLASSPATH` environment variable:

```
export HADOOP_CLASSPATH=$HADOOP_CLASSPATH:$HIVE_HOME/conf:$HIVE_HOME/lib/*
```

Next, generate tablespaces and tables. For the information tracking information system in my example, I have created a batch view (as a Hive table). I'll discuss steps to serve or deploy it using Splout SQL. First, for creating or generating a tablespace, you need to use the generate tool. This tool uses a JSON tablespace descriptor as I show next. You need to specify the input type and the Hive database and table names. Note that you don't need to specify input paths, since you have already specified directory for Hive installation, and therefore Splout can locate the appropriate Hive metastore and retrieve the necessary Hive tables from the appropriate database. The tablespace descriptor file can be created in the Splout SQL installation directory:

```
{
        "name": "AveCS1000Space",
        "nPartitions": 1,
        "partitionedTables": [{
                "name": "AveCS1000View",
                "partitionFields": "Corporation",
                "tableInputs": [{
                        "inputType": "HIVE",
                        "hiveTableName": "AveCS1000View",
                        "hiveDbName": "TrackInfo"
                }]
        }]
}
```

The information is provided in the file `AveCS1000Space.json`. The tablespace will be called `AveCS1000Space` and currently has only a single table `AveCS1000View` defined—that was created earlier in the last section. The database name is `TrackInfo` and I have chosen to create one partition for my data. I have used the name `Corporation` as a partitioning column, since this column will be a part of almost all the queries.

It is very important to partition the tablespace correctly becauseit is used for balancing data before indexing and deploying it. Usually, a frequently used key column for tables within a tablespace is used as a partitioning key. All the tables within a tablespace need to use columns of same type as partitioning key. For example, if tablespace A contains tables `Tbl1` and `Tbl2`, and if `Tbl11` is partitioned by a pair of (string, int) columns, `Tbl2` should also be partitioned by a pair of (`string`, `int`) columns.

Note that when a table is partitioned by a single or multiple columns, Splout concatenates the value of those columns to form a single string. Therefore, partitioning is a function of a row, and it is also possible to partition using arbitrary functions (such as a JavaScript function that takes the last five characters of a field).

Getting back to the deployment, the following command can be executed from command line to generate the tablespace AveCS1000Space (from the Splout SQL installation directory):

```
hadoop jar splout-*-hadoop.jar generate -tf file:///`pwd`/ AveCS1000Space.
json -o out-TrackingInfo_splout_example
```

For performance, you may need to add indexes to your tablespace, and Splout allows you to add indexes easily. You just need to modify the command used to generate the tablespace. For example, the following index will help performance:

```
TotalCustSup, Corporation
```

The following command will add the second index while generating the tablespace AveCS1000Space:

```
hadoop jar splout-hadoop-*-hadoop.jar simple-generate -it HIVE -hdb
TrackInfo -htn AveCS1000View -o out-TrackingInfo_splout_example -pby
Corporation -p 1 -idx "TotalCustSup" -t AveCS1000View -tb AveCS1000Space
```

I have not included the column Corporation since it is a partitioning column and is already indexed. The -idx option just adds more columns to the index. Also, note that I am using a different generator (simple-generate) instead of the one used earlier (generate), and therefore the command line options are different. There is no json configuration file and therefore, all the configuration (such as Hive database, table name, partitioning column, and so forth) has to be specified with the command.

A major disadvantage of using simple-generate instead of generate is that you can only have a single table in your tablespace, but that's usually the case. For the tracking information system example, you will need to generate four separate tablespaces for four batch views (or Hive/Splout tables)—if you need to supplement the indexes. If not, then you can simply create a single tablespace with all four tables in it (using the generate generator instead of simple-generate).

After the tablespace is generated successfully, deploy it as follows:

```
hadoop jar splout-hadoop-*-hadoop.jar deploy -q http://localhost:4412 -root
out-TrackingInfo_splout_example -ts AveCS1000Space
```

Note that localhost is the host QNode (to which the client is connected) is running on, and localhost will be automatically substituted by the first valid private IP address at runtime (as specified in the configuration file).

Once a tablespace is deployed, you can use it in any of your queries. For example, if you need to populate a web app using information for Toyota Motors, you can use the REST API, as follows:

```
http://localhost:4412/api/query/ AveCS1000Space?sql=SELECT * FROM
AveCS1000View;&key='Toyota Motors'
```

I have demonstrated how Splout SQL can be used successfully to serve your batch views for use by your applications. Next, I talk about how you can access data that's not yet processed by the batch layer and include it in your query results.

Speed Layer

You have seen that the latency of the batch layer makes it difficult to have up-to-date or near real-time data accessible for your queries. The purpose of the speed layer is to make that data available without any delays. In terms of functionality, a speed layer is very similar to the batch layer (since it also produces views based on master data too). The difference is that the speed layer only processes new or recent data (not yet processed by the batch layer), whereas the batch layer uses all the data for computing the views.

Another difference is that the batch layer updates a view by recomputing (or rebuilding) it, whereas the speed layer performs incremental processing on a view and only processes the delta (or new) transactions that were performed after the last time incremental processing was done. So, if your incoming data transactions are timestamped, and you extract them from your master dataset, then depending on whether a record was modified or added, you can modify your speed layer view accordingly.

Considering the differences in speed layer processing (compared to batch layer), you will realize that the architecture for the speed layer will differ depending on whether the speed layer (or near real-time) views are updated synchronously or asynchronously. What I mean by a synchronous update is applying any updates to master data directly to the speed layer views. Since a cluster will always have a fixed or predetermined capacity (for handling updates or any other dat-intensive operations), it can get overloaded with requests during peak usages. This can affect performance and functionality (if some requests are denied due to resource unavailability). In contrast, asynchronous update requests are placed in a queue with the actual updates occurring at a later time. The delay in applying asynchronous updates would depend on a lot of factors, such as volume of updates, processing resources required (and available), functional need for near real-time data, and so on, but it does offer an effective way to accommodate larger number of requests and is not affected by peak usage spikes.

Asynchronous updates provide many benefits, such as processing multiple messages from the queue and increasing throughput and handling varying load by buffering additional requests (till the load reduces and processing resources are available). You don't have these benefits with synchronous updates because there is no mechanism available to control the update volume and thus it can easily overload and crash your database system or lead to dropped requests, timeouts, and other errors that may disrupt your application.

The decision to use synchronous and asynchronous updates can also be based on the type of processing that your application performs. For example, synchronous updates can be used for transactional systems with user interaction that requires coordination with the user interface and completion of request needs to be guaranteed. Asynchronous updates can be more useful for analytics applications or applications that focus more on complex computations and aggregations rather than interactive user input. Looking at the benefits of asynchronous processing, I would suggest using it unless you have a very specific need for incorporating data at real-time in your speed layer views.

To summarize, you will need the following features supported while implementing the speed layer:

- Random reads and writes

- Support for wide range of data types including date/time

- Ability to perform scheduled or ad hoc updates

- Ability to support joins and any incremental update tasks (update, insert) with acceptable level of performance

- Support Indexing and provide SQL query interface for performance and ease of use

- Ability to interface with the Hadoop ecosystem with ease

- Provide scalability and fault tolerance

- Ability to provide in-memory processing for performance

After careful evaluation of choices, I short-listed Spark SQL and VoltDB. However, I quickly realized that VoltDB can't read from Hive (or HDFS) and hence discarded it. Although, while comparing these two choices, I realized that Spark SQL had its own shortcomings and even though they are not very relevant for the example I am demonstrating, they might be significant in some cases. They are:

- Transactional support is not offered by Spark SQL.

- Spark SQL DataFrames do not support indexes. Indexing is helpful for random Read/write performance.

- Spark SQL does not include storage natively, so you would need to use an external data store for storage.

I discuss Spark SQL in detail in Chapter 5 under "Query Tools" and the subsection "Spark SQL." That will help you understand the Spark architecture and where Spark SQL fits into it. For now, let me demonstrate usage of Spark SQL as the speed layer. I have demonstrated how to build batch and serving layers for tracking information system. Now I will build a speed layer.

The Lambda architecture defines the speed layer to be composed of records that are yet to be processed by the batch layer. So, as a first step, you need to determine what those records are. You might recall that a history record was inserted in table BatchProcHist after a batch view was built. So, the most recent record for a batch view can give us the date/time of most recent build and therefore help determine what the unprocessed records are. Because Hive doesn't support query results to be assigned to variables, I will write the most recent record for the first batch view to a table:

```
Create table MaxTable as select ViewName, max(CreatedAt) as MaxDate from
BatchProcHist group by ViewName having ViewName = 'ProfLFiveView';
```

But what happens if the speed layer has processed any new records from the master dataset since this batch view was built? Well, you need to check that and only consider the unprocessed records for updating the view (now a Spark data frame registered as a table). I'll call the speed layer view ProfLFiveView_S. Just like the batch views, speed layer views also write to the audit table BatchProcHist. So, I will write the most recent record for the first speed layer view to the same table (where I captured most recent record for the first batch view):

```
Insert into MaxTable select ViewName, max(CreatedAt) from BatchProcHist
group by ViewName having ViewName = 'ProfLFiveView_S';
```

Now I just need to determine which of these records is the most recent and use that as a basis to process the records for the first speed layer view:

```
Create table MaxTbl1 as select max(MaxDate) as MaxDate from MaxTable;
```

Finally, get the unprocessed records from the master data set and create the speed layer view. Also, add the timestamp and write a record to the audit history table:

```
Create table Profitemp1_S as Select a.ProfLastYear, a.AsOf, a.Corporation
from CorpProfitDetails a, MaxTbl1 b where a.AsOf > b.MaxDate;
```

```
Create table ProfLFiveView_S as select Corporation, sum(ProfLastYear) as
ProfLastFive from Profitemp1 group by Corporation
```

```
INSERT INTO TABLE BatchProcHist
  VALUES ('ProfLFiveView_S', from_unixtime(unix_timestamp());
```

Temporary tables MaxTable, Profitemp1_S, and MaxTbl1 can be dropped at this point. Also, note that I didn't use the condition having sum(ProfLastYear) > 0 while creating the view ProfLFiveView_S. The reason is that this sum is only for the new records of corporations that are profitable for last five years. To get the up-to-date sum, add it to the sum from the batch layer, and the updated profit will be determined automatically (taking into account the total profit or loss for the new records as indicated by a positive or negative number).

Let me assume that speed layer views are built every week. So, what happens when you need to update your speed layer views to accommodate new data and remove data that is already a part of the batch layer views (if batch layer views are rebuilt meanwhile)? There are two possible approaches:

- Rebuild the speed layer view considering the unprocessed records only (just like we built for the first time).

- Don't drop the temporary table Profitemp1_S after the first round of processing and delete expired (already part of rebuilt batch view) records from it and add the new records. Then just perform the aggregation and rebuild the speed layer view ProfLFiveView_S.

Remember, in order to perform a delete operation, you will need to change Hive configuration for CRUD support and add transactional support for table `Profitemp1_S` (discussed in the section for batch layer views).

I would consider the size of the speed layer view to decide between these options. If the view is not really huge and can be rebuilt quickly, I choose the rebuild option. However, if the view is huge and will take substantial processing and time to rebuild, I enable transactional support and simply add the new records and remove the processed (by batch layer) records from temporary table `Profitemp1`. The same logic (as discussed earlier in this section) can be used to retrieve the most recent processing date/times for batch and speed layer views and thereafter retrieve the unprocessed records from the master data set as needed. After the records in table `Profitemp1` are adjusted (expired records deleted and unprocessed records added), aggregation can be performed to build the updated view.

One more critical point to consider is the dependence of speed layer processing on batch layer processing. At a minimum, you need to expire or remove speed layer records that are processed by the batch layer. You can of course rebuild or add any new records also (to your speed layer view).

Next, I'll discuss building a speed layer view for the second batch view. As you may remember, it involves calculating an average (*Companies that have average customer support staff equal to or more than 1,000 for last five years*). I'll talk about how updated averages can be calculated for the corresponding speed layer view.

As a first step, let's get the most recent processing times (for batch and speed layer) for the view `AveCS1000View`:

```
Create table MaxTable as select ViewName, max(CreatedAt) from BatchProcHist
group by ViewName having ViewName = 'AveCS1000View';

Insert into MaxTable select ViewName, max(CreatedAt) from BatchProcHist
group by ViewName having ViewName = 'AveCS1000View _S';
```

Now I just need to determine which of these records is most recent and use that as a basis to process the records for the first speed layer view:

```
Create table MaxTbl1 as select max(MaxDate) as MaxDate from MaxTable;
```

Finally, get the unprocessed records from the master data set and create the speed layer view. Also, add the timestamp and write a record to the audit history table:

```
Create table CustSuptemp1_S as Select a.CustSuppStrength, a.AsOf,
a.Corporation from CorpCustSupDetails a, MaxTbl1 b where a.AsOf > b.MaxDate;

Create table CustSuptemp2_S as select Corporation, sum(CustSuppStrength) as
TotalCustSup, count(CustSuppStrength) as CountCustSup from CustSuptemp1_S
group by Corporation;
```

```
Create table AveCS1000View_S as select a.Corporation, (a.TotalCustSup +
b.TotalCustSup) as TotalCustSup, (a.CountCustSup + b.CountCustSup) as
CountCustSup, ((a.TotalCustSup + b.TotalCustSup) / (a.CountCustSup +
b.CountCustSup)) as AveLastFive from CustSuptemp2_S a, AveCS1000View b where
a.Corporation = b.Corporation and (AveLastFive >= 1000)
```

```
INSERT INTO TABLE BatchProcHist
  VALUES ('AveCS1000View_S', from_unixtime(unix_timestamp()));
```

Note that I had to use an additional temporary table so that I could add as well as count the CustSuppStrength numbers for the unprocessed records and the ones from the corresponding batch view—since this view calculates averages.

Having discussed all this logic for developing the speed layer, let me turn to the Spark interface and implementation of speed layer using Spark. As you may know, Spark uses dataframes and RDDs (resilient distributed datasets) as in-memory constructs that you can leverage for queries and performance. Spark also allows you to execute queries against Hive databases using the SQLContext. Both these concepts are useful for the speed layer implementation. You can use Scala, Python, or R within a Spark shell.

As a first step, you need to construct a HiveContext, which inherits from SQLContext and enables you to find tables in the Hive MetaStore and also supports queries using HiveQL. You do not have an existing Hive deployment for creating a HiveContext. If you don't have a hive-site.xml specifying Hive configuration and directories, the context automatically creates metastore_db and warehouse in the current directory. Here, I am using Scala, and sc is an existing SparkContext:

```
val sqlContext = new org.apache.spark.sql.hive.HiveContext(sc)
```

```
val sqlContext.sql("Create table MaxTable as select ViewName, max(CreatedAt)
from BatchProcHist group by ViewName having ViewName = 'AveCS1000View'")
```

```
val sqlContext.sql("Insert into MaxTable select ViewName, max(CreatedAt)
from BatchProcHist group by ViewName having ViewName = 'AveCS1000View _S'")
```

You can similarly execute all the HiveQL commands necessary to create the speed layer view AveCS1000View_S. For the last step (when the view is created), instead of creating the view, you can simply execute the select statement and read the result in a dataframe, as follows:

```
val resultsDF = sqlContext.sql("select a.Corporation, (a.TotalCustSup +
b.TotalCustSup) as TotalCustSup, (a.CountCustSup + b.CountCustSup) as
CountCustSup, ((a.TotalCustSup + b.TotalCustSup) / (a.CountCustSup +
b.CountCustSup)) as AveLastFive from CustSuptemp2_S a, AveCS1000View b where
a.Corporation = b.Corporation and (AveLastFive >= 1000)")
```

You can register the resultant dataframe as a temporary table and then execute any queries against it:

```
val resultsDF.registerTempTable("AveCS1000View _S")
val results = sqlContext.sql("SELECT Corporation FROM AveCS1000View _S")
```

You will need to use a query tool that can read from Hive and Spark to combine results from batch layer and speed layer views. There are enough choices, and of course you can also use Spark SQL as a query tool too.

There are a few things you need to note about Hive and Spark SQL integration. Because of the large number of dependencies that Hive has, it is not included in the default Spark assembly. You can enable Hive support by using the -Phive and -Phive-thriftserver flags to Spark's build. This will build a new assembly jar that includes Hive. Make sure this Hive assembly jar is present on all the data nodes, as they will need access to the Hive serialization and deserialization libraries (SerDes) for accessing data stored in Hive.

Also, Hive configuration is supplied by copying your hive-site.xml file in the $HADOOP_HOME/conf directory. Please note if you are using a YARN cluster (yarn-cluster mode), the datanucleus jars should be in the lib_managed/jars directory, and hive-site.xml under the $HADOOP_HOME/conf directory for the driver and all executors launched by the YARN cluster. The easiest way to achieve this is by adding them through the --jars option and --file option of the spark-submit command.

It is often said that the biggest issue with Lambda is maintaining two separate sets of code for batch and speed layers. By using Spark SQL and Hive, I think there's no need to maintain two sets of code—one is enough. That definitely simplifies the implementation.

Pros and Cons of Using Lambda

The Lambda architecture defines how batch and stream processing can work together to deliver a complete solution while using a NoSQL solution. Lambda architecture enables you to run ad hoc queries against all your data efficiently and in near real time. The idea is to precompute the results as a set of views and query the views instead of the master dataset. This architecture offers a number of benefits over the traditional NoSQL architectures (or the lack of) and redefines the role of NoSQL and Hadoop for data processing. However, there are issues with Lambda too. It can't solve all your data-processing problems. I discuss pros and cons of Lambda in this section, starting with the pros.

Benefits of Lambda

One of the most discussed benefits is data immutability. Also, how storage and query layers can have different storage structures. Another popular feature is Lambda's reprocessing abilities. Let me discuss all these features briefly:

- Lambda architecture emphasizes data immutability. Input data is retained without any changes to it. Processed and transformed data is written out separately, but it's always possible to access to input data received in its original form. This also saves data from corruption due to human errors or hardware faults and adds resilience to the architecture.

- Data is transformed in a series of modular stages, and that helps in debugging (each stage independently) as well as making the workflows tractable.

- It is easily possible to reprocess your data (processing input data again to re-derive output). Why is this needed? It is always possible that there are code changes within your application (due to change of functionality or discovery of an issue or a bug). If the modified code is used to derive output data from an input stream, you will need to reprocess your input using the new code. If you recall, a batch layer is rebuilt every time new data is processed. So, reprocessing of data is supported as well as performed by default.

- Lambda makes it possible to store your master dataset normalized, while offering the flexibility to denormalize your real-time and batch views as needed. This can help your queries perform better for NoSQL data, since NoSQL databases typically don't perform well for joins or sub-queries. The data separation also allows you to fine-tune each data layer as needed.

- The master dataset (being an immutable data store) can be used as a reliable source for analytics. Since it has a complete record or history of all the application data, it is possible to analyze any subsets of data or look for patterns within it.

- Lambda facilitates the use of near real-time data within your queries.

Issues with Lambda

Lambda has many useful features, but can it be used in all situations and for all kinds of data? Are there any inherent weaknesses or flaws that need to be addressed while using it? I'll talk about answers to these questions and more:

- Lambda (and Nathan) makes an assumption that real-time processing is less accurate, less powerful, and unnecessarily more complex compared to batch processing. That's not necessarily true. For example, many leading stream-processing systems (Storm, Spark, Amazon Kinesis) can provide a semantic guarantee as strong as any batch system.

- The claim that the Lambda architecture "beats the CAP theorem" is not true. Lambda is essentially an architecture for asynchronous processing. Therefore, the computed results are not immediately consistent with the incoming data.

- A big problem with Lambda architecture is that you need to maintain code (that needs to produce the same result) in two separate distributed systems (for batch and speed layers). Since you need to engineer your code specifically for the framework it runs on, the resulting operational complexity of systems implementing the Lambda architecture is huge.

One proposed approach for resolving this issue is to have a language or framework that abstracts over both the real-time and batch framework. That way, your code can be used for stream processing or MapReduce as needed. Kappa architecture and Butterfly architecture (by Milind Bhandarkar) are targeted at overcoming this issue. Both these architectures are discussed in this chapter.

- The operational burden of managing and tuning two operational systems (for batch and speed layers) is very high. Also, any time you plan to add new features, you can only consider features that can be supported by the intersection of the two systems. This may also prevent you from using popular Hadoop components and tools such as Hive, Pig, Crunch, Cascading, Oozie, and others.

Lambda has its pros and cons and is not suitable for all kinds of data or business objectives. There is already an alternative to Lambda called Kappa, which I cover in the next section.

The Kappa Architecture

In summer 2014, Jay Kreps coined the term Kappa architecture in an article for O'Reilly Radar. Jay was just commenting on Lambda architecture and issues with it. So, what is Kappa and how is it different from Lambda?

The concept is very simple. Use a stream-processing engine (Spark, Kafka, and so on) that allows you to retain the full log of the data you might need to reprocess. If there is a need to do reprocessing, start a second instance of your stream processing job that will process from the beginning of the retained data and write the output to a new destination (such as a table or file). When the second job completes processing, switch the application to read from the new output destination. After that, you can stop the old version of the job and delete the old output destination. Figure 9-8 illustrates the Kappa architecture.

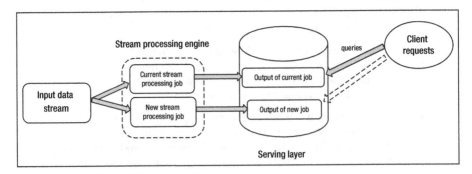

Figure 9-8. Kappa architecture

One of the reasons Kappa architecture was designed was to avoid maintaining two separate code bases for the batch and speed layers. Also, if batch and speed layers are replaced by a streaming layer (processed by a stream-processing engine), then a single stream-processing engine needs to handle real-time data processing as well as continuous data reprocessing (as data needs to be reprocessed when there are code changes).

Therefore, Kappa architecture has two layers: stream processing and serving. The stream-processing layer is responsible for executing the stream-processing jobs. Usually, a single stream-processing job takes care of real-time data processing. If there are code changes (to the stream-processing job) and data needs to be reprocessed, then a modified stream-processing job is executed additionally to complete that task. Serving layer is used to query the results.

Various open source technologies like Apache Kafka, HBase, HDFS, Spark, Drill, Storm, or Samza can be used to implement Kappa. For example, data can be ingested using a *publish-subscribe* messaging system like Apache Kafka. HDFS can be used for persistent storage. Any low-latency systems (such as Apache Storm, Samza, or Spark Streaming) can be used to implement the stream-processing layer in the Kappa architecture.

Now, it is possible to use Apache Spark to develop the batch and speed layers in the Lambda architecture (for a single code base). The serving layer can be implemented using Splout queries using Apache Drill. How do you choose one architecture over the other? Well, that depends on characteristics of the application that needs to be implemented.

For example, when the algorithms that need to be applied to the real-time data and to the historical data are identical, it is a good case to use Kappa architecture. But if the expected outputs for the real-time and batch algorithms are different, then the batch and real-time layers cannot be merged, and Lambda architecture must be used. Are there any situations where this happens? Consider a scenario where your batch layer needs to process a billion records and compute daily and weekly averages. Here, generation of the batch model will need so much time and resources that you will need to use approximation models for computing real-time views. So, you can't merge processing for your batch and real-time layers, and therefore you can't use Kappa—Lambda would be your only possible model.

I have highlighted several benefits of Kappa architecture, but you need to understand that it can't be used in every situation. It can't solve all your Big Data processing problems. There are of course other alternatives, such Zeta architecture or Iot-a, proposed by Michael Hausenblas. A number of architectural alternatives are available now, and you should evaluate your environment and make a prudent decision based on your data, processing needs, business objectives, and hardware resources available.

Future Architectures[1]

As we witness the current transformation in data architecture, where RDBMS is being supplemented by large scale non-relational stores, such as HDFS, MongoDB, Cassandra, and HBase, a more fundamental shift is on its way, which would require larger changes to modern data architectures. Although the current shift was mandated by business requirements for the connected world, the next wave will be dictated by operational cost optimization, transformative changes in the underlying infrastructure technology, and newer use-cases such as the Internet of Things (IoT), Deep Learning, and Conversational User Interfaces (CUI).

In order to hazard a guess about what the future of data architecture holds, let us take a brief tour of how we arrived at the current data architecture.

A Bit of History

Prior to the popularity of relational databases, multiple data models were being used and among those, hierarchical and navigational data systems were used extensively on mainframe-based systems. Because the number of clients for these data systems was limited, they remained monolithic, and more often than not, were offered by the mainframe manufacturer and bundled with hardware.

As the relational model was proposed (more than 40 years ago) and deemed suitable for a majority of data applications, it became very popular for prevalent use-cases in banking, insurance, and the financial services industry. Relational database systems became the default back-end data systems (as a store of record) in a variety of verticals. The advent of client-server systems (where multiple clients would access the data stored and served by the same server) created importance for up-front data modelling, SQL, formal data manipulation semantics (ACID) led to query concurrency improvements, rule-based and cost-based query optimization, and standard access methods (ODBC and JDBC), and resulted in a plethora of visual tools for building database-backed applications and data visualizations.

Clients' access to these operational databases was a mix of CRUD primitives on either single or very few records. To provide consistency across multiple CRUD operations, a notion of transactions was introduced (where either all the operations were carried out atomically or none at all). Thus, these data systems were known as OLTP (on-line transactional processing) systems, and their performance was measured in transactions-per-second.

Most business intelligence (BI) and reporting workloads used very different access patterns. These queries were mostly read-only queries on a large amount of historical data. Although the operational data systems were initially used to handle both transactional and analytical workloads, they could not fulfill the low-latency transactions and high-throughput analytics simultaneously. Thus, to serve this new class of applications, data systems specialized in OLAP (on-line analytical processing) were devised.

---

[1]This section was kindly contributed by Milind Bhandarkar, PhD, founder of Ampool, Inc. Milind's brief bio is included with the foreward he wrote

Because these OLAP systems had to handle large amounts of historical data, often they were built as MPP (massively parallel processing) systems on a shared-nothing distributed architecture. This created two silos of structured data in organizations—one for structured transactions and another for structured analytics. Even though both these systems were designed with relational data models in mind, often one would need to integrate multiple transactional data stores across multiple departments to provide the full historical data in the analytical data system. Thus, a notion of periodic ETL (extract-transform-load) was born, which would capture data changes across multiple transactional data stores, map their relationships, and structure them into fact/dimension tables with a star schema or snowflake schema. The analytical query engines and the storage for these analytical data were quite different from their transactional counterparts, since the analytical data once stored would almost never have to change (as it was a historical record of business transactions).

In the world of structured operational and analytical data stores, semi-structured data (such as server logs) and unstructured data (such as natural language communication in customer interactions) were either discarded or kept in an archival store for compliance reasons. Centralized file systems became a popular choice of data stores for semi-structured and unstructured historical datasets with specialized access layers (such as keyword search).

Apache Hadoop aimed to solve the semi-structured and unstructured data analytics workloads problem by providing HDFS on commodity hardware and collocating it with a batch-oriented flexible distributed data-processing paradigm called MapReduce. As the Hadoop ecosystem expanded, it was to tackle more and more data-processing workloads. Thus, there were scripting languages such as Pig, SQL-like query languages such as Hive, and a NoSQL store, HBase, that used HDFS for persistent storage.

Eventually, the compute resource management capability was separated from the batch-oriented programming model and allowed a proliferation of data-processing frameworks to run on top of data stored in HDFS. These included traditional MPP data warehouses (such as Apache HAWQ), streaming analytics systems (such as Apache Apex), and transactional SQL engines (such as Apache Trafodion). This gave rise to the notion of a data lake, where all the raw data across the enterprise and external data sources would be loaded and made available for flexible analytics, using best-of-breed data-processing engines on the same granular data.

Although Apache Hadoop and associated projects have rapidly evolved to promise a unified analytics platform, the key core component of Hadoop, the HDFS, has never been designed with interactive, streaming, and transactional workloads in mind and thus has become a hindrance in achieving that goal. As a result, multiple architectures, such as the Lambda and Kappa architectures, were proposed (to unify multiple data-processing workloads). Unfortunately, they remain quite difficult to implement.

For the Lambda architecture, the speed, serving, and batch layers need three different implementations of data-processing frameworks for the same functionality (depending on the speed and scale needed), and it is the responsibility of the implementer to transport data across these three layers—a non-trivial task. In addition, one cannot guarantee data consistency across the three layers without introducing yet another distributed transaction engine (between the data applications and the Lambda architecture).

The Kappa architecture, introduced by the creators of Apache Kafka, relies on a distributed log as the primary source of data. A *distributed log* provides decoupling between data producers and data consumers. It allows different batch analytics engines and streaming analytics engines to consume data from the same data bus, thus solving the data consistency problem introduced in the Lambda architecture. But the difficulty of implementing data processing in the speed, serving, and batch layers in three different engines remains.

The primary difficulty in implementing the speed, serving, and batch layers in the same unified architecture is due to the deficiencies of the distributed file system in the Hadoop ecosystem. If we were to provide a replacement for HDFS (or if we could augment the HDFS with a storage component that can serve the speed and serving layers while keeping data consistent with HDFS for batch processing), one could truly provide a unified data processing platform. This observation leads to the Butterfly architecture, described next.

Butterfly Architecture

The main intention of the Butterfly architecture is to unify data-processing tasks for batch, serving, and speed layers in a single platform. To implement the Butterfly architecture, we need to treat data with new, more general abstractions that are different from current abstractions (such as files, directories, or tables and indexes). In the Butterfly architecture, we organize data as a collection of three types of abstractions:

- *Datasets*: This is the most flexible abstraction, a partitioned collection of arbitrary records. No structure is imposed on records. In other words, interpreting what is in the records is left to the processing framework with the aid of a system catalog. This is equivalent to schema-on-read data, which is the only kind of data managed by current Hadoop/NoSQL data systems. The system catalog stores information about each dataset (as well as relationships among multiple datasets). Each dataset is given a unique identifier, and the catalog is a logical set of RDF triplets denoted by (Relation, Object1, Object2). For example, to indicate that dataset with ID 4596 is named SearchLog, the catalog has an entry (NameOf, 4596, "SearchLog"). As another example, to indicate the location of dataset 4596 to be in HDFS, an entry (Location, 4596, "hdfs://namenode:port/user/data/something") exists in the system catalog. Note that this is a logical representation of the system metadata about datasets and may be represented physically as a set of fixed-width tables, for reasons of efficiency. These datasets could be stored on multiple storage systems, and even multiple partitions from a single dataset may be stored across multiple storage back ends. In addition, when a dataset is stored as a stream of bytes in files or transferred across network, the serialization and deserialization formats are user-defined or operator-defined.

- *Dataframes*: Dataframes are structured datasets. They are partitioned with a user-specified partitioning key contained in the individual records. The dataframes could be mutable or immutable. *Immutable* dataframes may not be modified in any way (once they are created), while individual records of a mutable dataframe could be inserted, updated, or deleted. They are typically created by multiple computation frameworks by processing datasets. Dataframes are very similar to structured tables in relational database management systems (with predefined schema). Immutable dataframes are suitable for analytical workloads, whereas mutable dataframes are used for transactional CRUD workloads.

- *Event streams*: Event streams are unbounded dataframes. At least one of the fields in these records (events) is mostly monotonically increasing. Usually, this field is a timestamp or a sequence number. Optionally, streams may have a window size specified as either a number of records (in case of monotonically increasing field its sequence number), or time duration (in case the monotonically decreasing field its timestamp). Within a window, there could be some out-of-order arrival of events. However, across windows, the sequence number or timestamp is strictly monotonically increasing.

The main differentiating characteristic of the Butterfly architecture is the flexibility in computational paradigm on top of each of the preceding data abstractions. Thus, a multitude of computational engines, such as MPP SQL-engines (Apache Impala, Apache Drill, or Apache HAWQ), MapReduce, Apache Spark, Apache Flink, Apache Hive, or Apache Tez can process datasets, dataframes, and event streams.

These computation steps can be strung together to form *data pipelines*, which are orchestrated by an external scheduler. A resource manager (associated with pluggable resource schedulers that are data aware) is a must for implementing the Butterfly architecture. Both Apache YARN and Apache Mesos, along with orchestration framework (such as Kubernetes or hybrid resource management framework such as Apache Myriad (incubating)), have emerged in the last few years to fulfill this role. The Butterfly architecture and associated data flows are illustrated in Figure 9-9.

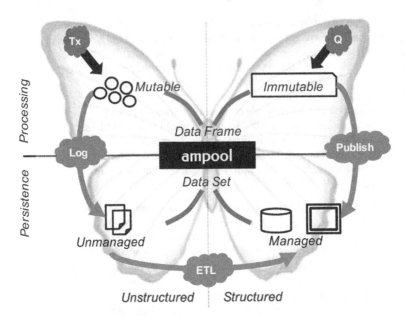

Figure 9-9. *Butterfly architecture*

Storage for Butterfly Architecture

In order to efficiently implement the Butterfly architecture, one needs a fast storage engine for data exchange across the data pipelines as well as streaming ingestion and analytics. Optimized implementations for immutable and mutable dataframes are needed for allowing fast batch-oriented queries and fast transactions, which allow coexistence of multiple workloads in a single system. Traditional disk-based storage systems make this unification extremely difficult. However, the emergence of NVMe-connected Flash, NVDIMMS (non-volatile dynamic memory modules), and a new class of persistent memory (SCM, or storage class memory) provides a perfect storage medium in which high-throughput scan-oriented workloads and low-latency random access workloads can coexist. Table 9-1 characterizes the current and projected performance of various storage layers, along with their approximate associated cost.

Table 9-1. *Types of Storage and Their Costs*

Storage Type	Approx. Cost per GB	I/O OPS/Sec	Throughput	Cost per GB for Billion IOPS	Cost per GB for GB/s Throughput
DRAM	$6	20 Million	50 GB/s	$300	$0.12
SCM	$2 (projected)	10 Million	10 GB/s	$200	$0.20
NAND Flash	$0.50	1 Million	1 GB/s	$500	$0.50
HDD	$0.03	100	100 MB/s	$30,000	$0.30

As you can see from Table 9-1, current generation of DDR4 DRAM is the most cost-efficient for throughput-oriented workloads, and the emerging Storage Class Memory (SCM) is the most cost-effective for random access workloads. Of course, cost is not the only consideration for building systems—storage density as well as power consumption are two other factors to consider. Since the new SCM promises to have much higher densities and much lower power consumption than DRAM, they have the potential of becoming the primary storage layer for a fast unified data platform.

Most existing databases and data-storage systems have been designed with the performance characteristics and storage densities of HDDs. Thus, they tend to avoid random access at all costs, and in order to avoid long latencies, they tend to parallelize their random access workloads either by spreading data across multiple hard disk drives in a disk array or by fetching all the data in expensive server-side DRAM while running sequential access workloads on data stored on hard disk drives. Thus, they introduce a lot of complexity to keep the data consistent and available across workloads (in case of disk failures). Also, hard disk drives (having mechanical parts) are much more prone to failure than solid state devices such as Flash, SCM, and DRAM.

For fully implementing the Butterfly architecture, one needs to cost-efficiently utilize the various classes of solid state memory. Ampool is building a novel storage technology for implementing the Butterfly architecture.

Ampool

Ampool's core product is a memory-centric, distributed, data-aware object storage optimized for both transactional and analytical workloads. These features of Ampool product are discussed in the following section:

> *Memory-centric*: Although DRAM costs have rapidly declined over the years, they are still very high compared to other storage media (such as SSD and hard disk drives). Fortunately, not all the data that needs to be analyzed in the enterprise needs the kind of performance that DRAM provides. Also, as the data becomes older, it is accessed less and less frequently. Thus colder data can be stored on hard disk drives, warm data can be stored on SSDs, and only data that is most frequently accessed (and needs fastest access) can be stored in DRAM. Manually moving data across these storage tiers is cumbersome and prone to error. Ampool implements smart tiering that monitors the usage of data and automatically moves the data across tiers, as it is accessed infrequently.

Distributed: Although the DRAM and storage density has increased dramatically over the years, adding more and more DRAM and storage to a single system (scaling up) does not scale the overall system performance proportionally with the cost. Thus, even memory-centric storage systems need to be clustered and distributed for linear scalability, fault tolerance, and disaster recovery. Ampool storage is designed as a distributed system from the ground up. Data is replicated across address spaces of various machines in the cluster (in order to be highly available). In addition, the changes in data are propagated via a scalable message bus across a wide area network (for disaster recovery).

Object store: Historically, the most common types of storage systems were categorized into a block store or file system. Each has its own advantages. A *block store* can be shared across different operating systems and has much lower overhead of accessing a random piece of data. However, network round-trips to fetch individual blocks are often insufficient for today's large-scale data workloads. In addition, since the basic unit of read and write is a 4 KB block, small updates (as well as small reads) result in a lot of unnecessary data traffic over the network or on the local disks. Filesystems are the most commonly used abstraction for storage and are available in various flavors across multiple operating systems.

In addition, several scalable distributed filesystems are available from multiple vendors. However, implementing filesystem semantics (which involves maintenance and navigation of a hierarchical name space structure), maintaining consistency and atomicity across filesystem operations, and providing random reads and writes in place in files, imposes a lot of overhead for the filesystem servers (as well as clients). Typically, the filesystem read/write access has 50–100 microsecond latency. When the filesystem was implemented on top of slow rotating disks (which had a 10 millisecond latency), the filesystem latency was negligible compared to the underlying storage media latency. However, with the new fast random access storage (such as SSDs and NVRAM), which have only a few microseconds latency, the filesystem abstraction has overwhelmingly high overheads.

In the last decade, because of the emergence of public clouds and their hostage storage solutions, a third kind of storage abstraction—object store—has become popular. Object stores have a flat hierarchy. To access an object, one only needs a bucket ID and an object ID (rather than navigating a hierarchical name space). In addition, object stores have rich metadata associated with each object and bucket, so that operations such as filters and content searches can be pushed down to the storage layer, reducing network bandwidth requirement and load on CPU. Object stores are ideal for the new classes of storage media because of the low CPU overhead, simpler semantics, and scalability—especially with a large number of data stored as objects.

Data-aware: Most of the existing object stores do not interpret the contents of the objects natively. Therefore, their utility is limited, and indeed, the most common use of object stores is as blob stores to store and retrieve multimedia (such as images or video). If one were to implement analytical workloads on data stored in an object store, it needs fetching the entire object (which may be megabytes or gigabytes in size) to the CPU, imposing a schema on it, deserializing it, and then performing the necessary analytical computations on it. The Ampool object store stores extensive metadata about objects (such as schema, versions, partitioning key, and various statistics about the contents of the objects), such that common operations like projections, filtering, and aggregates can be pushed down to the object store. This helps in speeding up most analytical computations and avoids network bottlenecks prevalent in other distributed storage systems. A block diagram for the current version of Ampool is shown in Figure 9-10.

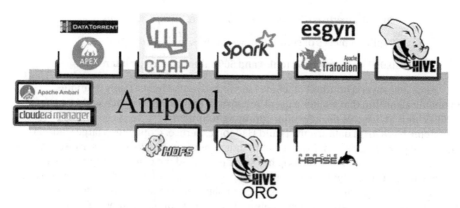

Figure 9-10. *Ampool architecture*

In addition to the core memory-centric object store, Ampool includes several optimized connectors that allow existing computational engines to efficiently store and retrieve data from the Ampool object store. Although the number of connectors is rapidly increasing with every version of Ampool, the current connectors provided out of the box include Apache Spark, Apache Hive, Apache Trafodion (in collaboration with Esgyn Corporation), Apache Apex (in collaboration with Datatorrent, Inc.), and CDAP (Cask Data Application Platform, in collaboration with Cask Data, Inc.). Although the Ampool system is in itself a fully distributed storage system able to maintain large volumes of operational persistent data, it provides several persistent storage connectors to load and store data. Connectors available include Hadoop Distributed File System (HDFS), Apache Hive, and Apache HBase. Ampool can be deployed as a separate system with Hadoop components or with an existing running Hadoop cluster (either with Apache Ambari or Cloudera Manager) and can be monitored and managed with provided tools or by connecting the JMX metrics produced by Ampool to any JMX-compatible monitoring system.

By providing fast analytical storage for (both immutable and mutable) dataframes, datasets, and for extensions for event streams, Ampool provides the missing piece for implementing the Butterfly architecture and allows unification of various transactional and analytical workloads.

Example Use Case: Ad Tech Data Pipeline

Acme.io is a very popular content aggregation company that has a web-based portal and also a mobile app with tens of millions of users, who frequently visit using multiple devices several times a day to get hyper-personalized content. Acme has several advertising customers who pay to display their advertisements on all devices. Acme is one of many "Web 3.0" companies and has a deep understanding of its users' precise interests as well as exact demographic data—based on which, it personalizes the content. It has an ever-growing taxonomy of its users' interests, and advertisers can target users by demographics as well as their precise interests. Here is Acme's business in numbers:

- 100 million registered users with 50 million daily unique users

- 100,000 advertisements across 10,000 advertising campaigns

- 10 million pieces of content (news, photos, audio, video)

- 50,000 keywords in 50 topics and 500 subtopics as user interests

Acme has several hundred machines serving advertisements. Using a unique matching algorithm that fetches a user's interests, it finds the best match within a few milliseconds and serves the ad within appropriate content.

Acme has a lot of data scientists and Hadoop expertise. It operates a large Hadoop cluster for providing personalized recommendations of content to its users. However, the batch-oriented nature of Hadoop has so far prevented the company from using that Hadoop infrastructure for real-time ad serving, streaming analytics on advertisement logs, and providing real-time feedback on campaign performance to its customers. Also, for its business and marketing analysts, who want to perform ad hoc queries on the advertising data to target larger pool of customers, Acme has set up a separate data repository apart from both the real-time analytics and batch analytics systems. As a result, the operating expenses of its data infrastructure has more than tripled. Worse, Acme incurs a huge overhead just trying to keep the data in sync across these three platforms. Since the same data is kept in multiple places, there is lag and discrepancies in the data, repetitive tasks for data cleansing, and ensuring data quality and maintaining data governance. This wastes more than 80% of valuable time of Acme data scientists and Big Data infrastructure specialists.

Acme architects and technologists decided to replace the entire data infrastructure with modern Flash and memory-based architecture and had a deep-dive with Acme data pipeline developers. They realized that they will have to rewrite the last five years' worth of data-analysis work with the new, unfamiliar, and immature technologies. Retraining the data practitioners alone would take several years. Instead, they decided to do incremental, piecemeal upgrades to the data infrastructure, moving towards the Butterfly architecture from their current Lambda architecture, using Ampool memory-centric storage.

The Data

Exactly four large data sets are used in Acme's data analysis pipeline: user profiles, advertisements, content metadata, and ad serving logs.

User Profiles

User profiles contain details about every registered user. The schema for user profile is as follows:

- UserID: UUID

- Age: 0..255

- Sex: M/F/Unknown

- Location: Lat-Long

- Registration timestamp: TS

- Interests: Comma-separated list of (topic:subtopic:keyword)

Advertisements

This dataset contains all the details about all the advertisements available for displaying within content. The schema for this data set is as follows:

- AdID: UUID

- CampaignID: UUID

- CustomerID: UUID

- AdType: {banner, modal, search, video}

- AdPlatform: {web, mobile}

- Keywords: comma-separated list of (topic:subtopic:keyword)
- PPC: $ per click
- PPM: $ per 1000 display
- PPB: $ per conversion

Content Metadata

The content dataset contains all the metadata about the content. The schema for the content dataset is as follows:

- ContentID: UUID
- ContentType: {news, video, audio, photo}
- Keywords: Comma separated list of (topic:subtopic:keyword)

Ad Serving Logs

This dataset is streamed continuously from the ad servers. Each entry in this log has the following fields, of which some may be null:

- TimeStamp: TS
- IPAddress: IPv4/IPv6
- UserID: UUID
- AdID: UUID
- ContentID: UUID
- AdType: {banner, modal, search, video}
- AdPlatform: {web, mobile}
- EventType: {View, Click, Conversion}

Computations

Following computational steps are performed on the data in Acme's advertisement analytics data pipelines.

Ingestion and Streaming Analytics

Ad servers produce ad click, view, and conversion events to Kafka brokers. Kafka consumers are embedded in the Apache Apex (DataTorrent) streaming analytics platform. For every event consumed, the following computations are done:

1. Parsing the event record
2. Extracting timestamp, ad ID, event type, and ad type

3. Looking up campaign ID from ad ID

4. Windowed aggregation of event types for each ad ID and campaign ID

5. Storing these aggregates in Ampool

6. Visualizing these aggregations in a streaming visualization dashboard of DataTorrent for a campaign ID and all ads in that campaign

7. The output of the streaming analytics is as follows:

    a. (Ad-ID, Time-Window, Number-Of-Views, Number-Of-Clicks, Number-Of-Conversions, Total-PPV, Total, PPC, Total PPConversion)

    b. (Campaign-ID, Time Window, Number-Of-Views, Number-Of-Clicks, Number-Of-Conversions, Total-PPV, Total, PPC, Total PPConversion)

Second streaming ingestion pipeline keeps the user table, ad table, and content table updated. While the ads are being displayed, clicked, and converted, new users are being registered, and existing users' information is being updated. New campaigns are created, existing campaigns are modified, new ads are created, and existing ads are updated. These inserts and updates are being done simultaneously, rather than periodically. In the second pipeline, we use Kafka consumers to get insert and update records and apply these inserts and updates to respective tables in Ampool in real time. The steps in this pipeline are as follows:

1. Ingest a {user, campaign, ad} {update, insert} event from Kafka broker.

2. Parse the event to determine which table is to be updated.

3. Update the respective table.

4. Keep track of total number of updates.

5. When 1% of the records are either new or updated, launch the batch computation and reset update counters.

Batch Model Building

In this batch-oriented computation, we build ad targeting models. The inputs for this pipeline are the user table, ad table, and content table. And output of this pipeline are two new tables:

1. (User-ID, Ad-Id1, weight1, Ad-Id2, weight 2, Ad-Id3, weight3)

2. (Content-ID, Ad-Id1, weight1, Ad-Id2, weight2, Ad-Id3, weight3)

These tables represent the top three most relevant ads for every user and for all content. These tables are then used for the ad serving systems, such that when a user visits particular content, the best match among these ads is chosen, based on one lookup each in the user table and content table.

Relevance of an ad for a user of a content is determined by cosine similarity in the list of keywords, and topics and subtopics. This batch model building pipeline, built using CDAP, has the following steps:

1. A MapReduce job to extract the relevant fields from user table and ad table, and join based on topics, subtopics, and keywords.

2. A Spark job to filter the top three matching keywords and compute the weights of ads for those keywords using cosine similarity.

3. Repeat the preceding steps for the content table and ad table.

Interactive and Ad Hoc SQL Queries

The interactive and ad hoc queries are performed on varying windows of the aggregates for campaigns and ads using Apache Trafodion (EsgynDB). Here are some examples of the queries:

1. What was the {per-minute, hourly, daily} conversion rate for an ad? For a campaign?

2. How many ads were clicked on as a percentage of viewed, per hour for a campaign?

3. How much money does a campaign owe to Acme.io for the whole day?

4. What are the most clicked ads and campaigns per hour?

5. How many male users does Acme have aged 0–21, 21–40?

The results of these queries can be displayed on the screen (interactively) and for the queries resulting in time-windowed data, visualized using a tool such as Tableau.

Summary

A few years back, when Nathan Marz first introduced Lambda architecture, there was a rush of excitement through the Big Data community because at the time there were no options for real-time processing of streaming data using Hadoop. The role of Hadoop and NoSQL was relegated to ETL or at the most batch processing. The introduction of Lambda changed that. For the first time, it was demonstrated that Hadoop had a possible use for real-time processing.

However, as the excitement wore off, problems with this architecture were soon noticed. Lambda is a good starting point, but you need to adapt it for your individual environment. Use of Lambda is also restrictive (in most cases) for choice of components of the Hadoop ecosystem you plan to use. Nathan has demonstrated his concepts by developing Java code for every small task related to Lambda, but that's not practical. If you plan to build your data lake (that's where I see the most use for Lambda) using the various production systems in your environment, developing fact-based model(s) for those systems will be a difficult and time-consuming task. I have already demonstrated the process using a real-world example. That should give you a good idea about the effort involved.

So, where can you use Lambda? And is there a real use for it? You can follow the "web-click" examples in Nathan's book and probably develop similar Java code to implement systems to gather and analyze social media data or data for your e-commerce systems or maybe IoT-related systems. But can you use Lambda to interface with relational systems? And more importantly, can you develop fact-based models for such interfaces? There is no absolute affirmative or negative answer to this question. It depends on the complexity of your source system and also your objective—what do you want to do with the data once it is in Hadoop?

Finally, is Lambda going to survive the onslaught of bleeding-edge, stream-processing engines like Spark that also remove the major hurdle of managing two distributed systems for providing batch and real-time functionality? I feel that only time will tell.

CHAPTER 10

■ ■ ■

Implementing and Optimizing the Transition

Recently, I have seen a number of organizations reversing their decision about using Big Data. These organizations represent diverse industries and therefore may not withstand the logic of Hadoop not being suitable for a particular industry. In most of these cases (apparently), performance and lack of usability were the main issues for deciding against using Big Data technologies. Granted that open source software does not have extensive and easy-to-understand documentation or means to troubleshoot, but these days, there are enough vendors selling supported Hadoop distributions and software with easy-to-use browser interfaces for performing all kinds of tasks starting with data ingestion to the end result: analytics.

So, why the hesitance and reluctance to invest money in Hadoop? Why has Hadoop not replaced a large number of data warehouses? Why is Hadoop still not a main application platform for big corporations? There is no short answer to any of these questions. I want to focus on the perceived lack of *huge* performance gain—a major factor for wanting to choose Hadoop to replace the older technologies. I will talk about how you can extract optimal performance from your Hadoop cluster using performance tuning at the hardware, operating system, Hadoop configuration, and data stages.

You've probably heard that Hadoop clusters can be built using commodity hardware, but that's not really true for production environments. I will discuss some typical hardware configurations for production and development environments. I will cover why you need to start with the operating system for performance tuning. I will also discuss the major configuration parameters that impact performance and explain how and why need to be tuned.

After you have your operating system tuned, you need to work on Hadoop configuration parameters and change them to gain optimal performance for your specific environment. And as you know, Hadoop holds data as files, so the storage format for these files is very important. There are reasons why a particular format needs to be used for storage, and I talk about the factors you need to consider while deciding a storage format. Also, considering the high data volumes, data compression is essential. I discuss the types of compression codecs and pros/cons. Finally, I cover special indexing and caching techniques that will help with performance.

© Bhushan Lakhe 2016
B. Lakhe, *Practical Hadoop Migration*, DOI 10.1007/978-1-4842-1287-5_10

Of course, as a first step for getting optimal performance from your Hadoop cluster, you need to run baseline stress tests and identify the problem areas or areas where performance is not as expected. I will start with Hadoop hardware configurations for production/development environments.

Hardware Configuration

You can't assume that a Hadoop cluster can be constructed using old, discarded, commodity hardware. You need to use servers with multiple CPUs (containing multiple cores) and with enough RAM. Your production cluster needs to have more powerful hardware than your development environment, and of course your NameNode (master node) needs to be more powerful than the DataNodes (worker nodes for either environment). This is just a quick summary.

Cluster Configuration

The HDFS master node (NameNode) needs to have more memory than the worker nodes. Also, the storage for the master node should be RAID, and because it's a SPOF (single point of failure), it needs to be replicated for failover scenarios. A NameNode needs to be configured based on the amount of data (as well as number of files you plan for the cluster to hold). And you need to consider growth projections and data compression while configuring.

Here's how you can calculate the cluster size for production usage. Let me start with spacing for a node and total number of nodes. Since operating system and other essential applications on a node need some space (roughly 25% of total space) and data blocks are replicated based on a replication factor (default 3):

```
HDFS space per node = (Raw disk space per node - 25% non-DFS local storage)/
(Replication Factor)
```

```
Number of Worker nodes = Total HDFS space/HDFS space per node
```

Consider the following for startup (individual) worker node configuration:

- Latest generation processor(s) with 12 to 16 cores (total)
- 4–8 GB memory per core
- 1–3 TB SATA disks per core
- 1GbE NIC

For a NameNode:

- 4–6 cores (total)
- Start with memory as follows: (3 GB + 1 GB for every 100 TB of raw disk space or 1 million file objects)
- Needs to be replicated (for failover)

- RAID-1 storage

- NameNode should run on a 64-bit OS to avoid 3 GB limit on JVM heap size

If you are using YARN, you can use 2 GB RAM and 1 core CPU as a starter configuration for the YARN master node, the Resource Manager (as a rule of thumb). But you might want to boost up the hardware for a really busy Resource Manager (a lot of scheduled jobs). Of course, you need to do workload profiling and review the resource usage at peak-time workloads. If there is maximum usage for a resource, adjust the resource allocation accordingly.

The size of your development environment depends on your application usage. If you are using a vendor product, then you might use your development environment only for version upgrades or customizations (to the vendor product). In that case, you can probably halve the hardware resources per node and may also want to reduce by half the number of worker nodes for your development environment.

However, if your application is home-grown (or developed within your corporation), then you might want to allocate 70–80% of hardware resources per worker node (as compared with production) and also use a count of 70–80% worker nodes (as compared with production), because you might have to process a larger number of enhancements (to the application) and may need to test out performance for them too. For a really dynamic development environment, you may need to match development resources (with production) and may need larger space to facilitate holding multiple versions of data (for testing).

Note that these are only guidelines for a generic cluster. You should consult your vendor (for Hadoop distribution) documentation or seek expert advice for your individual configuration needs.

Operating System Configuration

It is important to consult OS documentation before you start with performance tuning for your Hadoop cluster. Remember, HDFS is simply a file system (albeit distributed, fault tolerant, and with a lot of good features) that runs within the purview of the OS for your individual (master or worker) nodes. Some of the adjustments for your OS are intuitive, whereas others need a good understanding of it. Because RHEL (Red Hat Enterprise Linux) or CentOS are popular Linux flavors used for Hadoop clusters, I will assume the OS is one of them. I'll start with the intuitive adjustments:

- *Turn off the Power Savings option*: You need this BIOS setting to optimize performance for applications (instead of just switching off during idle time). Change this to PerfOptimized in your BIOS settings.

- *Turn off caching on disk controller*: Hadoop doesn't use it.

- *Mount disk volumes using the option NOATIME*: By default, the OS records the last accessed (read or write) date for a file. This option turns off that behavior and thereby speeds up access (since it is not used by Hadoop).

There are a number of advantages in using the ext4 filesystem (instead of ext3), such as multi-block and delayed allocation. Therefore, you should consider using it. And now, some not-so-intuitive settings:

- *Disable transparent Huge page compaction*: When enabled, this feature tells the Linux kernel to allocate 2 MB pages to a Linux process (whenever possible). But since the compaction part seems to cause a problem with Hadoop jobs and results in high CPU usage, it needs to be disabled. For RHEL, you can use the following command:

  ```
  echo never > sys/kernel/mm/redhat_transparent_hugepages/defrag
  ```

  In order to make that change permanent, add the following script in your /etc/rc.local file:

  ```
  if test -f /sys/kernel/mm/redhat_transparent_hugepage/defrag;
  then echo never > /sys/kernel/mm/redhat_transparent_hugepage/
  defrag ;fi
  ```

- *Reduce FS reserve blocks space*: There is 5% space reserved for special operations (such as file delete by root when the filesystem is full), but Hadoop doesn't need this space, so it can be removed. Use the following command:

  ```
  tune2fs -m 0 /dev/sdXY
  ```

- *Increase open file handles and files*: By default, the number of open file count is 1024 for each user, which might result in errors like java.io.FileNotFoundException: (Too many open files). Therefore, the *number of open file* limit needs to be set. For Linux, there are three limits: soft limit (can be set by a user), hard limit (only set by root or superuser), and system-wide limit (set by root in configuration file for the server). Choose a high value (like 4032) as your soft limit (that a user can set up to), a higher value (say, 32832) as the hard limit (that root can set up to), and a really high value (for example, 6544018) for system-wide file descriptors, since that's the total file descriptors possible for the whole system. Use the following commands:

  ```
  ulimit -S 4096
  ulimit -H 32832
  sysctl -w fs.file-max=6544018
  ```

- *Memory swapping*: In Hadoop, swapping (swapping in-memory data with filesystem) reduces job performance. So, keep maximum data in-memory and configure your OS to do a memory swap only if it is OOM (OutOfMemory). To achieve that, set the value for parameter vm.swappiness kernel to 0. Use the following command:

```
sysctl -w vm.swappiness=0
```

Note that the sysctl command will set the values for your session. To persist this value, add the following line to configuration file /etc/sysctl.conf:

```
vm.swappiness=0
```

For the file descriptor value (above) to persist, add the following line to configuration file /etc/sysctl.conf:

```
fs.file-max=6544018
```

Hadoop being a distributed file system, there is a lot of inter-node communication using the network. Subsequently, the network performance is important, so the network packet size is important too. Maximum transmission unit (MTU) indicates the packet size that can be sent using the TCP/IP protocol. The default size for MTU is 1500; you can increase it to 9000. A value of MTU that's greater than its default value is called *jumbo frames*. You can change the value of MTU by adding the following line in configuration file /etc/sysconfig/network-scripts/ifcfg-eth0 (or whatever your eth device name is):

```
MTU=9000
```

You must restart the network service for this change to take effect. Also, before modifying this value, make sure that all the nodes in your cluster (including switches) support jumbo frames. If not, don't make this change.

The next section discusses the Hadoop configuration parameters that are important to consider from a performance perspective.

Hadoop Configuration

Hadoop configuration can be broadly grouped into three categories: HDFS, JVM, and YARN (including MapReduce as a container). I discuss all these categories along with tunable parameters in each of them.

HDFS Configuration

HDFS holds your data and therefore is a key consideration for data access. You have to make sure that the data writes and reads are performed with optimal performance. I shared some configuration details for NameNode and DataNodes earlier, but note the details of some fast drives that you can use.

Also, you should perform some generic tasks like time synchronization, version control, and cluster balancing. It is important to synchronize time on all your cluster nodes. Failing to do so may result in errors, and it may even be difficult to know what the real time of those errors was. It is similarly important to use version control for configuration. You don't want to be in a situation where some nodes are at a particular version and others are at another. HDFS provides a utility (Balancer) to redistribute data in a uniform manner on your DataNodes. That helps in distributing processing (uniformly) as well and should be used after cluster expansion.

Getting back to configuration, you can consider key parameters such as block size or buffer size. Here's a complete list:

- *Drive type*: Even though RAID arrays are not required for DataNode storage (since HDFS replicates the data blocks as per specified replication factor), it will help to have fast SATA drives to hold your data. SSD (solid state drive) storage is ideal, but because it is expensive, you can use SSHD (solid state hybrid drive) storage that offers 7,200 RPM or SATA III drives offering 10,000 RPM.

- *Multiple disk mount points for your DataNodes and NameNode*: For DataNodes, the comma-separated list of mount-points (or directories) will spread the data across them and thereby provide optimal access performance. For NameNode, multiple directories (or mount-points) provide metadata redundancy. HDFS makes sure that data blocks for your files are replicated across DataNodes for redundancy. The relevant properties in hdfs-site.xml:

  dfs.datanode.data.dir
  dfs.namenode.name.dir

- *DFS block size*: This is a very important consideration. Review your expected file sizes and their usage. For example, if your data files are large but a large number of user queries retrieve small datasets (500 MB–5 GB), then you might want to start with a block size of 64 MB or 128 MB since you write once and read multiple times. You can override block size while writing new files and have different block sizes for files as per their expected use. The relevant property in hdfs-site.xml:

  dfs.block.size

- *Local filesystem buffer*: This is the buffer size (controlled by property io.file.buffer.size) used by HDFS for its I/O operations. It should be increased to 64 KB or 128 KB for performance gains. Also, depending on how much RAM you have available, you can set io.sort.factor (number of maps to merge while sorting a file) to 20 or 25 (the default is 10). Note that the value for io.sort.mb (the amount of memory used by a mappers to collect map output) should be 10 * io.sort.factor. So, 10 mapper task instances with io.sort.mb = 200 means your total RAM allocation for sorting is 2 GB. The relevant properties in core-site.xml:

  io.file.buffer.size

  And mapred-site.xml:

  io.sort.factor
  io.sort.mb

- *Short-circuit reads*: As a general rule, when a client requests a data block (for a file) from HDFS, the client contacts the appropriate DataNode and the data is sent to the client using a TCP connection. If the data block being requested resides on the same node as the client, then it is more efficient (for the client) to bypass the network and read the block data directly from the disk (termed a short-circuit read). Short-circuit reads can be enabled by setting the property dfs.client.read.shortcircuit to true. The relevant properties in hdfs-site.xml:

  dfs.client.read.shortcircuit

  You also need to set additional properties for this purpose. For details, see https://hadoop.apache.org/docs/r2.4.1/hadoop-project-dist/hadoop-hdfs/ShortCircuitLocalReads.html.

- *NameNode/DataNode concurrency*: For large clusters, it is imperative to have more threads for maximum concurrency. The parameter dfs.namenode.handler.count controls the number of server threads for the NameNode and should be increased from the default value of 10 to 50 or 100 (depending on the size of the cluster and available memory). The parameter dfs.datanode.handler.count similarly indicates the number of threads handling block requests for a DataNode. If you have multiple physical disks (for each of your DataNodes), you can increase the throughput by increasing this number from default value of 3 to 5 or more. The relevant properties in hdfs-site.xml:

  dfs.namenode.handler.count
  dfs.datanode.handler.count

- *DataNode Failed volumes tolerated*: This property is set to 0 by default. If a data volume fails, DataNode will shut down. Setting it to a higher value (2 or 3) will prevent the DataNode from shutting down when a single data volume fails. The relevant properties in hdfs-site.xml:

    dfs.datanode.failed.volumes.tolerated

The preceding list is not exhaustive. See the Apache documentation for a complete list of parameters defined in the files core-site.xml, hdfs-site.xml, and mapred-site.xml (or YARN configuration files if you are using yarn).

Also please visit www.odpi.org for complete details of the new ODPi standard that's being developed for standardization of core Hadoop components and certification of Hadoop distributions. Development of this standard will provide version control and harmony to the core Hadoop components and simplify their usage.

ODPi is a nonprofit organization that's developing a common reference specification called ODPi Core. Because Apache Hadoop, its components, and its distributions are evolving very quickly and diversely, it has resulted in slowing the Big Data ecosystem. The concept of a standard ODPi core will save on cost and reduce complexity and thereby accelerate the development of Big Data solutions by providing specifications for a common runtime and also assist in creating reference implementations and test suites.

JVM/YARN/MapReduce Configuration

All the Hadoop daemons are JVMs and therefore it is important to understand how you can get optimal performance for a JVM. There are some general guidelines and then means to facilitate troubleshooting, since there may be certain reasons or specific concerns for your environment that may drive certain configuration parameter values, and these values may not follow the generic guidelines.

Generic JVM Guidelines

Note that the following guidelines are generic and that your specific environment may have specific requirements that may not benefit from them.

- *Use 64-bit JVM for all daemons with compressed OOPS enabled*: It is important to use 64-bit JVMs for 64-bit environments because that enables you to use maximum possible hardware resources (memory).

    Using compressed OOPs (ordinary object pointers) is a technique for reducing the size of Java objects in 64-bit environments. A big benefit is that you can fit a bigger JVM using same amount of memory. A big drawback of this technique is that address uncompressing needs to be done before accessing memory referenced by compressed OOPs. This affects performance and uses valuable CPU resources. Starting from Java 6 update 18, Oracle (by default) enables the option UseCompressedOops in JVM based on maximum Java heap size.

- *Optimal Java heap size*: When a JVM starts executing, it gets some memory from the OS and uses this memory for all its needs. Part of this memory is called Java *heap memory*. It's a good idea to set the minimum (or starting) and maximum heap size to the same value (that is, set Xmx == Xms). Don't use Java defaults for parameters such as NewSize or MaxNewSize. For JVMs larger than 4 GB, you can use the ratio 1/8 to 1/6 (size of new JVM to old JVM) for MaxNewSize.

- *Using low-latency GC collector*: Garbage collection (GC) is re-use of heap space belonging to deleted objects or completed processes. You should use the concurrent algorithm or collector using option UseConcMarkSweepGC. That's because you need to keep the GC pauses shorter (even though that uses more CPU time for GC) in case of a JVM for Hadoop daemons, which have more dynamic memory usage. Note that the concurrent collector needs more RAM allocated to the JVM (than the serial or parallel collectors for GC).

  The option ParallelGCThreads=<N> sets the number of the GC worker threads. You should set the value of N to be same as the number of logical processors (up to 8). For more logical processors, set N to be approximately 5/8 of the number of logical processors (except for larger SPARC systems where N can be approximately 5/16 of the number of logical processors).

  Use a high number of GC threads for NameNode and JobTracker (ResourceManager for YARN), since you need the GC process without any latency for more effective memory utilization.

- *JVM configuration options for debugging*:

  - -verbose:gc -Xloggc:<file>: This option logs garbage collection event information to a file. In addition to the information -verbose:gc gives, each reported event is preceded by the time (in seconds) since the first garbage-collection event.

  - -XX:+PrintGCDetails: This option activates the "detailed" GC logging mode, which differs depending on the GC algorithm used. Here's a sample: [GC [PSYoungGen: 246648K->243136K(375296K), 0,0935090 secs]. This entry refers to a young generation GC instance, which reduced the occupied heap memory from 246648K to 243136K and took 0.0935090 seconds.

  - -XX:ErrorFile=<file>: The filename is used to specify a location for the fatal error log file (in case of fatal errors for JVM).

- -XX:+HeapDumpOnOutOfMemoryError: This command-line option tells the JVM to generate a heap dump when it can't allocate heap memory to a request. Since there is no overhead for using this option, it can be used for production systems (where it takes a long time to know that JVM is out of memory). The heap dump is in HPROF binary format, so it can be analyzed using any tools that can import this format (such as jhat). By default, the heap dump is created in a file called java_pid<JVM pid>.hprof, in the working directory of JVM.

Generic YARN/MapReduce Guidelines

MapReduce was the framework (for distributed processing of a job) Hadoop started with, but this was replaced by YARN (sometimes referred as *MapReduce 2*) in later versions. Many organizations still use MapReduce for various reasons. Therefore, I I'll give some tips for optimizing MapReduce configuration.

Optimizing MapReduce Applications

MapReduce is a programming model used for processing large datasets using a parallel, distributed algorithm on Hadoop clusters. A MapReduce program consists of a Map method that performs filtering and sorting (such as sorting sales by product names) and a Reduce method that performs a summarization or aggregation (for example, counting sales by products). The MapReduce framework distributes processing on various nodes of a cluster, runs tasks in parallel, manages all communication/data transfers between the various parts of the system, and provides redundancy and fault tolerance.

Here are some notes on optimizing the use of MapReduce:

- *Speculative execution*: All the nodes of your cluster may not be operating at the same speed—maybe one of the nodes is slower. To account for difference in machine capabilities, Hadoop schedules redundant copies of the same task across several nodes that do not have other work to perform, a process known as *speculative execution*. When a task completes, it notifies the JobTracker, and the copy of a task that finishes first becomes the definitive copy. Other copies that are executing speculatively are abandoned, and the reducers receive their inputs from mapper completing successfully first.

  Speculative execution is enabled by default. If you have identical nodes, you can save valuable resources by disabling this behavior. You can disable speculative execution for the mappers and reducers by setting the mapreduce.map.tasks.speculative.execution and mapreduce.reduce.tasks.speculative.execution options to false.

- *Combiner functions*: A *combiner* is a function that can be used for decreasing the amount of data be processed by reducers. A combiner needs to match the input/output key and value types of your mapper and can be used for a single mapper. By decreasing the data passed in to a reducer, a combiner also helps reduce I/O and network traffic, thereby improving performance.

- *Data compression*: You can use an appropriate codec for compressing data to reduce I/O and network traffic, thereby improving performance. Various codecs such as LZO, Snappy, and others can be used for compression depending on the format for your data (discussed later in this chapter).

- *Distributed cache*: Enables you to cache files frequently used by your applications. Once you cache a file for your job, Hadoop will make it available on all DataNodes (in HDFS, not in memory) where your map/reduce tasks are executing. So, you can access the cache file as local file for your job(s). This saves on valuable I/O and improves performance. See `http://hadoop.apache.org/docs/r2.6.3/api/org/apache/hadoop/filecache/DistributedCache.html` for more details.

  If you use Hive, you can develop a UDF (user-defined function) using Java and use this functionality. The command `ADD FILE <filename>` in Hive adds a distributed cache file that's distributed to every node.

- *Granularity for MapReduce tasks*: You can adjust the number of mappers depending on the data processed by your jobs and hardware resources available for execution. So, for example, if the average mapper running time is shorter than a minute, you can increase the `mapred.min.split.size`, so that fewer mappers are allocated and mapper initialization overhead is reduced. You can adjust the following parameters:

  - `Mapreduce.map.minsplitsize`

  - `Mapreduce.map.maxsplitsize`

  - Number of reducers

- **mapreduce.task.io.sort.factor:** For any of your jobs where a map task is running, each time the memory buffer reaches the spill threshold, a new spill file is generated. So, after the map task completes writing, there may be several spill files, and these spill files are merged into a single and sorted output file. This configuration property controls the maximum number of streams (files) to merge at once. The default value is 10, but it can be adjusted depending on your data volume along with the spill threshold (80% by default).

- **mapreduce.task.io.sort.mb**: When map task is executing, it writes to a circular in-memory buffer and the size of this buffer is defined by the `io.sort.mb` property. When this circular in-memory buffer is filled (spill threshold is reached), output is spilled to disk (in parallel using a separate thread). If the spilling thread is slow to write and the buffer is 100% full, then the map execution is stalled, so it's important to tune this property for optimal MapReduce performance. The default value is 100 MB and should be adjusted for your environment based on performance and spill files generated.

- **mapreduce.map.memory.mb/mapreduce.reduce.memory. mb**: These are the hard limits enforced by Hadoop for each mapper or reducer task and define the maximum memory that can be assigned to mapper or reducer's container. The default value is 1 GB, but you should set these values for your environment as needed.

- **mapreduce.map.java.opts/mapreduce.reduce.java.opts**: This is the maximum heap size of the JVM (-Xmx) for the mapper or reducer task and should always be lower than the value for property `mapreduce.[map|reduce].memory.mb`. Typically, this value should be 80% of the value for property `mapreduce.map. memory.mb/mapreduce.reduce.memory.mb`.

- **mapreduce.reduce.shuffle.parallelcopies**: As your job is executing, various mappers are executing on nodes (for your cluster), and their map output files are located locally (on the node that's executing the map task). These map tasks may complete at different times, and therefore the reduce task starts copying these outputs as soon as they complete. The number of copier threads that the reducer task can use to fetch map outputs in parallel, are defined by the property `mapreduce.reduce. shuffle.parallelcopies`. The default value is 5 and should be adjusted as per your data volumes and average number of mappers.

Optimizing YARN Execution

YARN (yet another resource negotiator) is the latest resource management framework for Apache Hadoop. This is essentially MapReduce version 2 with many new features like dynamic memory assignment (for mappers and reducers). Major components of YARN are as follows:

- *ResourceManager*: The master daemon process that communicates with the client (requestor), tracks resource availability on the cluster, and coordinates work by allocating tasks to NodeManagers.

- *NodeManager*: This is a worker daemon process that launches and manages processes executing on worker nodes.

- *ApplicationMaster*: Manages a task (or a process) spawned by NodeManager within a *container*, as requested by ResourceManager.

- *Container*: Represents a request to hold resources (CPU/RAM) on a worker node. For example, MapReduce is an application that runs within YARN, and ApplicationMaster will spawn mappers and reducers to run within a container (and request additional containers to ResourceManager as needed).

As shown in Figure 10-1, when a client process requests resources to ResourceManager, it locates a node with available resources and requests those resources to the NodeManager (on that node). NodeManager, in turn, spawns a container, and ApplicationMaster is invoked with it. ApplicationMaster manages the resources for the application (the client process) and requests additional resources (if needed) to ResourceManager.

Figure 10-1 shows details of the YARN architecture.

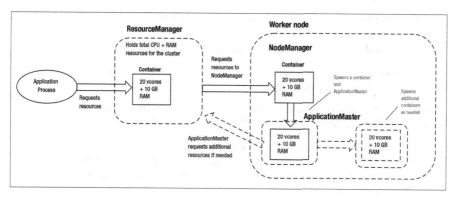

Figure 10-1. *YARN architecture*

Note the following:

- The total memory per node for a Hadoop cluster is determined by property yarn.nodemanager.resource.memory-mb.

- Maximum memory that ResourceManager can allocate to the ApplicationMaster container is determined by property yarn.scheduler.maximum-allocation-mb. The default minimum allocation is 1 GB but can be changed using property yarn.scheduler.minimum-allocation-mb.

- ApplicationMaster can only request resources from ResourceManager in increments of value for property `yarn.scheduler.minimum-allocation-mb` and can't exceed value for property `yarn.scheduler.maximum-allocation-mb`.

- In case of MapReduce (as application), ApplicationMaster will rounds off values for `mapreduce.map.memory.mb` and `mapreduce.reduce.memory.mb` to multiples of value for `yarn.scheduler.minimum-allocation-mb`.

So, to summarize, here are some YARN properties that you can tune:

- **yarn.scheduler.minimum-allocation-mb**: Minimum size of container that YARN will allow for running a job (default 1 GB).

- **yarn.scheduler.maximum-allocation-mb**: Largest size of container that YARN will allow for running a job (default 8192m).

- **yarn.nodemanager.resource.memory-mb**: Total amount of memory for containers on a worker node. This value should be: (total memory) – (memory allocation for OS, Hadoop daemons, and any other services).

- **yarn.nodemanager.vmem-pmem-ratio**: Defines ratio of virtual memory to available physical memory. The default of 2.1 means virtual memory will be double the size of physical memory.

- **yarn.app.mapreduce.am.resource.mb**: Memory allocated to ApplicationMaster.

- **yarn.app.mapreduce.am.command-opts**: Heap size allocated to ApplicationMaster (default (1 GB).

- **yarn.nodemanager.resource.cpu-vcores**: Number of cores that a node manager can allocate to containers. This value should be: (total number of cores on the node) – (cores allocated to Hadoop daemons and any other daemons).

This completes my discussion about YARN-related tuning and important parameters to consider. Next, I look at how to optimize your data model for usage with NoSQL solutions and also how to select a NoSQL solution for your environment.

Choosing an Optimal File Format

It is important to understand that the file format you choose to store your data can directly affect the performance of queries against that data. There are a number of parameters you need to consider while choosing the right format. The type of queries you plan to execute is of course the most important one. The next one is the amount of compression you need. And you need to make sure that the NoSQL solution you plan to use supports the storage format. Fortunately, most NoSQL solutions make it easy to convert data between formats.

File format affects query performance because it determines how quickly the dataset can be read by the system in response to a specific query. The speed of data retrieval is the biggest determinant of query performance. Now, the main (and most time-consuming) task for data retrieval is moving data from disk to memory and vice versa (unless you are using in-memory database). For example, if your dataset is 1 TB and you use 7200 RPM drives with hardware interface SATA 6 GB/s, since your disk read rate is close to 160 MB/s, it will take you about two hours to process a terabyte of data. For bigger datasets, similar performance will be unacceptable.

How can you improve your read performance? There are three ways. First, you can parallelize your read and write operations by leveraging distributed storage and computation technology. That will help you split up and distribute your data (and queries) across multiple nodes. HDFS offers distributed storage (with fault tolerance) and processing frameworks like MapReduce, YARN (or Spark) help you take *processing to data* or process data locally on each of the worker nodes. This constitutes distributing processing optimally on all the nodes (for a cluster) to complete a task (or a job) with optimal performance.

Secondly, you can reduce the total volume of data (that the query engine processes) by storing your data in a file format that efficiently uses compression. File formats support different compression algorithms and apply those algorithms to the data in many different ways. Note that the tradeoff between compression algorithms is between speed and the compression ratio. A higher compression ratio will take more time (and also consume more CPU resources) for the compression or decompression to occur. Of course, your file will be much smaller, and you will save on disk space.

How much compression can you achieve using the compression schemes for various file formats? Well, that depends on the combination of file format and compression scheme. For example, for a text (CSV) file of about 1 GB, Snappy or GZIP can compress the file to about 500 MB (if stored as a SequenceFile) or to about 300 MB (if stored using ORCFile or Parquet format). Table 10-1 specifies the compression schemes valid for various row-oriented and column-oriented file formats.

Table 10-1. File Formats and Compression Scheme Support

File Format	Compression Scheme				
	Snappy	GZIP	ZLIB	BZIP2	None
TextFile					X
SequenceFile	X	X			X
ORCFile	X		X		
RCFile	X	X		X	
Parquet	X	X			

The third way you can improve your read performance is by using stored statistics for aggregates. This is only supported by formats like Parquet and ORC and they can fetch aggregated statistics (for example, aggregations based on min/max values and null count) as pre-computed data. Also, Parquet and ORCfile formats optimize for read performance at the expense of write performance (because of the Hadoop philosophy of *write once read multiple times*).

Finally, organizational schemes impact performance for various types of queries. For example, queries that return a large number of columns (for a subset of rows) are faster when data is stored in row-oriented formats. From experience, queries returning more than 60% of columns benefit from row-oriented format. Alternatively, queries that summarize or aggregate a few columns across all rows within a table (or a subset of it) perform better, if data is stored in a column-oriented format. So, if you expect most of your queries to be of the form `select * from MyTable;` you should use a row-oriented format.

But if your queries are of the form `select sum(MyColumn)from MyTable` (that is, you are performing aggregations or generating summary statistics for only a few columns within your dataset), then you should probably use a column-oriented format. Next, I discuss a few row and column formats and their properties.

Row-based Formats

The most popular row-based storage formats within the Hadoop ecosystem are text files, sequence files, and Avro. I am sure you have worked with text files before. CSV files are easy to work with and supported by nearly all the tools within (and outside) the Hadoop ecosystem. Sequence files have also been used extensively within the Hadoop ecosystem. Avro files have a very small footprint and therefore provide much better performance (as compared with sequence files and text files). But Avro is not supported by many applications (compared with the other two row-based file formats).

Text Files

The simplest and most commonly used file format is text files. Most of the database systems or applications support exporting data to text formats like CSV or tab-delimited files. Usually, these text files contain ASCII or UTF characters with individual *fields* (or column values) separated by a special character called *delimiter* (such as comma, semicolon, ampersand, or tab), with new lines separating records.

Advantages of using text files are as follows:

- They are readable and very easy to work with.

- Large number of tools are available for manipulating them.

- Most applications and database systems can ingest (as well as output) text files.

Though text files are easy to work with, they don't provide optimal performance. Text files store all feld values (including numbers or Boolean values) as strings. So, if you need to store an integer value of 500, a text file will convert this value to a string equivalent (three characters "500") and then write it to your file.

There are a couple of issues with storing all data as strings:

- Numbers and Booleans need more space if stored as strings (for example, 50,000,000 as a string needs 8 bytes, but as an integer needs 4 bytes; the Boolean value "False" stored as a string needs 5 bytes, but as a Boolean needs only 1 byte). This increased space usage adds up and results in large files that take longer for retrieval (to memory) and impact query performance adversely.

- Converting strings to appropriate data types adds an extra task for your queries. This is especially important for Hadoop, where most of the tools in the Hadoop ecosystem follow the philosophy *schema on read* or resolve data types on read. So, every time you execute a query, this data-type conversion must be performed (unless all your data is really strings or text) and will slow down your queries as well as consume additional system resources.

Sequence Files

Sequences files are a popular file format for use with Hadoop ecosystem (after text files). Sequence files use a binary format that holds data as records consisting of key-value pairs. Here's how a sequence file is structured:

```
<File header><key1,(Doe,John,387-45-9876,1990-02-14,Chicago,IL)><sync marker>
```

So, a sequence file consists of a file header followed by records (represented as key-value pairs). The file header holds metadata about the file and data. A sync marker is used as record terminator. Hive (as well as Impala) uses a simplified version of sequence files that ignores the key portion of the record and encodes each row as a string with special character '\01' used as row delimiter.

For example, if you want to compress data for your Hive table that uses a sequence file using compression scheme Snappy, set the following at the Hive command prompt:

```
> set hive.exec.compress.output=true;
> set mapred.output.compression.type=BLOCK;
> set mapred.output.compress.codec=org.apache.hadoop.io.compress.
SnappyCodec;
```

The primary advantage of using sequence files is that all components within the Hadoop ecosystem support reads and writes to sequence files. Unfortunately, the way Hive and Impala use sequence files reduces many of this format's benefits and results in files that are similar in size to text files (and subsequently have the same issues as text files).

Hive and Impala (by default) store data in sequence files as strings. This means they use up as much space as text files, with numbers, Booleans, and other data types taking up more space than they need to. Also, the sync markers within the file add to the file size as well.

Avro

Avro is the most advanced row-based format currently available and differs from the text or sequence file formats as follows:

- Avro includes or embeds the schema of the data (corresponding to a table) within the file. This eliminates the need for redefining schema every time you share an Avro file between applications.

- Avro encodes fields based on their data type (as opposed to storing all fields as text). This reduces the (uncompressed) file size and also makes it possible to compress a file more effcectively. Subsequently, network transfer time and file-processing time (for data type conversions) is substantially reduced, providing your queries much better performance.

- Avro eases schema changes (and thereby schema evolution). Using Avro, it's much easier to add columns without re-writing the underlying data to match a new schema. If you need to add a new column to your data, you can implement it by including the additional field (in the end) and supplying a default value for old records. For older records missing this value, Hive will simply substitute the missing value by using the default value.

Here's how an Avro file is structured:

```
<File metadata><sync marker><data block(object count,object size,data)>
<sync marker>
```

The file consists of a file header (consisting file schema serialized as a JSON string and compression codec information) followed by one or more data blocks. Each data block consists of a number of records and metadata (such as record count, record size, and others) and the actual data, which can be compressed using any of the supported codecs. The following code creates a Hive table (Employee_avro) using the Avro file format:

```
> CREATE TABLE Employee_avro
(lastname STRING COMMENT 'Employee last name',
firstname STRING COMMENT 'Employee first name',
dept_code SMALLINT COMMENT 'Department code',
dob TIMESTAMP COMMENT 'Date of Birth',
zip STRING COMMENT 'ZIP CODE',
employee_since TIMESTAMP COMMENT 'Date of first visit')
ROW FORMAT SERDE 'org.apache.hadoop.hive.serde2.avro.AvroSerDe'
STORED AS INPUTFORMAT 'org.apache.hadoop.hive.ql.io.avro.
AvroContainerInputFormat'
OUTPUTFORMAT
'org.apache.hadoop.hive.ql.io.avro.AvroContainerOutputFormat'
TBLPROPERTIES ('avro.schema.literal'='{
```

```
"name": "employee_summary",
"type": "record",
"fields": [
{"name":"lastname", "type":"string"},
{"name":"firstname", "type":"string"},
{"name":"dept_code", "type":"int"},
{"name":"dob", "type":"string"},
{"name": "zip", "type": "string},
{"name": "employee_since", "type": "string"},
]}');
```

The part that starts with "name": "employee_summary" is the JSON schema definition and included in the file header (as part of file metadata). Compression codec can be specified exactly the same way as specified for sequence files.

Avro has some drawbacks as well:

- Using the Avro format can be more complicated than using any of the text formats and may involve longer development time

- Very few applications (outside of the Hadoop ecosystem) support this format or read it

- For Avro, you need to define your schema in advance, before you actually write it to a file, which isn't possible in some cases

To summarize, Avro is a great option for queries that use all or most of the columns and is therefore useful for data warehouses; especially the ones with wide fact tables consisting of hundreds of columns.

Column-based Formats

Columnar storage formats are more suited (and optimized) for analytic use cases because you need to aggregate or summarize a small subset of columns. Consider the Employee table from the last section and assume that there's an additional column called Salary that holds an employee's salary. With a columnar file format, it will be much faster to retrieve a list of employees with salaries more than double the average salary because a columnar format holds data in columns, which makes it easy (and fast) to aggregate.

The most popular columnar (or column-based) formats within the Hadoop ecosystem are RCFile, Parquet, and ORCFile. Each has its own strengths and weakness, and I discuss those in this section. Note that columnar storage formats aren't just used with the Hadoop ecosystem but also used by high performance analytic databases like Greenplum or Vertica.

So, to summarize, use a columnar format if:

- You frequently need to perform aggregation operations (for example, count, avg, min, max) as part of your queries

- Most of your queries select only a small subset of columns and also use a small number of columns as filters (in where clause)

Lastly, be sure that the preceding conditions apply for your environment (before choosing a columnar format), because if that's not the case, then data stored in columnar format and needing to retrieve the whole record will need to perform *row reconstruction* (the process of taking all the columns that belong to a single row and composing them back together). This involves a lot of work (non-contiguous data reads) for the system since each row is not stored contiguously and will impact performance really badly.

RCFile

The Row Columnar (RC) file format (introduced in 2011) is one of the most popular columnar formats used within the Hadoop ecosystem. It offers space efficiency and thereby speeds queries because they have to retrieve less data. Data within RCFile is structured as follows:

```
<Row group1(<Metadata header><column1(values)><column2(values)>
<column3(values)><Sync marker>)>,<Row group2(...)>,<Row group3(...)>
```

So, RCFile partitions data horizontally as well as vertically. First, data is partitioned into multiple row groups and then within every row group the data is organized by column. Also, the RCFile format ensures that all columns of a row are on a single node (they fit within a single HDFS block) to reduce the cost of row reconstruction (if needed). Finally, data in each row group is compressed by column (the compression codec can be specified exactly the same way as specified for sequence or Avro files).

As a major benefit (since RCFile was the first columnar format), almost all the tools within Hadoop ecosystem support RCFile. Also, a lot of tools outside Hadoop ecosystem support it, so it needs to be considered if you plan to use tools other than Hive or Impala for running analytic queries across your data.

However, compared to Parquet and ORCFiles, RCFile lacks a lot of advanced features. For example, ORCFiles and Parquet allow you to store more complex data types, have means for Hive to limit the data it loads into memory, and can encrypt data into smaller files.

ORCFile

The ORC file format was introduced as successor to the RCFile format and adds a number of features to it. For example, it uses complex data encoding schemes to further reduce data size. It also stores metadata to make it easier for skipping rows that don't fit common query criteria and stores basic statistics on columns. This results in significantly faster queries and highly compressed data. Data within ORCFiles is structured as follows:

```
<Index Data><Row group1(...)><Stripe footer>,<Index Data><Row group2(...)>
<Stripe footer>.........<File footer><Postscript>
```

The structure of a data row group is identical to RCFile, but there's an index data block preceeding each row group, followed by a stripe footer. At the end of a data file, there's a file footer and a postscript marker. These additional blocks provide the advanced functionality for ORCFile. The compression codec is specified as a table property.

ORCFile is one of the most advanced columnar file formats available. It uses complex functionality to reduce file space, making it easier for queries to identify critical parts of a file and avoid file scans. A major problem is the lack of support for this format. For example, Impala doesn't currently support ORCFiles. So, use of ORCFile format may limit the set of tools you can use with your data.

Parquet

The Parquet format was designed by engineers at Cloudera and Twitter. It is based on *the record shredding and assembly algorithm* described in the Dremel paper (Dremel is a scalable, interactive ad hoc query system for analysis of read-only nested data designed by Google).

Parquet providess very efficient compression and encoding schemes and uses three types of metadata: file metadata, column (chunk) metadata, and page header metadata. At the highest level, file metadata contains information about schema, number of rows, list of row groups, and list of keys/values. At the next level, rowgroup metadata contains list of column chunks for a row group, total byte size and number of rows. Column chunk metadata has the file path (for the chunk), file offsets, and column metadata (for columns that are part of that chunk). Column chunks may contain a number of pages, and page header metadata has the details (such as (un)compressed page size, Data page header(s), index page header(s), and so on. Data and index page headers have the details of values and encoding details. A Parquet structured file structure for M row groups and N columns would look like the following:

```
<FileMetaData><Row group1MetaData(<Column1MetaData(PageMetaData)>........
<ColumnNMetaData(PageMetaData)>).........<Row group2MetData(...)>......<Row
groupMMetData(...)><File footer>
```

To summarize, Parquet implements a complex data materialization engine incorporating advanced encoding techniques that achieves a balance between compression and speed. Also, Parquet decides the right encoding format for each of your data columns. You can choose the compression scheme for your Parquet file as following (for Hive):

```
> set parquet.compress=SNAPPY
```

Fortunately, Parquet is supported more widely (compared to ORCFile) and is certainly a recommended columnar format.

Indexing Considerations for Performance

Indexing is a very important consideration for query performance, and although Hadoop doesn't offer advanced levels of indexing (compared to RDBMS), there are some general guidelines that you can follow. First, the indexing guidelines such as optimal use of indexes (too many indexes will impact insert performance, or indexes should match frequent query patterns, and so on) are valid. Also, for Hive, index partitioning should match table partitioning (in terms of partitioning columns used). You can refer to Hive indexing documentation at https://cwiki.apache.org/confluence/display/Hive/ IndexDev for a comprehensive explanation of Hive indexing.

In this section, I focus on the two major types of indexes popularly used with Hadoop and their optimal usage: compact indexes and bitmap indexes.

Compact indexes

In general, a *compact index* can be used for columns that contain a lot of distinct or unique values (such as employee ID). You should use a compact index for columns that contain numeric values. Internally, a compact index is stored (for example, in Hive) as a sorted table with all the column(s) (to be indexed) values and the blocks where they are stored. Because the index is also a table, you need to store it using an optimal format (ORC, Parquet, Avro) matching your table format and compress it (if needed). If your table is partitioned, then the index is also partitioned, although you may change the partition structure for an index as needed. Make sure the index can be used for compact binary search by setting the property IDXPROPERTIES 'hive.index.compact.binary. search'='true'.

After you create the index, you need to refresh or update it (if data in your source table changes) as follows:

```
> ALTER INDEX <Index name> ON <Table name> REBUILD;
```

You can auto-update an index, but due to the high volume of data used with Hadoop, it is a better idea to schedule the index updates manually for times when the system is not in use.

Bitmap Indexes

A *bitmap index* is suitable for columns that have only a few distinct values (such as gender or logical (yes/no) or categories or types). For these columns, the ratio of the number of distinct values to the number of rows in the table is small. This ratio is known as the *degree of cardinality*.

Fully indexing a large table with traditional indexing can use a lot of disk space, and bitmap indexes only use a fraction of the size of the indexed data in the table. The reason is that an index provides a pointer to a data row (for a table) that contains a given key value and thus contains a list of row IDs for each key value (corresponding to the rows with that value).

However, for a bitmap index, a bitmap for each key value is used instead of a list of row IDs. Each bit in the bitmap corresponds to a row ID. If the bit is set, then the data row (with the corresponding rowed) contains the key value. A mapping function is used to convert the bit position to an actual row ID. Also, bitmap indexes compress the bitmaps. So, for a small number of distinct key values, bitmap indexes offer better compression. Since bitmaps from multiple bitmap indexes can be easily combined, you should use single-column bitmap indexes. Similar to a compact index, you need to sort the data in the column to be indexed for an effective bitmap index—otherwise, all the blocks containing values in the bitmap index would be read. Therefore you should set the property `hive.enforce.sorting` to `true` and describe in the `create table` statement which columns should be sorted.

Because a bitmap index (in Hive) is simply another table, you need to specify an effective storage format and compression (if the index is large).

Other index types are used for ORCFile and Parquest formats, such as *storage index* (a min/max index that lets you skip data blocks if a value is not contained in it and is suitable for numeric values and queries using the <, >, = operators), and *aggregate index* (similar to a table with predefined aggregations, like `count`, `sum`, `average` for a specific column, grouped by the same column).

To conclude, you need to know and evaluate your data for effective indexing and also develop mechanisms to update your indexes periodically based on data changes (to the source table).

Choosing a NoSQL Solution and Optimizing Your Data Model

The importance of selecting the correct NoSQL solution for your environment (and your data) is often overlooked. For example, if your data is mostly unstructured and your volume is small (about 2–5 TB), a columnar database won't be a suitable solution. First, you need to know about the major types of NoSQL databases, their characteristics, strengths/weaknesses, and how they perform for the type of processing you need (based on your business need). Your decision will have a huge impact on performance and supported functionality for your environment.

For details on the types of NoSQL databases, their features, and criteria for choosing the correct NoSQL database for your environment (based on your data), see Chapter 6 section "Selecting an Appropriate NoSQL Database".

An important point to note about NoSQL: it has really turned into (and will become more of) LimitedSQL, as the original NoSQL key-value, MapReduce-based databases are being replaced by the next-generation databases offering (simpler) SQL-based interfaces useful for analytics. Also, the performance and functional capabilities of these databases with LimitedSQL are improving constantly.

Getting back to NoSQL, after selecting an appropriate NoSQL solution, the next task is getting your data ready for migration to NoSQL. In most cases, OLTP or OLAP systems are migrated to NoSQL. Subsequently, you need to transform your data to work optimally with a NoSQL database. For example, data held in a relational OLTP environment has referential integrity defined and therefore you need to perform joins to retrieve the required data. Relational databases typically perform well for join operations and have features to enhance performance such as indexing, defining statistics, caching of data and query plans, and so on. If you move the relational data to NoSQL environment, most of the RDBMS features are not available. Also, NoSQL databases don't perform well for joins.

So, you have to redesign your data model and eliminate joins. You may have to denormalize your data for that purpose and may also need to combine some data tables to form larger tables. Different techniques need to be used for transforming your relational (OLTP) or Star schema (OLAP) design for NoSQL usage. See Chapter 6 for more.

Summary

Performance tuning is a vast topic in itself and is specialized enough to warrant its own book, considering the various subtopics involved. This chapter doesn't claim to be exhaustive in that respect. The purpose is to attract your attention to the different ways you can tune your NoSQL environment. For example, the list of MapReduce or HDFS parameters is not exhaustive. Refer to Apache documentation for a complete list of parameters and tune any other parameters that are more relevant to your environment. Or, if you consider indexing, carefully review your query needs and add the appropriate type of indexes that I may not have covered.

Also, consider the hardware aspect. A huge corporation like Teradata focuses largely on designing hardware for managing petabytes of data. A couple of years back, Intel came up with its hardware-based solution for facilitating encryption and decryption without sacrificing performance. You may not want (or have the resources) to go that far. The section on hardware optimization is meant to provide generic guidelines and also facilitate your thought process to optimize the hardware you plan to use for your implementation. You will have specific needs for your environment, but at least you have a good starting point. It is, of course, not possible to consider all types of scenarios for optimization.

There are different approaches adopted by organizations for performance tuning. Some organizations just start with generic guidelines and then think about performance tuning when they have specific problems. That way, they can focus on the problem area and save on valuable resources (time and money). The issue with that approach is that the immediate problem is fixed quickly, but does that guarantee there will be no additional issues in that area? Or some other area? Of course not. That's why you need to start with good planning. Perform stress testing, consider the data growth (and increased usage along with it), and also consider *boundary conditions* (minimum and maximum possible values). Boundary conditions may be applicable to your hardware resources, NoSQL solution, your network capacity, or even your technical support resources.

Having a good understanding of growth coupled with boundary conditions will enable you to plan effectively for any performance issues for the near future. As you know, with the dynamism of technology (especially in the NoSQL world), no system is guaranteed to have a very long life, but you can at least avoid issues in the immediate future if you are proactive and anticipate issues instead of responding to them as they appear.

## PART V

Case Study for Designing and Implementing a Hadoop-based Solution

CHAPTER 11

■ ■ ■

Case Study: Implementing Lambda Architecture

Lambda architecture was one of first definitive ideas in Big Data architecture and, like any new architecture, has its followers and detractors. How do you decide which side you are on? I have a simple answer: it depends on the architecture's applicability to your environment. Lambda is definitely not suited for all Big Data use cases. Maybe one of the newer architectures like Kappa or Fast Data architecture is more suited for your environment. Maybe you don't even need to have an architecture-based approach and can simply start with a data reservoir and design analytics as required. Every environment is unique in some ways and needs special design considerations, but the trick is to start with a generic approach—and the most appropriate one.

Why look for a new architectural approach towards data? Well, current RDBMS or NoSQL-based systems are not resilient. Because most data systems support create, read, update, and delete (CRUD) operations, there is a possibility of data corruption due to update and delete operations. For example, it is possible to delete a large number of rows when you actually intend to delete a single row. A software bug or hardware failure can also corrupt data. The immutability of master data within Lambda architecture provides an effective resolution to this issue.

Also, with current database systems, you always need to make a trade-off in your design, because you can either optimize for data storage (normalized design in third normal form) or query processing (denormalized design—usually first or second normal form). Lambda resolves this conundrum by separating your master data (stored using third normal form) from your query layer (stored as denormalized views).

So, how does an immutable data store capture changes to data? By dividing data in a number of "facts" and capturing changes to these facts in the time space. So, any changes to a fact are stored as a new fact record with a timestamp (to indicate when the change occurred). Consider an employee record. Address for an employee is a fact. Any time the employee moves, a new fact record can be added, along with a timestamp indicating when she moved. This preserves the employee's residential history (similar to type 2 dimension in data warehousing)—but more importantly, it preserves all the facts associated with an employee (in terms of his addresses). You can, of course, use the facts any way you need to.

Finally, how do the Lambda layers facilitate near-real-time data delivery? I discuss that using a real-world case study. I also briefly discuss the Kappa and Fast Data design changes for the same use case. I'll start by describing the business problem.

© Bhushan Lakhe 2016
B. Lakhe, *Practical Hadoop Migration*, DOI 10.1007/978-1-4842-1287-5_11

The Business Problem and Solution

Yourtown Insurance is an auto insurance company that recently has had to deal with a large number of fraudulent claims. Subsequently, it added stringent guidelines and a lot of extra processing for their claims. This resulted in tripling the processing time, and customers with genuine claims, being unhappy, moved their business to other insurance companies.

Yourtown Insurance hired experts in business processing (as well as software performance) who analyzed the past claims (using statistical models) and created a predictive model to determine whether a claim was possibly fraudulent. If a claim was determined to be possibly fraudulent, then it was directed to a special queue that performed additional processing and initiated an investigation if necessary. The rest of the claims (ones determined not to be fraudulent) were processed quickly, as they had been before additional processing was added.

This strategy reduced the processing time for (genuine) claims and still was able to identify (with about 80% accuracy) fraudulent claims. The consultants assured the IT department that with time, the predictive model they built would become more accurate and provide a larger percentage of accuracy. The model was built using a lot of factors for determining fraudulent claims, such as: number of claims filed by the customer during last year, filing time of the claim, weather conditions when claim was filed, age of the customer, customer's driving history, and more. As a result of the model evaluation, it was determined that certain values for the above factors indicated fraudulence (or the lack of it).

So, the claim parameters needed to be checked in real-time against aggregated (or calculated) customer data. Because the claim data volume was very large (30 TB with 1% monthly growth), it was decided to use Hadoop for data processing, and since there was a need for real-time processing, Lambda architecture was chosen. Based on the volume, it was agreed that the batch layer should be rebuilt every weekend and that the speed layer should hold data for the past six days. Fraudulence would be decided based on historical data (available through the batch layer) and the most recent data (available through the speed layer).

This chapter discusses the design and implementation of this solution using appropriate hardware, software, and programs that need to be developed.

Solution Design

I start with the hardware that's necessary for building the Hadoop cluster, because performance starts with appropriate hardware. Then I discuss the software components necessary and any customizations (as required).

Hardware

The data size for this system is 30 TB with 1% monthly growth. For the next four years, that's a total growth of about 50%, or 15 TB. Because the batch layer denormalizes data, you can assume that you will need roughly about 30% additional storage, taking the total space requirement to 60 TB. Now, if you want your system to be available while the batch layer is being rebuilt, then you will need to *double* your space (because you will need to build the new views before removing the old ones). For this example, you can assume that the system will be unavailable while the batch layer is being rebuilt. So, your final space requirement is 60 TB.

Chapter 10 discusses how to calculate the cluster size (for production usage). Here I will start with worker node configuration and total number of nodes. OS and other essential applications on a node need some space (roughly 2% of total space in this case, since 2% of 2 TB is 40 GB—quite enough for operating system and software. Though I have provided general guidelines and percentage of storage to reserve for operating system and software, you also need to consider disk drive size and approximately how much you need), and data blocks are replicated based on a replication factor (default 3). Consider:

```
HDFS space per node = (Raw disk space per node - 2% non-DFS local storage)/
(Replication Factor)
```

Start with the following for startup (individual) worker node configuration:

- Latest generation processor(s) with 12 cores (total)

- 4 GB memory per core

- 2 TB SATA disks per core

- 1GbE NIC

```
HDFS space per node = (2 TB - 2% non-DFS local storage)/3
```

HDFS space per node is 653 GB:

```
Number of Worker nodes = Total HDFS space/HDFS space per node
```

Number of worker nodes = 60 TB/653 GB = 92 .
For a NameNode:

- 6 cores (total)

- 4 GB RAM (3 GB + 1 GB for every 100 TB of raw disk space)

- Needs to be replicated (for failover)

- RAID-1 storage

- NameNode should run on a 64-bit OS to avoid 3 GB limit on JVM heap size

For YARN, you can use 4 GB RAM and a 4-core CPU as a starter configuration for Resource Manager. If there is maximum usage for a resource, adjust the resource allocation accordingly. To summarize, you need a 95-node cluster with 92 DataNodes, NameNode (two nodes in failover configuration), and a node for YARN Resource Manager.

You can calculate the size of your development environment based on guidelines provided in Chapter 10. For good performance, SSHD (solid state hybrid drive) storage that offers 7,200 RPM or SATA III drives offering 10,000 RPM can be used on DataNodes. Finally, network proximity or being a part of the same subnet will help reduce the intermodal network traffic and provide good performance.

Software

A browser-based application allows Yourtown's customers to enter claims. The claim data is stored using VoltDB and pushed to HDFS/Hive every hour. Batch layer views are built using this data. So, HDFS/Hive for the batch layer. For the serving layer, I will use a read-only database called Splout SQL. See Chapter 9 for more on Splout SQL. For the speed layer, I will use Spark (along with Spark SQL).

Database Design

The claim system has a large number of tables with a lot of columns to capture all the details. However, most of that data is not needed for fraud detection. Also, I don't want to oversimplify the predictive modeling process that uses a large number of parameters for deriving the predictions. So, I will demonstrate the concept of fraud detection using some parameters, but note that it's a complex process and needs much more information than I have room to provide here.

You might remember the logical model used as an example in Chapter 3 (Figure 3-5). Since the model is fairly generic, I'll reproduce it here as an example.

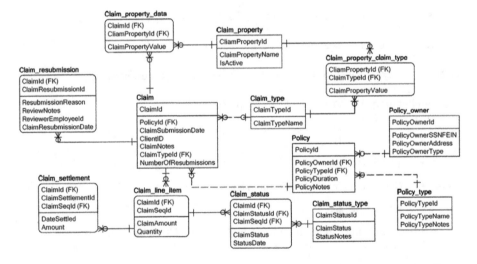

For our purposes, we can use the following tables (master data stored in HDFS) for building batch views on:

- Claim
- Claim_status_type
- Policy
- Policy_owner
- Claim_line_item

- `Claim_status`
- `Claim_type`
- `Policy_type`

Also, we can assume that the `Policy_owner` entity has additional columns `PolicyOwnerDOB` and `PolicyStartDate`, and the `Claim` entity has an additional column `ClaimWeatherCond` (to hold weather condition at time of filing a claim). An additional entity, `PO_Drv_Hist`, holds the policy owner's driving history details and has the attributes shown in Figure 11-1.

PolicyOwnerId (FK)
ViolationNum
ViolationSeverity
ViolationDate
ViolationDetails

Figure 11-1. *The PO_Drv_Hist entity*

There is a *one-to-many* relation between `PolicyOwner` and `PO_Drv_Hist` entities (as you can see from the design). A policy owner may have one or more violations. If there are no violations, then there won't be a record for a `PolicyOwner` in the `PO_Drv_Hist` entity. As you see, the master data is in a normalized form, but Lambda architecture allows you to hold your master data normalized. You can, however, denormalize your data for the batch (and subsequent) layers.

Considering a Fact-based Model

Let's consider applying a fact-based model to this data. As mentioned in Chapter 9, a data model in third normal form that has timestamps (for preserving history) within appropriate data tables can constitute a fact-based model.

In this case, the data model being considered is already in third normal form. The dynamic tables that will have records added frequently (`Claim`, `Claim_resubmission`, `Claim_settelement`, `Claim_status`) already have a column to capture date/time. For `Policy`, I have added the column `PolicyStartDate` to hold the date when a policy is added. The static tables holding application metadata (`Claim_type`, `Claim_status_type`, and so on) don't have a timestamp column (and for a fact-based model, they should). But you can assume (for this example) that the static data is not changing and therefore you can denormalize the data (utilizing existing static data) and use it for your batch layer views. In other words, the master data can be viewed as a fact-based model.

Data Conditions for Fraudulence

Discussing the data conditions for determining fraudulence will help you design the batch layer views (since you can then determine what data you need for your views):

1. If a customer has filed more than 5 claims during last 12 months, there is a possibility of fraud (for his next claim).

2. Claim filing time after 10 p.m. indicates possibility of fraudulence.

3. Weather conditions such as snow, rain, storm, avalanche, tornado indicate possibility of fraudulence.

4. Teenage drivers with at least 2 severity 1 violations in the last 12 months may file fraudulent claims.

5. Drivers with at least 3 severity 1 violations in the last 12 months may file fraudulent claims.

The insurance company (based on its predictive model) determined that claims satisfying condition (1) along with two more of the other conditions needed to placed in *additional evaluation/investigation* queue. Also, claims satisfying conditions 2, 3, and either 4 or 5 also needed to be placed in the *additional evaluation/investigation* queue.

All the other claims were processed rapidly without any additional constraints, since they were considered genuine.

Batch Layer Design

First, we denormalize the data. I will start with the Claim entity, and as you can see, I have included columns from entities Claim_line_item, Claim_status, Claim_status_type, and Claim_type. Also, I have only included columns that I need. This will be used for batch views related to claims.

As a next step, I will denormalize the Policy entity and include columns from entities Policy_owner and Policy_type. This will be used for policy-related batch views. Note that I have added a LastModified attribute to both views (since they don't have attributes for time variance). The denormalized entities are shown in Figure 11-2.

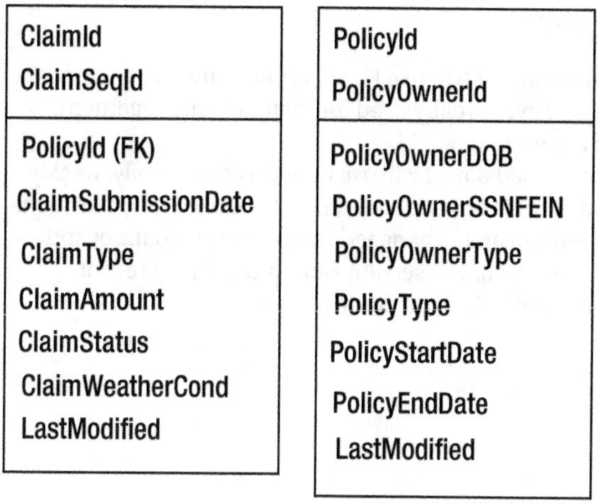

ClaimId	PolicyId
ClaimSeqId	PolicyOwnerId
Policyld (FK)	PolicyOwnerDOB
ClaimSubmissionDate	PolicyOwnerSSNFEIN
ClaimType	PolicyOwnerType
ClaimAmount	PolicyType
ClaimStatus	PolicyStartDate
ClaimWeatherCond	PolicyEndDate
LastModified	LastModified

Figure 11-2. *Denormalized Claim and Policy entities*

I will start with claim-related batch views:

1. The first step for this batch view will count the number of claims for a policy for the last 12 months and have a temporary table with counts greater than 5. As a second step, this temporary table will be joined with the denormalized Policy entity to get the policy owner details, constituting the batch view.

2. The second batch view will filter claims by weather conditions such as snow, rain, storm, avalanche, or tornado.

Next, the policy-related batch views:

3. The third batch view will list teenage drivers with at least 2 severity 1 violations in the last 12 months. As a first step, a temporary table will be populated with drivers with 2 or more severity 1 violations in the last 12 months using the PO_Drv_ Hist entity. Then the entries will be filtered using DOB (date of birth) from the denormalized Policy entity for drivers with ages less than or equal to 19.

4. The fourth batch view will use the temporary table created for the third batch view and filter the entries for drivers with age greater than 19 years.

As a next step, you need to derive these views from the master data held in HDFS. Please note that these *views* are really Hive tables. I will describe the processing in the next section.

Implementing Batch Layer

As explained in Chapter 9, for several reasons, I will use HDFS for holding the master data and the batch-layer views (Hive tables). Hive is really used for metadata management, and you may use MySQL for holding the metadata.

Also, for appending vertical or time-based data, I will use Hive partitions (daily, weekly, or monthly as your application may warrant) to append new data. I have used Hive partitions to demonstrate the concept of how new data can be managed for your master dataset and processed in the batch views that are created. I have used timestamp LastModified for partitioning the tables. Here are the Hive tables that constitute master data:

```
CREATE TABLE ClaimsMaster(
ClaimId INT,
ClaimSeqId INT,
PolicyId INT,
ClaimSubmissionDate TIMESTAMP,
ClaimType STRING,
ClaimAmount INT,
ClaimSTATUS STRING,
ClaimWeatherCond STRING
)
PARTITIONED BY (LastModified TIMESTAMP)
ROW FORMAT DELIMITED FIELDS TERMINATED BY "\;";
CREATE TABLE PolicyMaster(
PolicyId INT,
PolicyOwnerId INT,
PolicyOwnerDOB DATE,
PolicyOwnerSSNFEIN STRING,
PolicyOwnerType STRING,
PolicyType STRING,
PolicyStartDate TIMESTAMP
PolicyEndDate TIMESTAMP)
PARTITIONED BY (LastModified TIMESTAMP)
ROW FORMAT DELIMITED FIELDS TERMINATED BY "\;";
CREATE TABLE PO_Drv_Hist(
PolicyOwnerId INT,
ViolationNum SMALLINT,
ViolationSeverity TINYINT,
ViolationDate TIMESTAMP,
ViolationDetails STRING)
PARTITIONED BY (LastModified TIMESTAMP)
ROW FORMAT DELIMITED FIELDS TERMINATED BY "\;";
```

Next step is adding new data to these tables holding master data. As you know, these tables are stored as files within HDFS, and Hive holds the metadata to manage data modifications more effectively. New data can be added on a daily basis (or any other necessary frequency) using dynamic partitions. You can create a staging table (pointing at the file holding new data) and add the new partition to a table as follows:

```
CREATE EXTERNAL TABLE ClaimsMaster_stg(
ClaimId INT,
ClaimSeqId INT,
PolicyId INT,
ClaimSubmissionDate TIMESTAMP,
ClaimType STRING,
ClaimAmount INT,
ClaimSTATUS STRING,
ClaimWeatherCond STRING,
LastModified TIMESTAMP
) ROW FORMAT DELIMITED FIELDS TERMINATED BY "\;"
LOCATION "/InsuranceExample/ClaimsMaster/staging";

FROM ClaimsMaster_stg INSERT OVERWRITE TABLE ClaimsMaster PARTITION
(LastModified) SELECT ClaimId, ClaimSeqId, PolicyId,
ClaimSubmissionDate, ClaimType, ClaimAmount, ClaimSTATUS, ClaimWeatherCond,
LastModified;
```

Note that the staging table has an additional column, pointing to a staging directory (holding the new data) for table ClaimsMaster. The same principle can be applied for adding new data to tables PolicyMaster and PO_Drv_Hist. Also, the process of copying new data file to the appropriate staging directory, creating staging table and adding the new partition to base table, can be automated and scheduled.

Now I create the batch views. I will first create a table BatchProcHist to maintain a history of batch views created:

```
CREATE TABLE BatchProcHist(
ViewName STRING,
CreatedAt timestamp)
ROW FORMAT DELIMITED FIELDS TERMINATED BY "\;";
```

I will create the first view now in order to list policy owners with more than 5 claims in the last 12 months. As a first step, I will get a list of policies with more than 5 claims (in last 12 months) and write to a temporary table:

```
Create table ClaimDeftemp1 as Select PolicyId, count(ClaimId) as
Claimcount from ClaimsMaster where datediff(current_date, add_months
(to_date(ClaimSubmissionDate),12)) <= 0
group by PolicyId having count(ClaimId) > 5
```

Note that I have only considered the date part of ClaimsubmissionDate and compared with current date after adding a year to it.

For the next step, I will join this temporary table with the denormalized Policy entity to get the policy owner details, constituting the batch view:

```
Create table ClaimDefView as Select P.PolicyOwnerID, P.PolicyId,
C.Claimcount from PolicyMaster P, ClaimDeftemp1 C where P.PolicyId =
C.PolicyId;
```

Last, writing to the history table:

```
INSERT INTO TABLE BatchProcHist
  VALUES ('ClaimDefView', from_unixtime(unix_timestamp()));
```

The second batch view filters claims by weather conditions such as snow, rain, storm, avalanche, or tornado:

```
CREATE table ClaimWeatherView as Select distinct ClaimId,
ClaimWeatherCond from ClaimsMaster where ClaimWeatherCond in
('Snow','Rain','Storm','Avalanche','Tornado');
```

Writing to the history table:

```
INSERT INTO TABLE BatchProcHist
VALUES ('ClaimWeatherView', from_unixtime(unix_timestamp()));
```

The objective of the third batch view is to list teenage drivers with at least 2 severity 1 violations in last 12 months. First, I populate a temporary table (listing drivers with 2 or more severity 1 violations in the last 12 months):

```
Create table TeenageVioltemp1 as Select PolicyOwnerId,
count(ViolationSeverity) as TotalViolations
from PO_Drv_Hist where (datediff(current_date, add_months(to_
date(ViolationDate),12)) <= 0) and (ViolationSeverity = 1)
group by PolicyOwnerId
having count(ViolationSeverity) > 2
```

Next, the entries (from temporary table) will be filtered using DOB (date of birth) from the denormalized Policy entity for drivers aged 19 and under:

```
Create table TeenageViolView as Select T.PolicyOwnerId, T.TotalViolations
from TeenageVioltemp1 T, PolicyMaster P  where T.PolicyOwnerId =
P.PolicyOwnerId and
(datediff(current_date,add_months(P.PolicyOwnerDOB,228)) <= 0)
```

Writing to history table:

```
INSERT INTO TABLE BatchProcHist
VALUES ('TeenageViolView', from_unixtime(unix_timestamp()));
```

I have used the add_months function to add 228 months, or 19 years, to the date of birth (for drivers) and checked the difference (to determine if a driver is a teenager).

The fourth batch view lists adult drivers with three or more violations. So, I will create a new temporary table (similar to the third batch view) and filter the entries for drivers with age greater than 19 years:

```
Create table Violtemp1 as Select PolicyOwnerId, count(ViolationSeverity) as
TotalViolations
from PO_Drv_Hist where (datediff(current_date, add_months
(to_date(ViolationDate),12)) <= 0) and (ViolationSeverity = 1)
group by PolicyOwnerId
having count(ViolationSeverity) > 3
```

Filtering for adult drivers:

```
Create table AdultViolView as Select T.PolicyOwnerId, T.TotalViolations from
Violtemp1 T, PolicyMaster P  where T.PolicyOwnerId = P.PolicyOwnerId and
(datediff(add_months(P.PolicyOwnerDOB,228),current_date) < 0)
```

Writing to history table:

```
INSERT INTO TABLE BatchProcHist
VALUES ('AdultViolView ', from_unixtime(unix_timestamp()));
```

Important: Don't forget to remove the temporary tables you created—otherwise, your scripts will abort with an error.

So, having created the batch views, the next step is presenting or serving them.

Implementing the Serving Layer

I discuss the functionality and characteristics of serving layer in Chapter 9. Basically, it "serves" the batch views or provides fast access with minimum latency. That's why the serving layer needs to be a specialized distributed database that can:

- Host the batch views and support good performance for random as well as sequential data access (reads only)

- Be capable of quickly swapping a batch view with a newer version when it is rebuilt by the batch layer (that is, support batch updates)

- Error-tolerance (since views can be quickly redeployed from the batch layer)

- Indexing capability for fast retrieval

Splout SQL was a solution in Chapter 9—I will use that again. See Chapter 9 for architectural and operational details of Splout SQL. Splout SQL can be used to deploy batch-layer views as tables within tablespace(s). A *tablespace* is used for grouping tables that have the same key column. The advantage is that you can partition multiple tables using the same partitioning key. For Splout SQL, partitioning is important, because it is used for balancing data before indexing and deploying it. Note that when a table is partitioned by a single or multiple columns, Splout concatenates the value of those columns to form a single string. Therefore, partitioning is a function of a row, and it is also possible to partition using arbitrary functions (for example, a JavaScript function that uses only the first eight characters of a column).

For my example, observe that batch views 1, 3, and 4 use `PolicyOwnerId` as a key column. So, you can design a tablespace with these three batch views (or Hive tables). The other tablespace can hold the second batch view that uses `ClaimId` as a key column. So, as a next step, you need to generate tablespaces and tables.

For creating or generating a tablespace, you need to use the "generate" tool. This tool uses a JSON tablespace descriptor, as shown in the following code. You need to specify the input type and the Hive database and table names. The tablespace descriptor file can be created in the Splout SQL installation directory:

```
{
        "name": "PolicyTblspace",
        "nPartitions": 12,
        "partitionedTables": [{
                "name": "ClaimDefView",
                "partitionFields": "PolicyOwnerId",
                    "tableInputs": [{
                        "inputType": "HIVE",
                        "hiveTableName": "ClaimDefView",
                        "hiveDbName": "MyHiveDB"
                }]
        },
        {
                "name": "TeenageViolView",
                "partitionFields": "PolicyOwnerId",
                "tableInputs": [{
                        "inputType": "HIVE",
                        "hiveTableName": "TeenageViolView",
                        "hiveDbName": "MyHiveDB"
                }]
        },
        {
                "name": "AdultViolView",
                "partitionFields": "PolicyOwnerId",
                "tableInputs": [{
                        "inputType": "HIVE",
                        "hiveTableName": "AdultViolView",
                        "hiveDbName": "MyHiveDB"
                }]
        }]
}
```

Let me quickly review the information provided in this file (`PolicyTblspace.json`). The tablespace will be called `PolicyTblspace` and currently has three tables (or batch views) defined, `ClaimDefView`, `TeenageViolView`, and `AdultViolView`, that were created in the last section. The database name is `MyHiveDB` (you need to use the database name where you have created the Hive tables), and I have created 12 partitions for my data. I have used `PolicyOwnerId` as a partitioning column since this column will be a part of almost all the queries.

To deploy this tablespace, the following command can be executed from the (Linux) command line to generate the tablespace `PolicyTblspace` (from the Splout SQL installation directory):

```
hadoop jar splout-*-hadoop.jar generate -tf file:///`pwd`/ PolicyTblspace.
json -o out-MyHiveDB_splout_example
```

For performance, you may need to add indexes to your tablespace, and Splout allows you to add indexes easily. The catch is that you have to use a different generator called `simple-generate` instead of the generate tablespace generator that was used to generate the `PolicyTblspace` tablespace. The limitation of using the `simple-generate` generator is that your tablespace can only have a single table. Since the other tablespace for my example only has one table (or batch view), I will demonstrate the `simple-generate` usage for that tablespace. The following command will create an additional index while generating the tablespace `ClaimTblspace`:

```
hadoop jar splout-hadoop-*-hadoop.jar simple-generate –it HIVE –hdb MyHiveDB
–htn ClaimWeatherView -o out-MyHiveDB_splout_example -pby ClaimId -p 1 -idx
"ClaimWeatherCond" -t ClaimWeatherView -tb ClaimTblspace
```

Note that I have not included the column `ClaimId` since it is a partitioning column and is already indexed. The `-idx` option just adds more columns (in this case, `ClaimWetaherCond`) to the index. Also note that there is no `json` configuration file, and therefore, all the configuration (such as Hive database, table name, partitioning column, and so on) is specified with the command.

After the tablespaces are generated successfully, you need to deploy them as follows:

```
hadoop jar splout-hadoop-*-hadoop.jar deploy -q http://localhost:4412 -root
out-MyHiveDB1_splout_example -ts PolicyTblspace
```

```
hadoop jar splout-hadoop-*-hadoop.jar deploy -q http://localhost:4412 -root
out-MyHiveDB2_splout_example -ts ClaimTblspace
```

`localhost` is the host QNode (to which the client is connected) is running on, and `localhost` will be automatically substituted by the first valid private IP address at runtime (as specified in the configuration file).

Once a tablespace is deployed, you can use it in any of your queries. For example, if you need to check whether a specific claim (ClaimId=14124736) was filed during inclement weather conditions, you can use the REST API, as follows:

```
http://localhost:4412/api/query/ClaimTblspace?sql=SELECT * FROM
ClaimWeatherView;&key=14124736
```

You can use Splout SQL (or any other database solution of your liking) to deploy the batch-layer views as demonstrated in this section. Next, I will discuss how you can access data that's not yet processed by the batch layer and include it in your query results.

Implementing the Speed Layer

To recapitulate, the purpose of the speed layer is to make data unprocessed by batch-layer views available without any delays. Another difference (between speed-layer and batch-layer views) is that the batch layer updates a view by recomputing (or rebuilding) it, whereas the speed layer performs incremental processing on a view and only processes the delta (or new) transactions that were performed after the last time incremental processing was done. So, if your incoming data transactions are timestamped, and you extract them from your master dataset, then depending on whether a record was modified or added, you can modify your speed-layer view accordingly.

The next thing you need to consider is whether you need to update the speed layer synchronously (applying any updates to master data directly to the speed-layer views) or asynchronously (queuing requests and actual updates occurring at a later time). For this example, asynchronous updates will more useful because analytics applications focus more on complex computations and aggregations rather than interactive user input. Also, considering the high data volume, it would he beneficial to have more control on the updates (for example, handling varying load by allocating additional requests temporarily.

I will use Spark to implement the speed layer. More specifically, I will use the Spark processing engine and Spark SQL.

Since the Lambda architecture defines the speed layer to be composed of records that are yet to be processed by the batch layer, you need to determine what those records are. You may recall that a history record was inserted in table BatchProcHist after each of the batch views was built. So, the most recent record for a batch view can give us the date/time of most recent build and therefore help determine what the unprocessed records are. I will write the most recent record for the first batch view to a table (since Hive doesn't support query results to be assigned to variables):

```
Create table MaxTable as select ViewName, max(CreatedAt) as MaxDate from
BatchProcHist group by ViewName having ViewName = 'ClaimDefView';
```

That gives you the most recent date/time when the batch layer view was built. However, since speed layer views are processed more often, you also need to determine the date/time of records last processed by the speed layer (since you only need to consider the unprocessed records) for updating the *view* (here, a Spark dataframe registered as a table). I'll call the speed layer view ClaimDefView_S. Because speed-layer views also write to the audit table BatchProcHist, I will write the most recent record for the first speed-layer view to the same table (where I captured most recent record for the first batch view):

```
Insert into MaxTable select ViewName, max(CreatedAt) from BatchProcHist
group by ViewName having ViewName = 'ClaimDefView_S';
```

Now, I just need to determine which of these records is most recent (just in case the batch layer was rebuilt after the last speed-layer build) and use that as a basis to process the records for the first speed layer view:

```
Create table MaxTbl1 as select max(MaxDate) as MaxDate from MaxTable;
```

Finally, get the unprocessed records from the master data set and create the speed-layer view. Also, add the timestamp and write a record to the audit history table:

```
Create table ClaimDeftemp11 as Select PolicyId, ClaimId from ClaimsMaster a,
MaxTbl1 b where where a.LastModified > b.MaxDate;
```

```
Create table ClaimDeftemp12 as Select PolicyId, count(ClaimId) as
Claimcount from ClaimDeftemp11 where datediff(current_date, add_months
(to_date(ClaimSubmissionDate),12)) <= 0
group by PolicyId having count(ClaimId) > 5
```

As a final step, I will join this temporary table with the denormalized Policy entity to get the policy owner details constituting the batch view and write a record to the history table:

```
Create table ClaimDefView_S as Select P.PolicyOwnerID, P.PolicyId,
C.Claimcount from PolicyMaster P, ClaimDeftemp12 C where P.PolicyId =
C.PolicyId;
```

```
INSERT INTO TABLE BatchProcHist
  VALUES ('ClaimDefView_S', from_unixtime(unix_timestamp()));
```

Drop the temporary tables now (since we may recreate some of them for the next speed-layer views):

```
Drop Table MaxTable;
Drop Table MaxTbl1;
Drop Table ClaimDeftemp11;
Drop Table ClaimDeftemp12;
```

Other speed-layer views can be similarly created as follows:

```
--View 2;
Create table MaxTable as select ViewName, max(CreatedAt) as MaxDate from
BatchProcHist group by ViewName having ViewName = 'ClaimWeatherView';

Insert into MaxTable select ViewName, max(CreatedAt) from BatchProcHist
group by ViewName having ViewName = 'ClaimWeatherView_S';

Create table MaxTbl1 as select max(MaxDate) as MaxDate from MaxTable;
CREATE table ClaimWeatherView_S as Select distinct a.ClaimId,
a.ClaimWeatherCond from ClaimsMaster a, MaxTbl1 b where a.LastModified >
b.MaxDate and a.ClaimWeatherCond in ('Snow','Rain','Storm','Avalanche',
'Tornado');

INSERT INTO TABLE BatchProcHist
VALUES ('ClaimWeatherView_S', from_unixtime(unix_timestamp()));
Drop Table MaxTable;
Drop Table MaxTbl1;
--View 3;
Create table MaxTable as select ViewName, max(CreatedAt) as MaxDate from
BatchProcHist group by ViewName having ViewName = 'TeenageViolView';

Insert into MaxTable select ViewName, max(CreatedAt) from BatchProcHist
group by ViewName having ViewName = 'TeenageViolView_S';

Create table MaxTbl1 as select max(MaxDate) as MaxDate from MaxTable;

Create table TeenageVioltemp11 as Select a.PolicyOwnerId,
a.ViolationSeverity from PO_Drv_Hist a, MaxTbl1 b where a.LastModified >
b.MaxDate;

Create table TeenageVioltemp12 as Select PolicyOwnerId,
count(ViolationSeverity) as TotalViolations
from TeenageVioltemp11 where (datediff(current_date, add_months
(to_date(ViolationDate),12)) <= 0) and (ViolationSeverity = 1)
group by PolicyOwnerId
having count(ViolationSeverity) > 2
```

```
Create table TeenageViolView_S as Select T.PolicyOwnerId, T.TotalViolations
from Teenagevioltemp12 T, PolicyMaster P  where T.PolicyOwnerId =
P.PolicyOwnerId and
(datediff(current_date,add_months(P.PolicyOwnerDOB,228)) <= 0)

INSERT INTO TABLE BatchProcHist
VALUES ('TeenageViolView_S', from_unixtime(unix_timestamp());

Drop Table MaxTable;
Drop Table MaxTbl1;
Drop Table TeenageVioltemp11;
Drop Table TeenageVioltemp12;

--View 4;
Create table MaxTable as select ViewName, max(CreatedAt) as MaxDate from
BatchProcHist group by ViewName having ViewName = 'AdultViolView';

Insert into MaxTable select ViewName, max(CreatedAt) from BatchProcHist
group by ViewName having ViewName = 'AdultViolView_S';

Create table MaxTbl1 as select max(MaxDate) as MaxDate from MaxTable;

Create table Violtemp11 as Select a.PolicyOwnerId, a.ViolationSeverity from
PO_Drv_Hist a, MaxTbl1 b where a.LastModified > b.MaxDate;

Create table Violtemp12 as Select PolicyOwnerId, count(ViolationSeverity) as
TotalViolations
from Violtemp11 where (datediff(current_date, add_months
(to_date(ViolationDate),12)) <= 0) and (ViolationSeverity = 1)
group by PolicyOwnerId
having count(ViolationSeverity) > 3

Create table AdultViolView_S as Select T.PolicyOwnerId, T.TotalViolations
from Violtemp12 T, PolicyMaster P  where T.PolicyOwnerId = P.PolicyOwnerId
and
(datediff(add_months(P.PolicyOwnerDOB,228),current_date) < 0)

INSERT INTO TABLE BatchProcHist
VALUES ('AdultViolView_S', from_unixtime(unix_timestamp());

Drop Table MaxTable;
Drop Table MaxTbl1;
Drop Table Violtemp11;
Drop Table Violtemp12;
```

Chapter 9 discusses all the operational details about interfacing Spark with Hadoop. Here, I will briefly discuss using Spark SQL for getting data from Hive (into DataFrames) and also executing DML (Data Manipulation Language—update, insert, or delete commands) statements against Hive tables from Spark.

As you may know, Spark uses dataframes and RDDs (resilient distributed datasets) as in-memory constructs that you can leverage for queries and performance. Spark also allows you to execute queries against Hive databases using the sqlContext. To start with, you need to construct a HiveContext, which inherits from SQLContext and enables you to find tables in the Hive MetaStore and also supports queries using HiveQL. Here, I am using Scala, and sc is an existing SparkContext (you can use Python or R within a Spark shell):

```
val sqlContext = new org.apache.spark.sql.hive.HiveContext(sc)
```

```
val sqlContext.sql("Create table MaxTable as select ViewName, max(CreatedAt)
from BatchProcHist group by ViewName having ViewName = 'ClaimDefView'")
```

```
val sqlContext.sql("Insert into MaxTable select ViewName, max(CreatedAt)
from BatchProcHist group by ViewName having ViewName = 'ClaimDefView_S'")
```

You can similarly execute all the HiveQL commands necessary to create the speed-layer view ClaimDefView_S. For the last step (when the view is created), instead of creating the view, you can simply execute the select statement and read the result in a dataframe, as follows:

```
val resultsDF = sqlContext.sql("Select P.PolicyOwnerID, P.PolicyId,
C.Claimcount from PolicyMaster P, ClaimDeftemp12 C where P.PolicyId =
C.PolicyId;")
```

You can register the resultant dataframe as a temporary table and then execute any queries against it:

```
val resultsDF.registerTempTable("ClaimDefView_S")
val results = sqlContext.sql("SELECT PolicyOwnerId FROM ClaimDefView_S")
```

You will need to use a query tool that can read from Hive and Spark to combine results from batch-layer and speed-layer views. There are enough choices, and of course you can also use Spark SQL as a query tool too.

Storage Structures (for Master Data and Views)

Chapter 10 discusses how to select an optimal file format. In this section I will apply the concepts discussed in Chapter 9. So, let me briefly consider the parameters to choose the right format:

- The type of queries (you plan to execute) is first and the most important one. As you have seen from the batch views, the queries for building master data involve choosing a small subset of columns (from a larger set) with few filters. Also, there are multiple aggregations required to build the batch-layer views.

- The amount of compression you need. With a dataset sized at 30 TB (and 1% monthly growth), compression is a necessity.

- Ensure your NoSQL solution supports the storage format you plan to use.

Now, you may recall from Chapter 9 that a columnar format offers good compression and is more suited for data needing aggregation operations (such as count, avg, min, max). Also, columnar format provides good performance for use cases that involve selecting a small subset of columns and also use a small number of columns as filters (in the where clause).

Subsequently, you will benefit from using columnar format for storing data. The next decision is which columnar format you should choose. The popular formats include RCFile, ORCFile, and Parquet.

The RCFile format is the first columnar format to be introduced and is supported most widely within the Hadoop ecosystem (almost all the Hadoop tools support it) as well as by tools outside Hadoop. Compared to Parquet and ORCFiles, RCFile lacks a lot of advanced features such as support for storing more complex data types or providing encryption. However, for the current example, there are no complex data types that need to be supported, and there is no need for encryption. So, RCFile format can be used.

If you see performance issues, switch to Parquet, which offers better compression and achieves a balance between compression and speed. Also, Parquet is supported widely by Hadoop as well as external (to the Hadoop ecosystem) tools.

You should use an advanced distributed-processing framework like YARN (or Spark) to help you speed up processing of this data and provide optimal performance (since the data volume is fairly high).

Other Performance Considerations

I have not considered the tuning of OS configuration for this example because of the availability of a large number of options for OSes. Since the configurations will change (based on what OS or framework you choose), I don't think it's possible to provide finer details. You can, however, refer to the HDFS and YARN tuning guidelines from Chapter 10 as a starting point (if you plan to use YARN). And if you use Spark, there are specific guidelines for tuning JVMs, in addition to the generic guidelines from Chapter 10.

Because Spark may hold large amounts of data in memory, it relies on Java's memory management and garbage collection (GC). So, understanding and tuning Java's GC options (and parameters) can help you get the best performance for your Spark applications. A common issue with GC is that garbage collection takes a long time and thereby affects performance for a program, sometimes even crashing.

Java applications can use one of two strategies for garbage collection:

- *Concurrent Mark Sweep (CMS) garbage collection*: This strategy aims at lower latency and therefore does not do compaction (to save time). It's more suited for real-time applications.

- *ParallelOld garbage collection*: This strategy targets higher throughput and therefore performs whole-heap compaction, which results in a big performance hit. This is more suited for asynchronous or batch processing (for programs performing aggregations, analysis, and so on).

JVM version 1.6 has introduced a third option for garbage collection called Garbage-First GC (G1 GC). The G1 collector aims to achieve both high throughput and low latency and is therefore a good option to use.

To start with, note how Spark uses JVM. Spark's executors divide JVM heap space in two parts. The first part is used to hold data persistently cached into memory. The second part is used as JVM heap space (for allocating memory for RDDs during transformations).

You can adjust the ratio (of these parts) using the `spark.storage.memoryFraction` parameter. This lets Spark control the total size of the cached RDD (less than (RDD heap space volume * `spark.storage.memoryFraction`)). You need to consider memory usage by both the parts for any meaningful GC analysis.

If you observe that GC is taking more time, you should first check on usage of memory space by your Spark applications. If your application uses less memory space for RDDs, it will leave more heap space for program execution and thereby will increase GC efficiency. If needed, you can improve performance by cleaning up cached RDDs that are no longer used.

It is preferable to use the new G1 collector, as it better handles growing heap sizes that usually occur for Spark applications. It is of course not possible to provide a generic strategy for GC tuning. You need to understand logging (by Spark) and use it for tuning in conjunction with other parameters for memory management.

Indexing is another area I have not considered, since indexing in your environment will depend on the types of queries and their frequencies. Finally, I have used a generic solution for storage (HDFS with Hive) for two reasons. First, Lambda has multiple layers, and compatibility of multiple components needs to be ensured through usage of components with widespread support. Second, the actual NoSQL solution you use will depend on your specific type of data and also on what you want to do with it (in terms of processing). So, me using a specific NoSQL solution may be useful only to a few people. I have listed these areas (that I have not considered) more as a reminder for you to consider for your specific environment.

Reference Architectures

In this chapter, I have discussed all aspects of designing and implementing a Hadoop-based solution for a business requirement using the Lambda architecture. I started with hardware, software, and then discussed design as per Lambda framework. Finally, I discussed the steps for implementation. Of course, a production implementation has many additional components, such as network, monitoring, alerts, and more, to make the implementation a success. So, it will be helpful for you to review some complete architectures to get an idea of what's involved for production implementation of a Hadoop-based system. The components (of course) change depending on the vendor (for example, Microsoft, AWS, Hortonworks, Cloudera, and so on). For example, Figure 11-3 shows a Lambda implementation using AWS components. You can see the use of Kinesis to get streaming data and use of a Spark cluster (implemented using EC2s) to process that data. The batch layer is implemented using EMRs that form a Hadoop cluster with a MasterNode and four DataNodes. The speed-layer views can be delivered using DynamoDB and combined with batch-layer views to any reporting, dashboard (visualizations), or analytics solutions. Since this is a production implementation, you can observe usage of security, monitoring, and backups/archival using appropriate AWS components.

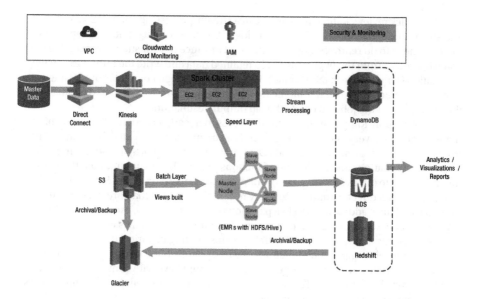

Figure 11-3. *Lambda implementation using AWS components*

Similar architectures can be built using Microsoft components or Hortonworks/Cloudera components.

Changes to Implementation for Latest Architectures

Kappa architecture, Fast Data architecture, and Butterfly architecture are some of the latest or *future state* architectures. If you have to implement the system (from my example in earlier sections) using these architectures, certain changes will be needed. I will not discuss complete re-implementations but just focus on component-level changes to the architecture. I will start with Kappa architecture.

Re-Implementation Using Kappa Architecture

First thing to note is the possibility of applying Kappa architecture instead of Lambda. Note that Kappa can only replace Lambda where the expected outputs for the speed layer and batch layer are the same. If the expected outputs for the speed and batch algorithms are different, then the batch and speed layers cannot be merged, and Lambda architecture must be used. In my example from previous sections, the expected outputs for the speed layer and batch layer are same, and therefore, it is possible to use Kappa architecture.

As a quick review, Kappa involves use of a stream-processing engine (Spark, Kafka, and so on) that allows you to retain the full log of the data you might need to reprocess. If there is a need to do reprocessing, start a second instance of your stream-processing job that will process from the beginning of the retained data and write the output to a new destination (for example, a table or file). When the second job completes processing, switch the application to read from the new output destination. After that, you can stop the old version of the job and delete the old output destination.

You can apply Kappa for the example discussed in earlier sections. To start with, there is only one layer—the streaming layer. File streams can be created for reading data from master data files, and appropriate DStreams can be created. Spark Streaming can apply transformations and aggregation functions to these DStreams and hold them in memory or write out as files (to HDFS). For processing new data, Spark Streaming will monitor the data directory and process any new files created in that directory. Since new master data is added as new Hive partitions (for my example), those files can be copied from the staging location to the Spark data directory. New files will be streamed as new DStreams and can be joined with DStreams holding historical data, and the same transformation and aggregation functions can be applied on the resulting DStreams to have an up-to-date dataset (the same as what you would have with combined batch-layer views and speed-layer views). The resulting DStream can be served to client applications as a dataframe or a Hive table as required.

In case of changes to the transformation functions or discovery of a data or processing issue, a new Spark Streaming job can be started to apply the transformations again to a new DStream (created from master data), and when it completes, the new destination can be used to serve the client applications. Figure 11-4 has the architectural details.

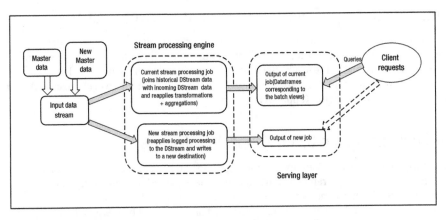

Figure 11-4. *Kappa architecture applied for Lambda case study*

Changes for Fast Data Architecture

You may need to implement Fast Data architecture. *Fast Data* is defined as data created (almost) continuously by mobile devices, social media networks, sensors, and so on, and a data pipeline processes the new data within milliseconds and performs analytics on it.

For my example, it will mean joining the new data stream captured in real time with the historical data stream and applying transformation as well as aggregation functions on it.

The Kappa architecture defined in Figure 11-4 will be mostly valid along with some changes to it. The part that will change is the processing for new data. Instead of looking for new files in the data directory, there will be an additional mechanism like Kafka to capture multiple data streams and combine them before passing on to Spark Streaming to process as a new DStream for the stream-processing engine. The new DStream will then be joined with the historical DStream and transformation/aggregation functions applied to it.

Changes for Butterfly Architecture

The Butterfly architecture is discussed at length in Chapter 9 along with a real-world example. It offers a huge performance advantage due to the nexus of hardware with software (software effectively driving the hardware resources). If you were to use Butterfly architecture for implementing the example discussed in this chapter, you would need to follow these steps:

- Ingest the input data stream using events (insert) from Kafka broker

- Parse the event to determine which speed-layer views the data belongs to

- Update respective speed-layer view

- Keep track of total number of updates

- When 1% of the records are new (for a speed-layer view), launch the batch computation, update batch views, and reset update counters

Summary

In this chapter, I have tried to address all the aspects of a Hadoop-based implementation using Lambda architecture. Note that this is a generic implementation to give you some idea about the steps involved in implementing Lambda for your environment. Also, observe that my approach discusses data from a relational database instead of a clickstream-based web application. There are several reasons for this approach. The major reason is that most of the production systems are based on relational data. The new social media–based or sensor-driven or mobile device–based data is still not mainstream. It is mostly used as supplementary or auxiliary data. Also, most of the clickstream applications have semi-structured (or unstructured) data that varies greatly, and therefore a single example may not be very representative.

This chapter (and this book) is more about migrating, integrating, or transitioning your relational technology–based systems to Hadoop. Therefore, I have used RDBMS data an example of source data that you will be working with. In reality, that will mostly be the case. So, where and how can you use Hadoop? You can use Hadoop for moving, transforming, aggregating, and getting the data ready for analytics. What kind of analytics? That totally depends on your specific use case.

There are applications of Hadoop ranging from discovering historical trends in buying trends for retail goods to accurately predicting birth conditions based on biological pre-birth data. A hospital in Australia uses Hadoop to analyze a large amount of pre-birth data to predict what possible conditions a child may have and to have the resources ready to counter them. Insurance and credit card companies use Hadoop for establishing predictive models for possible fraud. Hadoop is used for traffic analysis and prediction of optimal routes. The possibilities are endless.

But remember that Hadoop is just a powerful tool, and optimal use of it depends on the skill level (and creativity) of the user or designer. New technologies, architectures, and applications are added on a daily basis. It's truly an emerging technology right now. Hopefully, I have provided some useful information and direction to your thought process to make use of this technology.

When you implement a migration or integration for your environment, you will need to use additional tools or technologies. Some of the legacy systems won't allow you to extract the data easily. Fortunately, there are enough forums and user groups to help out. It rarely happens that you ask a question and no one answers it. The spirit of collaboration and sharing knowledge is one of the biggest strengths of Hadoop and any open source solutions that are built around it. I wish you good luck in implementing Hadoop-based systems and hope you can interface your existing systems successfully with them!

Index

© Bhushan Lakhe 2016
B. Lakhe, *Practical Hadoop Migration*, DOI 10.1007/978-1-4842-1287-5

Get the eBook for only $5!

Why limit yourself?

Now you can take the weightless companion with you wherever you go and access your content on your PC, phone, tablet, or reader.

Since you've purchased this print book, we're happy to offer you the eBook in all 3 formats for just $5.

Convenient and fully searchable, the PDF version enables you to easily find and copy code—or perform examples by quickly toggling between instructions and applications. The MOBI format is ideal for your Kindle, while the ePUB can be utilized on a variety of mobile devices.

To learn more, go to www.apress.com/companion or contact support@apress.com.

Printed in the United States
By Bookmasters